AF334710

his is Number 3 in a series of monographs in the history of tech-
ology and culture published jointly by the Society for the History
f Technology and the M.I.T. Press. The members of the editorial
oard for the Society for the History of Technology Monograph
Series are Melvin Kranzberg, Cyril S. Smith, and R. J. Forbes.

Publications in the series include:

History of the Lathe to 1850
Robert S. Woodbury

English Land Measuring to 1800: Instruments and Practices
A. W. Richeson

The Development of Technical Education in France 1500–1850
Frederick B. Artz

The Development ‹
Technical Education in
1500–1850

The Development of
Technical Education in France
1500–1850

Frederick B. Artz

Oberlin College

Published jointly by

THE SOCIETY FOR THE HISTORY
OF TECHNOLOGY

and

THE M.I.T. PRESS
Massachusetts Institute of Technology
Cambridge, Massachusetts, and London, England

To the
Memory
of
Georges Weill
1865–1943

Preface

The French, in the three and a half centuries between about 1500 and 1850, developed all, or nearly all, the basic forms of modern technical education. And in the course of time, from Russia across western Europe and the United States to Japan, all countries modeled their technical schools on those of France. So, in the gradual transfer of technical training from an apprenticeship system where one learned a calling on the job to one where one learned much of his technical profession in a school, France played the dominant role.

I first became interested in French technical education years ago when making a close study of France during the Bourbon Restoration. There I found the leading businessmen and many of the more forward-looking government officials greatly interested in the improvement and extension of technical education. This led me to an interest in the whole story of the subject as a vital chapter in the history of French civilization.

During a sabbatical leave of absence, I worked up the fundamentals of the subject in a series of American libraries at Harvard and Yale Universities, in the New York Public Library, and at the Library of Congress. This was followed by the work of several summers in Paris in the *Bibliothèque Nationale* and the National Archives, and in a series of special libraries, such as those attached to the *Conservatoire des arts et métiers,* the *École polytechnique,* the *Société d'encouragement pour l'industrie nationale,* the *Chambre de Commerce de Paris,* and, finally, the Army and Navy Libraries.

Unfortunately for purposes of comparison, the story of technical education in countries other than France has been little studied; a full comparison of French experience and practice with what was going on elsewhere was therefore not possible. However, wherever material on technical education in other states was available it has been used, for comparative purposes, in this account.

Parts of the earlier portions of this study have appeared in the *Revue d'histoire moderne* and the *Revue historique.* These portions are here revised, and the rest is new. I am grateful to my colleague, Robert E. Neil, for reading the proofs.

Oberlin, Ohio   FREDERICK B. ARTZ
1 June, 1966

Contents

CHAPTER THREE

CHAPTER FOUR

*The Development of
Technical Education in France
1500–1850*

The Beginnings
1500–1700

The structure of modern society is in large degree the result of technological change. Only the growth of pure science, to which this change has often been closely related, can be compared with it as a basic cause for the transformation of the western world since the Middle Ages. Yet it was only in an irregular and casual fashion that changing technology affected the course of educational theory and the organization of the schools. The practical training given to apprentices and workers under the old guild system sufficed both for passing on acquired techniques and for improving them; its general excellence was a hindrance to the growth of other types of education. Hence, until the nineteenth century the training of the worker, of the engineer, and of the military and naval officer was largely left to such practical experience with tools and machines as could be acquired in the shop, field, mine, regiment, or ship. Organized higher education, which by the thirteenth century had reached an unusual degree of excellence, was mostly confined to the professions of medicine, law, and theology, and to the general cultural enrichment of the leisure classes.

Technical education thus did not assume anything like its contemporary forms before the first half of the nineteenth century. A study of its earlier development shows that its origins were extraordinarily diverse. No single thinker, schoolman, or statesman envisaged all or even any large section of its problems. Even those aspects of the subject that were considered by the educational and economic theorists and reformers of the sixteenth, seventeenth, and eighteenth centuries had only slight and haphazard influence on the practice of the schools. Viewing the whole period down to 1800 makes it evident that in order to get any just idea of the origins of modern technical education one must consider the various and often widely unrelated fields of general educational theory and practice, of economic thought and economic policies of governments, and of early military and naval instruction. And to understand these three main currents one must frequently go further afield to consider the general history of education, science, technology, and government.

1. Technical Education in Utopia

An extended interest in the use of the school for some systematic instruction in agriculture and in industrial processes appears first in the descriptions of a series of ideal commonwealths of the sixteenth and seventeenth centuries. It is a very significant fact that, although these utopias propose vast schemes that include all human activities, "whenever in these a system of education is described the curriculum is found to be more or less industrial in character. In some instances instruction in the industries is introduced for economic reasons; in others the industries are studied as belonging to the realities to which men turn with such relief from the abstractions of the medieval schools."[1] The ideal commonwealths show clearly that society was passing beyond the ideals which had served it for centuries and that the more daring thinkers were striving to conceive new educational ideals to meet new conditions.

The great interest of Thomas More, in his *Utopia* (1516), is to relieve the wretchedness of the poor who suffer both from wars and from the meanness and stinginess of the rich. If the lower classes were educated to make a living they could, he believed, better their own condition. So More proposes that every citizen in Utopia be taught the common methods of agriculture and also some one handicraft.[2] Like most of the descriptions of ideal commonwealths of the period, More's treatise was first published in Latin and thus had an extended circulation among the intellectual classes all over Europe.[3] Rabelais, who wrote in the vernacular and in a far livelier style, presented his ideas in the form of a novel rather than of an ideal state. His was the first plea for educational reform that was widely read in France. Impatient with all things medieval, he lashed into the educational practice of his day —

[1] L. F. Anderson, *History of Manual and Industrial School Education* (New York, 1926), p. 6. The suggestions of educational reform in these ideal commonwealths show interesting contrasts with the Renaissance idea of educating a gentleman. Cf. the three excellent studies by W. H. Woodward, *Vittorino da Feltre and Other Humanist Educators* (Cambridge, 1897), *Studies in Education During the Age of the Renaissance, 1400–1600* (Cambridge, 1906), and *Erasmus, Concerning the Method and Aim of Education* (Cambridge, 1904). Erasmus, though he had a strong bias in favor of the use of the classics in education, found a place in his scheme for the teaching of physics and mathematics.

[2] The Utopians were to be so instructed in agriculture from "their childhood, partly by what they learn at school and partly by practice, they being led out often into the fields about the town, where they not only see others at work, but are likewise exercised in it themselves." H. Morley, ed., *Ideal Commonwealths* (New York, 1901), p. 40.

[3] Two translations of *Utopia* appeared in French in the sixteenth century, one by Jean Leblond (Paris, 1550) and one by Barthélemy Aneau (Lyons, 1559). An English version appeared about the same time.

the formalism of its curriculum and the stupid brutality of its discipline — and demanded a training that would develop all the latent capacities of the natural man. Such technical training as he proposes is not intended, as with More, to improve the lot of the masses but to form a new type of individual, an individual guided by his reason, one who could think independently.[4] It is still the Renaissance idea of the gentleman: a gentleman, though, sharing richly in every human experience. He extended the whole ideal of training by his emphasis on education through the senses, practical lessons in things and processes which he deemed quite worthy of the attention of the governing classes. His general influence on educational thought was great and came down through Montaigne and Locke to Rousseau.[5]

In *The City of the Sun* (1623), the Italian, Campanella,

[4] Rabelais writes of the training of youth, "They went likewise to see the drawing of metals or the casting of great ordnance, how the lapidaries did work, as also the goldsmiths and cutters of precious stones; nor did they omit to visit the alchemists, money-coiners, upholsterers, weavers, velvet-workers, watchmakers, looking-glass framers, printers, organ builders, and other such kind of artificers, and everywhere giving them somewhat to drink, did learn and consider the industry and invention of the trades." Urquhart and Le Motteux's translation of *Gargantua,* Book I, Chap. 24. Cf. A. Coutaud, *La pédagogie de Rabelais* (Paris, 1899). Montaigne also believed that sciences should be studied to enlarge the cultural experience of the gentleman; like Rabelais, he attacked the pedantry of both the old scholastics and the new classicists. Montaigne, likewise, thought the schools made a mistake in neglecting the training of the man of affairs, busying themselves too much with scholars, doctors, and lawyers. Cf. P. Villey, *L'influence de Montaigne sur les idées pédagogiques de Locke et Rousseau* (Paris, 1911), and A. M. Boase, *Fortunes of Montaigne; History of the Essays in France 1580–1669* (London, 1935). P. Porteau, *Montaigne et la vie pédagogique de son temps* (Paris, 1935) refutes some of Montaigne's strictures on the schools of his time.

[5] Similar ideas are to be found in Charron, *De la sagesse* (Paris, 1601), Livre III, "Devoirs des parents et enfants." There is an excellent bibliography of sixteenth-century educational treatises, *Répertoire des ouvrages pédagogiques du XVI siècle* (Paris, 1886), and a general bibliography covering material to the Revolution, A. Silvy, *Essai d'une bibliographie de l'enseignement secondaire et supérieur en France avant la Révolution* (Paris, 1894).

describes a city divided by its walls into seven concentric circles. The surfaces of these walls are to be utilized for public instruction, each wall to be covered with pictures and diagrams in some field of science. The sixth wall is to be reserved for "the mechanical arts, with the several instruments for each and their manner of use among different nations." The city magistrates are to act as teachers of the handicrafts, and their instruction is to be supplemented by visits to workshops. Throughout the commonwealth the highest rewards are to go to those who practice the industrial arts with the greatest success.[6] In another ideal city, *Christianopolis* (1619), J. V. Andreä, a German scholar, describes a system of education partly vocational and industrial, with part of the day "devoted to manual training and domestic art and science as each one's occupation is assigned according to his natural inclination." In a second work, *Theophilus,* published thirty years later, Andreä proposes that every school should provide, through different sorts of handiwork, for the cultivation of mechanical skills.[7]

Finally, in the *New Atlantis,* Francis Bacon envisages science as the primary civilizing agency of society, and in his description of "Solomon's House" he outlines a great technological school and museum which, besides many other features, is to contain laboratories for the demonstration and improvement of most of the mechanical processes used in industry.[8]

[6] T. Campanella, *The City of the Sun,* in Morley, ref. 2, pp. 145–51. Cf. L. Blanchet, *Campanella* (Paris, 1920). The idea of putting plans on walls may have come from the placing of large maps on walls by the Romans and from the Renaissance practice of frescoing huge pictures on walls.

[7] J. V. Andreä, *Christianopolis,* ed. by F. E. Held (Oxford, 1916), pp. 210, 260; F. Henam and W. Moog, *Geschichte der neueren Pädagogik,* 6th ed. (Osterwieck, 1919), p. 120.

[8] F. Bacon, *New Atlantis,* in H. Morley, ref. 2, pp. 129–37. For Bacon's influence in France, cf. Ch. Adam, *Philosophie de Bacon* (Paris, 1890), pp. 335ff. The first French translation of the *New Atlantis,* by Raguet, did not appear until 1702 but, like More's *Utopia,* the Latin edition had an extended circulation in France. Bacon used the term "manual arts" in his first work, published in 1605.

It was clear to Bacon that the great need of the age was scientific research, carried out on a scale so extensive that only the state could support it, and so organized as to employ the most capable scholars. In his *Advancement of Learning,* Bacon proposes that, instead of insisting on a uniform course of study in all schools, a variety of educational institutions be established which would permit a choice of studies adapted to the needs of different types of students.[9] Through his writings runs an enthusiasm for scientific method which can and must be applied to the practical needs of society; in this he clearly represents the early modern craze for new inventions which it was believed would make over the whole life of man.[10] "The pioneers of modern science," says Wolf, "certainly wished and expected the relations between science and technology to be most intimate. The notion of knowledge for its own sake had no glamour for them. In fact, it was their great expectation that the new science, unlike the old book learning, . . . would confer power. . . . All the early scientific academies busied themselves with useful inventions."[11] Bacon's influence is difficult to define with any exactness, but the great popularity of his writings undoubtedly helped widen the scope of learning, particularly in the direction of increased study of the sciences and their application.

[9] Joseph Moxon, in the preface to the single-volume edition of his *Mechanick Exercises* (London, 1683), says, "Bacon in his *Natural History* reckons that philosophy would be improved by having the secrets of all trades lie open, not only because much experimental philosophy is couched among them, but also that the trades themselves might by a philosopher be improved."

[10] Cf. G. N. Clark, "Early Capitalism and Invention," *Economic History Review* (April 1936); E. F. Heckscher, *Mercantilism* (2 vols., London, 1935), Vol. 2, pp. 126ff. The idea of science as being of both educational and practical value was becoming common after the middle of the sixteenth century; as Montaigne said, "C'est un grand ornement que la science et un outil de merveilleux service." There is a brief but penetrating explanation of the fundamental ideas back of these changes in E. Durkheim, *L'évolution pédagogique en France* (2 vols., Paris, 1938), Vol. 2, Chap. 9.

[11] A. Wolf, *A History of Science, Technology and Philosophy in the 16th and 17th Centuries* (London, 1935), pp. 451–52.

The utopian theorists were not themselves teachers, nor were they connected with educational institutions, and their writings had little immediate influence on the practice of the schools. Their ideas are chiefly of interest because they show the direction in which the most daring thinkers were moving.

2. Technical Education in Educational Theory and in the Schools

Although it led to few tangible results, the educational theorizing of the seventeenth century both in France and in the rest of western Europe shows everywhere the assumption that manual and technical education can be incorporated in the curriculum of the schools. Such reforms ceased to be considered only as part of the society of a dreamland. The industrial arts and the practical applications of science to industrial, naval, and military training began to be reckoned among the essential fields of knowledge. The theoretical writers on education, however, continued throughout the century to consider the teaching of drawing and all types of handiwork in the schools as a means of furthering general education and not as a means of producing better artisans. Much more practical were the economic writers and the statesmen. All of these changing attitudes may be traced in the thought of educational reformers, in the gradual reorganization of primary and secondary schools — most of which in France were still under ecclesiastical control — in the writings of the mercantilist economists, and finally in the active intervention of the state in offering better training for industry and for service in the army and navy.

Educational reform was one of the chief concerns of many of the great thinkers of the seventeenth century. From Descartes and Comenius to Locke an increasing emphasis is placed on the ideas that sensory impressions form the basis of education and that one learns best by doing. Out of the first grew the object method of teaching and later the laboratory method of instruction, and out of the second came the concept of working through a process with tools as a means of learning agricultural and industrial techniques and, beyond this, of enriching and enlarging human experience and usefulness.

The educational system of the Moravian educator and bishop John Amos Comenius (1592–1670), like that of the earlier Renaissance theorists of education, was directed toward the formation of the whole personality and character of the child though, like other Protestant educators, Comenius had more interest in knowledge for knowledge's sake than had the Catholic educators. Only indirectly and by implication could his theories be applied to the problems of technical education. In the training of youth he believed the course of nature should be followed; the child should first be taught to recognize the objects about him and to understand their nature and uses. So the hand, the mind, and the tongue would be trained together, the first to do, the second to think, and the third to interpret. "Artisans," he says, "do not detain their apprentices with theories, but set them to do practical work at an early stage; thus they learn to forge by forging, to carve by carving, to paint by painting. . . . Mechanics do not begin by drumming rules into their apprentices. They take them into the workshop and bid them look at the work that has been produced, and then, when they wish them to imitate this (for man is an imitative animal) they place tools in their hands and show them how they should be held and used. Then, if they make mistakes, they give them advice and correct them, often more by example than by mere words." [12] If the objects themselves are not obtainable, pictures are to be used. In all subjects general, concrete, and easy problems should be pre-

[12] J. A. Comenius, *The Great Didactic,* ed. by M. W. Keatinge, 2nd ed. (London, 1910), Chap. 21, secs. 5 and 7.

sented first; then the teacher may move on to the particular, the abstract, and the more difficult.

As to the manual arts, he says that children between the ages of six and twelve "should learn the most important principles of the mechanical arts, both that they may not be too ignorant of what goes on in the world around them, and that any special inclination toward things of this kind may assert itself with greater ease later on."[13] Curiously enough, though he suggests that young pupils, during their recreation periods, "be given tools and allowed to imitate the different handicrafts, by playing at farming, at politics, at being soldiers or architects,"[14] he does not, in more advanced schools, pro-

[13] Comenius, *op. cit.*, Chap. 29, sec. 6. Comenius' plan for an organized hierarchy of schools from the most elementary to the university was first instituted at Halle, chiefly due to the efforts of August Francke. Cf. F. Sommer, *Francke und seine Stiftungen* (Halle a. d. Saale, 1927).

[14] Comenius, *op. cit.*, Chap. 19, sec. 49. Cf. A. Heyberger, *Comenius* (Paris, 1928), the best study of Comenius. Cf. also J. Needham, ed., *The Teacher of Nations* (*Addresses and Essays in Commemoration of the Visit to England of . . . Comenius*) (Cambridge, 1942) and M. Spinka, *Comenius* (Chicago, 1943). The influence of Comenius on manual education was more marked in England and in middle Europe than in France. Cf. G. H. Trumbull, *Samuel Hartlib, a Sketch of his Life and his Relations to Comenius* (Oxford, 1932). The growth of interest in new technical processes was evident in England; from 1677 on Joseph Moxon published in two series of monthly parts his *Mechanick Exercises,* one of the earliest treatises on tools and their uses in any vernacular language. It dealt merely with practical methods used in blacksmithing, building, etc., "entirely uninfluenced by the investigations of Galileo, Descartes, and the scientific societies." Wolf, ref. 11, p. 480. Several pages of it are produced in C. A. Bennett, *History of Manual and Industrial Education up to 1870* (Peoria, Ill., 1926), pp. 51–60. John Milton in his essay *On Education* shows a similar interest: "And having thus passed the principles of arithmetic, geometry, astronomy, and geography, with a general compact of physics, they may descend in mathematics to the instrumental science of trigonometry, and from thence to fortification, architecture, engineering, or navigation . . . They may procure . . . the helpful experience of . . . architects, engineers, mariners, . . . [for the training of soldiers who should], with much exactness and daily muster, serve out the rudiments of their soldiering in all the skill of embattling, marching, encamping, fortifying, besieging and battering." *Se-*

vide shopwork for such training; these mechanical arts were to be learned from a book. Comenius presented in his *Great Didactic* (Latin edition, 1638) a complete intellectual ladder, from a school for young children to advanced research establishments supported by the state, a scheme extraordinarily modern in its breadth and insight. Many of his ideas had been advocated earlier by Bacon, Campanella, Andreä, and others, but the comprehensiveness of his view of the whole field of education and the many friends he made on his endless travels — he taught in twenty cities — created a great audience for his ideas.

Descartes considered the problems of education more incidentally, though his influence in seventeenth-century France

---

lected Prose of John Milton (Oxford, "World's Classics" 1934), pp. 151–52, 156. Cf. O. M. Ainsworth, *Milton on Education* (New Haven, 1928). J. J. Becker, a German, published in 1668 his *Methodus didactica,* in which he projected a system of state schools, one of which was to offer training in handicrafts and was to be joined to a museum of natural history and industry. Spinoza — himself a lens-grinder — in his *Tractatus de intellectus emendatione* (Amsterdam, 1677) called attention to the value of studying mechanics for supplying practical conveniences; Leibniz in his *Projet de l'éducation d'un prince* (1693), suggested the establishment of trade schools for the large class of boys not fitted by nature for intellectual pursuits. There was urgent need for such schools "in order that youths might not be kept back many years uselessly by the flogging of the schoolmaster, and to the great injury of the state . . . ; the youths might have been useful, . . . while now their skill has been delayed by just so many years." L. F. Anderson, ref. 1, pp. 19–20. In his *Nova methodus docendi discandique juris* (Leipzig, 1697), Leibniz recommended the teaching of handicrafts and commercial methods as part of the plan for educating boys between the ages of twelve and eighteen. Cf. A. Krüger, *Leibniz als Pädagog* (Leipzig, 1900) and P. P. Wiener, "Leibniz's Project of a Public Exhibition of Scientific Inventions (1675)," *Journal of the History of Ideas* (April 1940). Leibniz's project differs somewhat from Bacon's *Solomon's House* and from Descartes's museum in that one of its chief purposes was to interest the general public in the possibilities of applied science. Thomas Budd published in 1685, in Philadelphia, a concrete plan for a trade school, *Good Order Established in Pennsylvania and New Jersey in America.* Another interesting plan is that of J. Bellers, *Proposals for Raising a College of Industry of all Useful Trades and Husbandry* (London, 1698; republished by Robert Owen in 1818). Of all these writers Leibniz was the only one read to any extent in France, but he was read by philosophers and scientists rather than by schoolmasters.

was far greater than that of Comenius. In the first chapter of the *Discours de la méthode* (1637) and in others of his writings he attacked the emphasis on training in rhetoric, which was especially prevalent in the Jesuit secondary schools. It would be better if the students spoke only the worst of Breton dialects and knew no Latin but could reason well than if they were trained in this "new scholasticism of words and rhetoric." In training students to reason, the teacher should instruct them to observe and analyze the world about them before they turned to abstract ideas. The inequality of men's minds is due to the difference in their education, not to some social or intellectual predestination. Man's dignity consists in his power of thought, and man's power and capacities need a factual and rational type of education for their development. He believed, moreover, that the vernacular should replace Latin as the language of learning. To further scientific inquiry and also technological improvement he proposed, in a letter written about 1648, the founding of technical museums and schools in Paris. A contemporary who saw the epistle described it as follows: "He persuaded him to found excellent establishments in Paris for the perfectioning of the arts, . . . in the royal college and in other places, which would be open to the public: various large rooms for artisans, each to be devoted to one craft, and to each would be joined a room filled with all the mechanical instruments necessary or useful to the craft taught. Sufficient funds should be furnished not only to conduct experiments, but also to support teachers. . . . These professors should be skilled in mathematics and physics so as to be able to answer all questions. . . . They need not give public lessons except on holidays and Sundays."[15] This is one of the first definite proposals for what about a century and a half

---

[15] R. Descartes, *Projet d'une école des arts et métiers,* made to d'Albert, Treasurer-General of France about 1648, in A. Baillet, *La vie de Monsieur Descartes* (2 vols., Paris, 1691), Vol. 2, pp. 433–34. Cf. J. Boorsh, *État présent des études sur Descartes* (Paris, 1937).

later became the *Conservatoire des arts et métiers* and the first *écoles des arts et métiers* in France.

The immediate educational influence of Descartes was shown in the Oratorian and Jansenist schools, where mathematics, mechanics, and logic were commonly taught, and in the Jesuit schools, where they were introduced into the curricula. His influence was also evident in the growing taste among wealthy scientific *dilettanti* for model making and collecting. One such collection, described in *Recueil d'ouvrages curieux de mathématique et de mécanique ou description du cabinet de M. Grollier de Servière* (Lyons, 1719), was made up of both models and drawings.[16] A number of such collections which came into the hands of the royal government in the later part of the eighteenth century were combined during the Revolution to form the *Conservatoire des arts et métiers*.

The seventeenth century in France saw a remarkable growth of new religious orders, the Jansenists, the Oratorians, and the *Frères des écoles chrétiennes*. All the orders, including the older one of the Jesuits — whose *collèges* gave free instruction and whose students outnumbered those of all the other orders — had to recognize the growing domination of the state, which exercised its control by granting or refusing to grant royal honors and favors. In turn, the teaching orders obtained from the political authorities the defense and enforcement of their ecclesiastical views.[17] Most of them also show in their

---

[16] Wolf, ref. 11, p. 539. Treatises with elaborate descriptions of mechanical processes, illustrated by diagrams, became common from the later Middle Ages on; after the development of printing they became more elaborate. A good idea of their contents in the late sixteenth and seventeenth centuries can be derived from an examination of J. Besson: *Théâtre des instruments mathématiques et mécaniques* (Lyons, 1578). In 1582 Latin and Italian editions of this work appeared, and it became well known all over Europe. On early scientific collections and museums, cf. D. Murray, *Museums, their History and Use* (3 vols., London, 1904), especially Vol. 1.

[17] G. N. Clark, *The Seventeenth Century*, 1st ed. (Oxford, 1929), pp. 301–304.

curricula a greater emphasis on the use of French instead of Latin, on the teaching of science, particularly mathematics and physics, and on the object method of teaching.

The earliest of the new seventeenth-century teaching orders, the Oratorians, was founded in 1611 and soon opened schools for the education of priests. The number of their schools increased rapidly — fifty were established in twenty-five years — and they soon undertook the instruction of children not studying for the priesthood; after the expulsion of the Jesuits in 1762 they took over some of the Jesuit *collèges*. The discipline was mild, French was used instead of Latin for instruction in some of the courses, Latin was taught as literature rather than as mere language — their standard Latin grammar, the *Nouvelle méthode* (1640) of de Gondrem, had all the explanations in French — history and geography were given much attention, and the teaching of mechanics and higher mathematics was superior to that offered in any secondary school in Europe.[18]

[18] The methods of the Oratorians are best studied in Père Lamy, *Entretiens sur les sciences* (1683) and Père Thomassin, *Méthode d'étudier et d'enseigner* (1681). The fundamental purpose of education, according to the Oratorians, was first to acquire knowledge, so as to be able to form correct judgments, and then, finally, to act as a Christian man: "The study of letters is only to form the judgment, and judgment is not worth anything except in regulating the will." G. Compayré, *Histoire critique des doctrines de l'éducation en France,* 5th ed. (2 vols., Paris, 1885), Vol. I, p. 226. Cf. P. J. Lallemand, *Histoire de l'éducation dans l'ancien Oratoire de France* (Paris, 1888). In the eighteenth century the number of Oratorian *collèges* declined; there were about 1100 pupils in 1700 but only 389 in 1753; however, the taking over of some of the Jesuit *collèges* after 1764 arrested the decline of the Oratorians. Cf. H. C. Barnard, *The French Tradition in Education* (Cambridge, 1922), p. 176. There is an excellent map on pp. 300–301 of this work, showing the distribution of the Oratorian *collèges*. For French secondary education in the seventeenth century there is a good general introduction in H. E. Lantoine, *Histoire de l'enseignement secondaire en France au XVIIe siècle* (Paris, 1874): cf. also G. Carré, *L'enseignement secondaire à Troyes du moyen-âge à la Révolution* (Paris, 1888), V. Chauvin, *Histoire des lycées et collèges de Paris* (Paris, 1866), and C. Muteau, *Les écoles et collèges en province depuis les temps les plus reculés jusqu'en 1789* (Dijon, 1882).

The Jansenists founded their first schools in 1643, about half a century after the Jesuits had started their institutions. They used French in the instruction, an important innovation, whereas the Jesuits used Latin and the Oratorians employed both Latin and French. They followed the ideas of Comenius of moving from the known to the unknown, and from the concrete to the abstract. "Reason, not routine" was their ideal. They also held Descartes's idea that the dignity of man lay in his ability to think, though their bias was always in favor of moral education; the founders' original aim was to provide recruits for holy orders. Like the humanists of the sixteenth century, the religious orders of the seventeenth and eighteenth centuries regarded the teaching of science — or any other sort of mere knowledge — as ancillary, as a kind of scaffolding which an engineer puts up to aid in constructing a building. Nowhere in their system, moreover, do they provide for manual training for their pupils, and the Jansenist teaching of mathematics and mechanics was inferior to that in the Jesuit and Oratorian schools.[19] In the few years they existed, the (Jansenist) Port-Royalist schools never had more than a thousand pupils. But the writings of their educational theorists[20] had an important influence in spreading the ideas and attitudes of Descartes and in introducing those of Comenius in France, thus bringing into French educational theory a wider use of French in instruction and a greater emphasis on the concrete in teaching.[21]

[19] Cf. H. C. Barnard, *The Little Schools of Port-Royal* (Cambridge, 1913) and, by the same author, *The Port-Royalists on Education* (Cambridge, 1918).

[20] Cf. the chief Jansenist textbooks: A. Arnauld and P. Nicole, *Le logique* (Paris, 1662); A. Arnauld, *Nouveaux éléments de géométrie* (Paris, 1667); P. Coustel, *Les règles de l'éducation des enfants* (2 vols., Paris, 1687); P. Nicole, *Traité de l'éducation d'un prince,* 2nd ed. (Paris, 1671); and G. Lancelot, series of *Méthodes* (Paris, 1670ff.), for learning different languages.

[21] Nicole says, "Since the intelligence of the child is always very dependent upon his senses, it is necessary, as far as possible, to communicate

The schools of the *Frères des écoles chrétiennes* also used French instead of Latin in instruction and, since their foundation by the Abbé de La Salle in 1688, gave instruction in reading, writing, and mathematics, as well as in manual training, gardening, mechanical and freehand drawing, and metalworking. The boys were also taught business forms, such as receipts for payments, promissory notes, and simple accounting. All this instruction was of an elementary order. In Paris they took over from the priests of Saint-Sulpice (1699) a workroom established to teach poor children to work with their hands, and a continuation school for young artisans, in which mathematics, drawing, and trade subjects were taught.[22] In the course of the eighteenth century the numbers attending their schools increased; by the time of La Salle's death in 1721 they had nine thousand pupils, and by the beginning of the Revolution the number had risen to thirty-six thousand. Many of the students came from the poorer classes in the towns; the majority were taught elementary subjects and a trade. In time special schools were established in which was given more

---

through the senses the information which is given them, and to make it enter not merely by the hearing but by the sight." P. Nicole: *Essais de morale et instructions théologiques* (2 vols., Paris, ed. of 1714), Vol 2, p. 279.

[22] The first French schools to give instruction in manual arts to poor children were for girls, who for centuries had been taught needlework, usually in connection with nunneries. There are frequent references among English, French, and German writers on theology, politics, and economics in the seventeenth century to the necessity of educating the poor; typical is a statement of the Archbishop of Lyons written in 1666, "that schools must be established for the education of the children of the poor, in which, along with the fear of God and good manners, they will be taught to read, write, and figure, by teachers capable also of teaching them things that will put them in a position to work in the arts and professions." Cf. the article, "Frères des écoles chrétiennes," F. Buisson, *Dictionnaire de pédagogique* (2 vols., Paris, 1887); and the study of G. Rigault, *Histoire générale de l'institut des Frères des écoles chrétiennes* (2 vols., Paris, 1937–1939). In the eighteenth century the schools of the *Frères* gave instruction in mechanical processes to adults every Sunday afternoon. E. Bertrand, *L'enseignement technique en Allemagne et en France* (Montpellier, 1913), p. 213.

advanced instruction in geography, hydrography, mechanics, and physics. In contrast with the manual training given in their primary schools, this advanced instruction — as in the projects of Comenius — was largely theoretical.[23]

Much of the experience of the teaching orders in summed up in the Abbé Fleury's *Traité du choix et de la méthode des études,* which he published in 1686 while he was tutor to the children of the Prince de Conti. He attacked the overemphasis of the Jesuits on literary and rhetorical studies and the abstract methods they used in teaching sciences: "what one calls studying physics, is reasoning in the air, as if nature were no longer in the world to be consulted."[24] He refused to recognize Latin as the essential basis of education; still, in spite of many protests, Latin studies continued to dominate the curriculum in the church schools down to the Revolution.[25] Fleury speaks of the necessity of teaching "the knowledge of the arts which use ingenious machines . . . as chemistry, the smelting of metals, glass-making, leathermaking, and dyeing." Like most of the schoolmasters of the later seventeenth century and of the eighteenth, he believed that the study of geometry not only had practical value but would also teach the youths to think. "It forms the mind in general," he wrote, "and strongly fortifies the reason. It accustoms one not to be contented with appearances, to hunt for solid proofs." Fleury also saw that science should be taught apart from philosophy. One purpose of the

[23] The school methods of the *Frères des écoles chrétiennes* are described in Abbé de La Salle, *Conduite des écoles,* written between 1670 and 1695; a useful edition is that brought out by J. Moronval (Paris, 1838). Cf. F. Laudet, *La Salle, instituteur des instituteurs* (Tours, 1929). There is an English version of La Salle's *Conduite des écoles,* ed. by F. de La Fontainerie (New York, 1935). The work of the *Frères des écoles chrétiennes* in helping the poor to aid themselves is paralleled by the work of Pietist reformers in the German states.

[24] Compayré, ref. 18, Vol. 1, p. 373.

[25] F. Vial, *Trois siècles d'histoire de l'enseignement secondaire* (Paris, 1936), pp. 8–10, and D. Mornet, *Les origines intellectuelles de la Révolution française* (Paris, 1933), p. 328.

education of a youth should be to develop him as a gentleman; but more important than that is to train his intellect. He saw clearly that new types of instruction were necessary for the training of businessmen and "practicioners" (which includes engineers) and others "who have no need of Latin."[26]

Besides the *collèges* of the teaching orders, a large number of small academies for young gentlemen were run by private individuals. These had been started in the sixteenth century, on Italian models, and by the middle of the seventeenth century were scattered all over France. Such a school had only a few pupils. From seven to fourteen years the boys were taught mathematics, languages, history, and geography; after fourteen the instruction included work in law, mathematics, mechanics, and the principles of fortification, but apparently much of this was sacrificed to instruction in horsemanship and dancing. Often the pupils entered these schools only after they had completed a course in a *collège;* Richelieu was trained in one of these. The English diarist, John Evelyn, traveling in France in 1644, speaks of visiting such a private school and of seeing the teaching in fencing, dancing, and music. The curriculum, he adds, contained "something in fortifications and mathematics." These private schools never had either the uniformity of organization or the number of pupils of the schools run by the religious orders. Private schools of this type were often aided by the royal or the municipal government, especially to help support the riding stables they had to maintain. Some of the pupils in these academies later entered the army; indeed these schools, where emphasis was on training gentlemen for military careers, are ancestors of the state military schools of the eighteenth century. This type of school declined with the

---

[26] A. Dartigues, *Le traité . . . de l'Abbé Fleury* (Paris, 1921), pp. 232–33. Lamy, the Oratorian, wrote, "There is no study better fitted to train judgment than geometry. . . . It furnishes models of clarity and order . . . it accustoms the mind insensibly to reason well." Compayré, ref. 18, Vol. 1, p. 237. On Fleury, besides Dartigues' edition of the *Traité,* cf. L. Genay: *Un pédagogue oublié du XVIIᵉ siècle* (Paris, 1879).

founding of the *École militaire* in 1751; there were eight in Paris in the first half of the eighteenth century, but only three were left by 1780.[27]

3. Some Scientific Textbooks in the Schools of Seventeenth-Century France

The teaching of mathematics had been greatly furthered in the sixteenth century by the work of Petrus Ramus (Pierre de la Ramée, 1515–1572). A humanist, Ramus had insisted that mathematics was "the first of the liberal arts without which all other philosophy is blind." He wrote some excellent textbooks and at his death left an endowment for a chair of pure and applied mathematics at the University of Paris. The steady improvement in the teaching of mathematics in the French higher schools dates chiefly from his extraordinary work as writer, teacher, and propagandist.

The improvement in the instruction in mathematics and

[27] John Evelyn: *Diary,* ed. by W. Bray (London, n.d.), pp. 56, 64; G. Hanotaux et de La Force: *Histoire du Cardinal de Richelieu* (Paris, n.d.), Vol. 4, p. 378, and A. de Pluvinel, *L'instruction du roy en l'exercise de monter à cheval* (Paris, 1625). De Pluvinel (p. 206) concludes his discussion of such schools thus, "Here then, sir, are the best methods I know for suppressing the vices that prevail among the nobility of your kingdom, powerful remedies to cure the pernicious maladies which have robbed this monarchy of so much courage." The author was trained in such a small gentleman's school in Italy. The best discussion of these private academies, especially those that emphasized military training, is in de la Roche, "Les académies d'équitation sous l'ancien régime," *Revue des études historiques* (1920). The history of one such academy from the early seventeenth century to the Revolution is given in P. Reigneaud, "L'Académie royale de Riom," *Mémoires de l'académie des sciences, belles-lettres et arts de Clermont-Ferrand* (1881); cf. also, L. Picard, *Origines de l'école de Cavalerie,* (2 vols., Saumur, 1889). For the influence of these academies on English education, cf. J. W. Adamson, *Pioneers of Modern Education 1600–1700* (Cambridge, 1905), Chap. 10, and Foster Watson, *The Beginnings of the Teaching of Modern Subjects in England* (London, 1909), pp. xxxii–xxxvi; and for their influence on German schools, cf. F. Paulsen, *Geschichte des gelehrten Unterrichts auf den deutschen Schulen und Universitäten,* 2nd ed. (2 vols., Leipzig, 1896), Vol. 1, book III.

mechanics in French schools continued steadily during the seventeenth century. In the vague and indefinite science of the period there was great need of introducing some exact standards, which was precisely the service that mathematics could render. Moreover, in improving technical skills, mathematics was of first importance; good maps, accurately adjusted instruments and machines, artillery with accurate and uniform calibers, and many other sorts of technical apparatus either themselves involved higher mathematics in use or could be constructed only through a familiarity with mathematics made possible by improved teaching. In all these changes the influence of Descartes continued and augmented that of Ramus.

In the field of technics, Descartes showed clearly the mathematical nature of physical processes and laid the foundation for the extension of standards of mathematical measurement. Although the new mathematics and mechanics had to make their way gradually and alongside the older scholastic and humanist studies, the very substantial progress in mathematical teaching was a great advance beyond the late medieval scholastic education and also beyond the humanistic curricula of the Renaissance. Such changes were a fundamental prerequisite for the later growth of higher technical education.

The standard introductory work in mathematics used in the French schools of the seventeenth century was a volume of three hundred pages, entitled *Institutio totium mathematicæ*. It opened with the four rules of arithmetic, fractions, and proportions; geometry had then two parts: an elementary, theoretical set of the propositions of Euclid, and a more extended section on practical or applied geometry which included methods of measuring distances, heights, plane surfaces, and solids. A final section was devoted to astronomy, theoretical and applied, a mixture of the systems of Aristotle, Ptolemy, and Tycho Brahe, the Copernican hypothesis being rejected.[28] Another

---

[28] C. de Rochemontieux, *Un collège des Jésuites au XVIIe et XVIIIe siècles, le collège Henri IV de la Fléche* (4 vols., Le Mans, 1889), Vol. 4, pp. 36–49;

typical textbook in French was that of Père J. François, the Jesuit teacher of Descartes, *L'arithmétique et la géométrie pratique, c'est-à-dire l'art de compter toute sorte de nombres avec la plume et les jetons, et l'art de mesurer . . . toute sorte de lignes, de surfaces et de corps et particulièrement d'arpenter les terres et d'en contre-lever les plans et ensuite de faire des cartes géographiques . . . hydrographiques . . . typographiques.*[29] The use of textbooks of this sort in the schools of the various teaching orders of seventeenth-century France shows that instruction in mathematics, mechanics, and the simple principles of engineering was common, and was quite beyond the offerings of the earlier schools.[30]

---

also R. Descartes: *Discours de la méthode,* ed. by E. Gilson (2nd ed., Paris, 1926), pp. 129–30. On Ramus, cf. G. Boissier, "La réforme des études au XVIe siècle," *Revue des deux mondes* (Dec. 1882), and F. P. Graves, *Ramus* (New York, 1912).

[29] Père François also wrote *La science des eaux qui explique en quatre parties, leur transformation, communication, mouvement et mélange, avec les arts de conduire les eaux et mesurer la grandeur tant des eaux que des terres,* etc. (Rennes, 1653). Another commonly used textbook of mathematics and mechanics was the work of another Jesuit, Père Bourdin: *Le cours de mathématiques, contenant en cent figures une idée générale de toutes les parties de cette science, l'usage de ses instruments, diverses manières de prendre les distances, l'art d'arpenter, divers moyens de lever et tracer un plan, la réduction des figures par les triangles de rapports, la trigonométrie, les fortifications regulières et irregulières, leurs dehors, profil, élévation, et sciographie. Contenant de plus un traité de l'usage du globe terrestre,* etc. (3rd ed., Paris, 1661).

[30] The *Ratio studiorum* (1599) of the Jesuits emphasized the practical side of mathematics: "Let him [the professor of mathematics] explain in class to the students of physics . . . the elements of Euclid, in which explanations . . . let him add something of geography or of the spheres or of other matters." *Monumenta Germanica paedagogica* (Berlin, 1897), Vol. 5, p. 348. The high regard in which the Jesuit teaching was held is neatly stated by Bacon: "As for the pedagogical part, the shortest rule would be, 'Consult the Jesuits,' for nothing better has been put into practice." Francis Bacon: *De dignatate et augmentis scientiarium* (London, 1623), Book VI, Chap. 4. Had Bacon lived to know the schools of the French teaching orders of the seventeenth century, he would have been even more impressed by their curricula and their methods of teaching.

The material in the textbooks came partly from Euclid and partly from ancient works like Aristotle's *Mechanical Questions,* his *Physics,* and his *Treatise on the Heavens.* Galileo's law of falling bodies, Descartes's and Leibniz's theories of force, Descartes's theory of optics and his analytical geometry, the hydrostatic laws of Torricelli and Pascal, Pascal's principles of the calculation of probabilities, and Leibniz's differential calculus — all found their way into the textbooks during the course of the seventeenth century. Practical descriptions of the wheel, the pulley, the wedge, the screw, the lever, and the balance were given; new instruments and machines were also described: the pendulum, the calculating machine, the telescope, the barometer, and the thermometer. The education given to Louis XIV about the middle of the seventeenth century included, besides the old trivium and quadrivium, the "mechanical arts": agriculture, war, architecture, surgery, weaving, and the art of piloting a ship; the instruction of the Grand Dauphin, supervised by Bossuet, included fortification and the drawing of machines.[31]

The tendency was to drop the general metaphysical implications and to teach the more mathematical side of mechanics, defined by one seventeenth-century writer as "the art of making machines draw, push or carry bodies, which are beyond human force," by another as "the art of forcing bodies as

[31] C. Fremont, "Origines de la poulie, du treuil, de l'engrenage, de la roue de voiture," *Bulletin de la société d'encouragement pour l'industrie nationale,* 2 articles (Paris, 1921). C. Fremont, "Évolution des méthodes et des appareils employés pour l'essai des matériaux," *Comptes rendues, Congrès international des méthodes d'essai des matériaux de construction* (Paris, 1900). On technical methods, cf. also three works by L. Olschki: *Die Literatur der Technik und der angewandten Wissenschaften vom Mittelalter bis zur Renaissance* (Leipzig, 1919), *Bildung und Wissenschaft im Zeitalter der Renaissance in Italien* (Leipzig, 1922); and *Galilei und seine Zeit* (Halle, 1927). Concerning the education of Bourbon princes, cf. H. C. Barnard, *The French Tradition in Education* (Cambridge, 1922), pp. 132–33, and H. Druon, *Histoire de l'éducation des princes dans la maison des Bourbons de France* (2 vols., Paris, 1897).

far as it is possible to act against their nature," by a third as "the science which examines the property of movements." It was also said that "in the movements one must consider the mass, speed, direction . . . , and the amount of the movement." The textbooks of mechanics, on the other hand, used fewer concrete illustrations of principles than had those of the sixteenth century, though some still contained descriptions of the methods used in setting up the great obelisk in front of Saint Peter's in Rome, those employed in constructing the Pont Neuf in Paris (finished in 1604), as well as the methods of making clocks, printing machines, and other mechanisms. As many of the students were young aristocrats who intended to enter the army, such training proved very practical. The Oratorians gave the best intruction in physics, algebra, geometry, plane and spherical trigonometry, analytical geometry, calculus, and mechanics.[32] It was from such courses that the teaching of engineering in the military schools of the eighteenth century derived.

The seventeenth and eighteenth centuries also saw the publication of many descriptions of technical processes connected with engineering, military, naval, and manufacturing problems; many of these books, pamphlets, and articles were subsidized by the state. Few of them were probably ever used in the secondary schools, but as the technical school developed they were studied there, and among skilled workers they formed an important medium of technical education. Among the most interesting of these practical manuals are those written by A. Bosse, especially his *La pratique du trait à preuves du M. Desargues, Lyonnais, pour la coupe de pierre en architecture*. The Desargues referred to in this title was a distinguished mathematician whose work laid the foundation

---

[32] F. E. Farrington, *French Secondary Schools* (New York, 1910), p. 13. Cf. also P. Boutroux, "L'enseignement de la mécanique en France au XVIIe siècle," *Isis* 4 (1922), pp. 276–94; this article contains many interesting details.

of synthetic descriptive geometry, a science whose implications were not developed till the time of Gaspard Monge more than a century later.[33]

4. The Economists and Statesmen

The writers on economics had a much clearer conception of the need for industrial and technical training than had the professional educationalists. As early as the fifteenth century they had begun to launch attacks on the indifference of the French state to the developing commercial and industrial activity of the towns; the doctrines of mercantilism had begun to take form.[34] France — so the argument ran — is endowed with extraordinary natural resources and economic advantages, and yet the French, through ignorance, poor management, laziness, and carelessness, allow themselves to be dependent on other nations not only for luxuries but even for many of the necessities of life. This is all wrong for a country that is the

[33] L. F. Maury, *L'Ancienne académie des sciences* (2d ed., Paris, 1864); D. N. Lehmer, *An Elementary Course in Synthetic Projective Geometry* (Boston, 1917), especially Chap. 10; H. T. Pledge, *Science since 1500* (London, 1939), pp. 74–75. Cf. also A. Blum, *Abraham Bosse et la société française au dix-septième siècle* (Paris, 1924).

[34] "Mercantilism . . . was not an abstract entity like the idea of divine-right monarchy, nor was it a well-knit system of economic philosophy with the parts fitting into each other and properly subordinated to the whole, such as Marxian socialism . . . [It] is, rather, the name applied by later students to an agglomeration of more or less related practices, theories, beliefs and hypotheses. . . . The syllogistic exposition current today are fictions of over-simplification created for pedagogic purposes. . . . Progressing from the scattered concepts of the fifteenth and sixteenth centuries mercantilism achieved in the early seventeenth century the status of an organized though some-what amorphous body of postulates, convictions, and precepts." C. W. Cole, *French Mercantilist Doctrines before Colbert* (New York, 1931), pp. 213–14. The most useful books on French mercantilism are two elaborate studies by P. Boissonade, *Le socialisme d'état 1453–1661* (Paris, 1927) and *Colbert 1661–1683* (Paris, 1932); C. W. Cole, *op. cit.*, also *Colbert and a Century of French Mercantilism* (2 vols., New York, 1939), and *French Mercantilism 1683–1700* (New York, 1942 and 1965). Cf. also J. U. Nef, *Industry and Government in France and England 1540–1640* (Philadelphia, 1940).

most populous in Europe and which is coming to command the greatest military and diplomatic power. The state must be strengthened by curbing feudal rights and municipal privileges and must bring the whole of France under a centralized government with a strong administration and a powerful army and navy. This government should then devote itself to increasing the national wealth, primarily by increasing the supply of gold and silver. To accomplish this, production must be greatly increased, imports must be kept down, colonies developed, and national needs supplied with articles manufactured at home. Importation of foreign luxuries should be reduced through tariffs and through sumptuary laws, and finally — by putting everyone to some useful employment — even the lowest and the poorest classes should be made useful to the state. France would become a perfect hive of industry. This meant the fullest co-operation of the state with industry and commerce; every economic activity was to be under state direction. There was nothing the government might not do to promote national wealth; every expedient was held legitimate. To increase both the quality and the quantity of French manufactures, especially of silk and woolen cloth, tapestry, lace, ribbon, furniture, glassware, and metalwork, the state must not only protect these industries by tariffs but it must go further and develop, alongside the traditional system of apprenticeship, some better methods of training workers. The theorists gradually came to see that this was to be accomplished best by the extension of state manufactures and manufactures under state patronage, and by the creation of new ones, on none of which the guild regulations would be binding and in which the training of the workers could be under the direction of the most skilled artists and craftsmen to be found in Europe.

Among the economic theorists the role to be played by technical education is always a minor theme. In view of their concern for improving and extending French manufactures, it is curious that they were so slow in conceiving the benefits that might be derived from new types of instruction. Laffemas, the earliest of the French economic writers who attempted to work the scattered mercantilist ideas into a complete system, proposed the organization of *Chambres des manufactures* which should instruct youth in "sciences" and teach them to study scientific treatises.[35] In his *Économies royales* (published in 1638, long after he was out of office), the Duc de Sully, who had been the principal finance minister of Henry IV, proposed an industrial museum like that suggested by Descartes; there should be set up in the Louvre a collection of models of machines used in industries. A. de Montchrétien, who had traveled in Holland, Germany, and Switzerland, proposed the establishment in France of the sort of elementary industrial training which he had seen abroad. Schools, he believed, should be organized in every province in France "to instruct the poor in handicrafts, and train them in workshops in the most essential elements of the trade; . . . each craftsman would thus be formed in the excellent practice of the [industrial] arts and crafts, according to his natural capacity."[36] Such work schools for children and workhouses for the unemployed would greatly increase the productivity of French industry.

Cardinal de Richelieu declared in his *Testament politique* that trade schools were more important to France than schools

---

[35] On Laffemas, cf. Cole, *French Mercantilist Doctrines before Colbert,* Chap. 2; H. Hauser, "Le système social de Laffemas," *Revue bourguignonne 12,* pp. 113–31; and P. Mongrédien, "Laffemas," *Revue des questions historiques* (1928). Laffemas lists a series of the products of Italy and the Low Countries that the French should produce at home: Milanese gold thread; Piedmontese steel; Turkish carpets, Bruges satins, Flemish tiles, Italian glass, and tapestries, and linens in the style of Flanders and Brabant (Cole, *op. cit.,* p. 103).

[36] A. de Montchrétien, *Traité de l'économie politique,* ed. by F. Funck-Brentano (Paris, 1889), pp. 27, 38, 102, and 119. Montchrétien also called attention (p. 119) to the superior tools and machinery used in Dutch manufactures. On Montchrétien, cf. A. Vène, *Montchrétien et le nationalisme économique* (Paris, 1923).

of liberal arts.[37] He founded at Langres a school for children orphaned by wars; the instruction included mathematics, theories of construction, and practical training in several types of cloth and shoe making. By 1640 the municipalities had opened a number of such workshops for the training of the pauperized lower classes near certain poorhouses in Paris and in the provinces. In 1657 letters patent instituted a trade school for young men in the parish af Saint-Germain-des-Prés in Paris. Scattered efforts of this sort continued to be made down to the French Revolution, but only in the nineteenth century was any serious attempt made to develop such training on a scale sufficient to meet the problem.

The growing interest in business produced a number of treatises on wholesale and retail merchandising; most interesting of these is Savary's *Parfait négociant* (1st ed., 1675). There is no profession, he declares in speaking of business, "where intelligence and good sense are more necessary." A parent who has a child he wishes trained for business should see that, beginning at the age of seven or eight, he be taught writing, arithmetic, accounting, and the living languages: Italian, Spanish, and German. The boy should also learn to know not only the customs of other peoples but the merchandise to be found abroad and what are the products desired by foreign countries. It is useless to teach boys Latin, grammar, rhetoric, and philosophy. If France has few businessmen, he says, it is because she has too many classical *collèges*. Savary complains that the French nobility, unlike the aristocracies of Italy and England, take little interest in commercial undertakings. The greatest weakness of the French merchant is his ignorance. Most of the book discusses in a detailed fashion commercial law and the actual methods of wholesale and retail merchandising, and the author tries to solve the innumerable problems of the

---

[37] Richelieu, *Testament politique* (The Hague, 1740), p. 129. On Richelieu, cf. G. von Carlow, *Richelieu als merkantilischer Wirtschaftspolitiker und der Begriff des Staatsmerkantilismus* (Jena, 1929).

businessman. The whole treatise is written in a lively and attractive style, and the work had an enormous vogue. Besides many French editions which appeared down to 1800, it was translated into Italian, Dutch, English, and German.[38]

More significant than these theories were the efforts of the government to stimulate French industry and commerce through the development of various types of state industries. These date from the second half of the fifteenth century, when the royal government became active in the economic field; mercantilism in practice thus antedates the theoretical elaboration of its doctrines. Gradually a large number of state industries and industries receiving state patronage were set up; these were granted important privileges and subsidies and were protected from the competition of the guilds. In these organizations all sorts of new tools and improved technical processes were introduced, and most of them included the training of skilled workers. Such training resembled that given by the guildmasters to their apprentices; it was almost entirely practical and was largely based on rule-of-thumb methods. It differed, however, from the older industrial training given to apprentices in that it allowed for more experimentation in industrial processes. The purpose of the royal government in such enterprises was to raise the quality of French manufacturers toward the high level of excellence attained by the Flemish and Italian craftsmen of the later Middle Ages and

[38] H. Hauser, "Le parfait négociant de Savary" in his *Les débuts du capitalisme* (Paris, 1927), pp. 266–308. The best introduction to the history of business education is E. Gottmann, *Die Wirtschaftsoberschule und ihre Entwicklung* (Eisfeld, 1932); for England, cf. F. Watson: *The Beginnings of the Teaching of Modern Subjects in England* (London, 1909), pp. xxxvi–xlii, xlix–l. Business education had developed in Italy and Flanders in the later Middle Ages; cf. H. Pirenne, "L'instruction des marchands au moyen âge," *Annales d'histoire économique et sociale,* Vol. 1, 13–28; A. Evans, ed., *Pergolotti's La Pratica della Mercatura* (Cambridge, 1936); A. Sapori, "La Cultura del Mercante Medievale Italiano," *Rivista di Storia Economica,* 1937; and E. Weber. "Literaturgeschichte der Handelsbetriebslehre" in Ergänzungsheft XLIX of the *Zeitschrift für die gesamte Staatswissenschaft,* 1914.

the Renaissance. As a result of these efforts, much of the work in the French state manufactures, from the later fifteenth century on, was directed by able artists who designed furniture, fabrics, and many other types of *articles de luxe* as well as carried on their own work in sculpture and painting. For this reason the new styles of the Renaissance penetrated French industries very rapidly, affecting not only painting, sculpture, and architecture but also the slightest details of furniture, fabrics, and costume.

The best of the manufactories under royal patronage were in the shops of the Louvre, which lasted until the Revolution. J.-B. Colbert (1619–1683), Louis XIV's chief finance minister, reorganized another great center, the Gobelins, which was run directly by the state. Here, as in the workshops of the Louvre, were manufactured a multitude of different objects, including furniture, tapestries, fabrics, especially fine types of silk and woolen figured cloth, fine chandeliers and hardware, and glassware. All these things were intended for use in the many royal residences or as gifts to be made by the king. In the same way, Colbert brought about remarkable improvements in the shipbuilding trades. As a result of all these activities, which affected thousands of skilled workers but which antedate any real technical education in a modern sense, a great technical revival took place in France. The stimulus given to French industries, especially in the luxury manufactures — lace, hosiery, ribbons, silk cloth, woolens, clocks, furniture, faience, and tapestry — between the end of the Hundred Years' War and the Revolution (1453–1789) pushed French manufactures into the leading position in Europe. Ever since that time France has commanded the most important place in the world's luxury trades.[39]

[39] P. Boissonnade, *Le socialisme d'état, conclusions,* pp. 151–52, 309–10. Cf. Cole, *Colbert and a Century of French Mercantilism,* especially Vol. 1, Chap. 6, on general ideas of Colbert, and Vol. 2, Chaps. 10–12, on manufactories and their regulation. Besides improving the quality of manufactures, the industries under state patronage were also to alleviate unemployment

The reforming efforts of Colbert from 1661 to 1683 show clearly that he realized the necessity for extending and improving technical instruction; especially did he believe that the intellectual and artistic elite must be more intimately associated with industry. Colbert wanted to accomplish rapidly, by new types of training, what had been achieved slowly in Italian and Flemish industry under the old guild system. Besides the practical training given to skilled workers in the French state manufactures, the government established academies for the teaching of art and design. Letters patent of 1648 and 1655 had founded the *Académie royale de peinture* with twelve professors, each of whom had charge of the school for a month. The faculty soon included Lebrun, Philippe de Champagne, and Lemoyne. In 1665 Colbert organized the *École de Rome* for twelve students, supported for three years by the French government; they were taught arithmetic, geometry, and drawing. On their return they were employed

and to convert the masses to a more industrious attitude. In 1603 Henry IV declared, "The establishment of [industrial] arts is an easy . . . remedy for ridding the kingdom of the many vices which idleness produces." A few years later Montchrétien wrote, "Work and industry are the restraints against . . . civil war," and Richelieu declared, "The people is a mule which indulges itself in idleness." E. Levasseur, *Histoire des classes ouvrières et de l'industrie en France avant 1789* (2nd ed., 2 vols., Paris, 1900), Vol. 2, p. 174. Cf. also Bellers, ref. 14, pp. 29–32. Eight manufactories under royal patronage were established from the reign of Louis XI through that of Henry III; forty were created by Henry IV; there were 113 under Colbert, 243 in the first half of the eighteenth century, 158 in the period 1753–1789 (Levasseur, *op. cit.,* Vol. 2, pp. 175–77). Levasseur (Vol. 2, p. 239) gives an excellent summary account of the principal methods of administering these royal manufactories. The two works of Boissonnade and Cole's *Colbert* (ref. 34) give in elaborate detail the history of these industries—both those under royal patronage and those, like the Gobelins, the Savonnerie, and the *Imprimerie royale,* which were run by the state. On the state industries and those under royal patronage during the eighteenth century, cf. also Levasseur, *op. cit.,* Vol. 2, pp. 519–21; H. Sée, *L'évolution commerciale et industrielle de la France sous l'ancien régime* (Paris, 1925), pp. 255–60; G. Fagniez, "L'Industrie en France sous Henri IV," *Revue historique 23* (1883), and Germain Martin, *La grande industrie sous le règne de Louis XIV* (Paris, 1899), pp. 102ff.

by the state as architects, painters, sculptors, and engravers. In 1676 the *Académie de peinture et de sculpture* (a reorganization of the *Académie royale de peinture*) was placed over the *École de Rome*. Colbert organized several small industrial museums, and in 1675 he sketched a plan for a reform of the curriculum in secondary schools, in which he introduced the study of geography and history and the "sciences employed in commerce."

In 1671 the *Académie royale d'architecture* was founded.[40] In the Middle Ages the mason was often also architect, contractor, and foreman, but from the fifteenth century on there was a growing tendency to distinguish between the mere workman and the architect or the engineer. Moreover, the introduction of Italian Renaissance architecture in the early sixteenth century and the revival of Vitruvius' treatise on architecture had led to an adherence to the new classical rules and proportions. These could be studied either in Italy or through printed books, plans, and elevations. The older methods by which the builders worked — ground plans and occasionally models[41] — did not change greatly, but to introduce the neo-

---

[40] The *Académie de peinture et de sculpture* and the *Académie d'architecture* were installed in the Louvre and the Palais-Royal from 1692 to 1807, in which year they were moved to the *Institut de France*. By 1816 they had been combined and reorganized as the *Académie des beaux arts*. Between 1819 and 1830 their various departments were transferred to the present buildings on the Rue Bonaparte. E. Müntz, *Guide de l'école nationale des beaux arts* (Paris, 1889), p. 3; cf. L. Vitet, *L'académie royale de peinture et de sculpture,* 2nd ed. (Paris, 1880), with essential documents; H. Lapauze, *Histoire de l'académie de France à Rome* (2 vols., Paris, 1924), and N. Pevsner, *Academies of Art, Past and Present* (Cambridge, 1940). In Boissonnade, *Colbert,* pp. 25–26, there is a comprehensive bibliography of the whole subject of Colbert's relations to technical education; this should be used in connection with the general bibliography, pp. 371–384. On the place of the architect and the *Académie d'architecture,* cf. M. S. Briggs, *The Architect in History* (Oxford, 1927), Chap. 6, which contains many interesting details and an excellent bibliography, though it fails to emphasize the continuity of medieval architectural methods with those of the Renaissance; cf. also Wolf, ref. 11, Chap. 21.

[41] J. S. C. Bridge, *A History of France from the Death of Louis XI*

classical features of design there was required a somewhat different technical and artistic training than that of the medieval master-mason, who had served well enough so long as style and construction methods had remained traditional. At the same time a few original minds were pushing out to discover new structural principles. Leonardo da Vinci was among the first to go beyond the traditional, late-medieval handling of structural problems. He carried on experimental investigations on the behavior of materials under stress, particularly on the relation of size to the strength of beams and columns. He concluded from his experiments that the maximum load that could be supported by a column of given height was proportional to the cube of its diameter, and that the carrying capacity of a beam of given section varied inversely with its span.[42] Galileo carried this type of investigation much further and, unlike Leonardo, published his results, though not until 1638, in his *Discourses concerning two new sciences,* in large part a study of the measurement of the resistance of materials to fracture.[43]

Before 1550, French professional architects had begun to replace both Italian architects and native master-builders. One of the earliest important French Renaissance architects was Philibert de l'Orme, who began his training with his father, a builder in Lyons. Later, he tells us, he devoted himself "to new inventions, consulting the most learned men in Europe in geometry and the sciences necessary to architecture," and he went to Italy to measure ancient buildings.[44] Besides buildings,

---

(Oxford, 1936), Vol. 5, p. 219, and C. Enlart, *Manuel d'archéologie française,* 2nd ed. (4 vols., Paris, 1919), Vol. 1, pp. 66–81.

[42] Wolf, ref. 11, p. 467. Cf. P. Duhem, *Études sur Leonardo da Vinci* (3 vols., Paris, 1906–1913); I. D. Hart, *The Mechanical Investigations of Leonardo da Vinci* (London, 1925); and C. Fremont, *Évolution des méthodes et des appareils employés pour l'essai des matériaux de construction* (Paris, 1900).

[43] Excellent edition by H. Crew and A. de Salvio (New York, 1933). The first French translation of Vitruvius, by J. Martin, appeared in 1547.

[44] De l'Orme tells us how, in measuring buildings in Italy, "I did with

these professional French architects designed parks and gardens and planned whole sections of towns and cities; thus the new *Académie royale d'architecture* became as much a school of engineering as of the fine arts. The purpose of Colbert's *Académie* was to extend the study of sound principles of classical architectural design and of practical construction and to teach these to young men who entered as students. It was also to act as an advisory body on state buildings, on canal, road, and bridge construction, on fortifications, on the exploitation of mines, and on the technical processes used in industry.

---

great labor . . . and expenses . . . not only in ladders and ropes, but also in excavating foundations," study the principles of Roman architecture (Briggs, ref. 40, 206). Vasari's *Lives,* Bohn edition (London, 1907), shows that the Renaissance architect was supposed to spend years measuring and drawing ancient buildings, and studying carefully all the methods of construction used. "Architecture," says Vasari, "is to be adequately pursued only by such men as possess an excellent judgment, a good knowledge of design, or extensive practice in some such occupation as painting, sculpture, or woodwork, and have been thereby led to the habit of measuring figures, edifices, and bodies of similar character . . . such as . . . columns, cornices, and basements, and to examine all these in their relative proportions, even to the most minute particulars." (Vasari, Vol. 3, p. 458.) Again, in speaking of Brunelleschi, Vasari says he studied antique buildings so that "he took no time either to eat or sleep; his every thought was of architecture, which was then extinct. I mean the good old manner, and not the Gothic and barbarous one, which was much practised at that period." (Vol. 1, p. 423.) There was in all this, says Briggs, "no hard line between 'science' and 'art': mathematics, mechanics and geometry were an essential part of the architect's equipment, and even in his researches into antiquity he was as much concerned with the composition of Roman stucco and the bending of Roman masonry as with the proportions of cornices and the details of mouldings." (Briggs, ref. 40, p. 148.) For further details about the training of Italian architects, particularly in the later, neoclassical period, cf. G. Giovannoni and P. d'Achiardi, "Architectural education in Italy in the past," *Proceedings of the International Congress on Architectural Education* (Royal Institute of British Architects, London, 1925). There is a list of the principal French artists and architects of the Renaissance, with some indication of their training, in Enlart, ref. 41, Vol. 1 pp. 791–96. A fundamental work for the whole subject is W. B. Parsons, *Engineers and Engineering in the Renaissance* (Baltimore, 1940). Cf. also the important article by E. Zilsel, "The Sociological Roots of Science," *The Am. Jour. of Sociology,* 1942.

Within a few years after its foundation it gave to a small group of apprentice architects courses in applied mechanics, hydraulics, stone cutting, and civil and military engineering. It rarely had more than fifty students, but in organizing such a curriculum the *Académie d'architecture* takes rank as the first higher technical school in France. By the end of the seventeenth century most important buildings were designed by professional architects, though in 1665 a façade for the Louvre was designed by a medical man, Claude Perrault. The practice of holding competitions for designs had become common by the latter part of the seventeenth century.

The training given in the art academies in the end improved the quality of French architecture, engraving, and manufactures. To hasten this advance many of the younger men trained in the academies were employed in the Savonnerie and the Gobelins tapestry works, in the mint, the royal press, and the royal manufactory in the Louvre. The teachers trained in the art academies acted as instructors for the apprentices in the state manufactories. At the Gobelins works, Lebrun and a staff of instructors gave a six-year course of theoretical and practical training in design and manufacture. In 1676 Colbert proposed to establish art schools in the provinces, modeled after two opened by the government at Lyons and Reims in the later sixteenth century. The direct result of Colbert's effort led only to the establishment of an art school in Bordeaux (1688); in the eighteenth century the royal and municipal governments set up a number of such schools.

In order further to stimulate interest in improving industrial techniques, a series of new royal institutions was established. The universities were hostile or indifferent to science, which had to depend on private or on state aid. "The theological spirit," says Caullery, "dominated the universities until the Revolution, and in France it is not to them that one must look, before the nineteenth century, for the sources of scientific progress. This is one of the principal characteristics of the history of science in France."[45] When Rollin became rector of the University of Paris in 1694, he made the most vigorous efforts to reform the backward ways of the faculties, but to little avail. The old lethargy continued through the eighteenth century. In 1704 the professors were obliged "to teach nothing contrary to the faith or the decrees of the councils." In 1713 professors suspected of Jansenism were expelled. A few years later, when they were allowed to return, they persecuted their former oppressors with the same stupid bitterness. A satire of the time presents Truth trying to gain admission to the Sorbonne. She is turned away with the advice, "Flee or I shall accuse you of impiety."[46]

Science, neglected by the universities, got aid from the state. The *Académie des sciences,* established in 1666, gave subsidies for scientific work and stimulated publication; in 1665 the

[45] M. Caullery, *La science française depuis le XVII* siècle* (Paris, 1933), p. 13. The interest in science, in spite of the hostility of the universities, was nevertheless great; as the Englishman, Thomas Sprat said in 1667, the interest in science was so strong "that there seems to be nothing more in vogue throughout Europe." H. J. Laski, *The Rise of Liberalism* (New York, 1936), p. 151.

[46] Preserved Smith, *History of Modern Culture* (2 vols., New York, 1930–1934), Vol. 2, pp. 408–09; cf. C. Jourdain, *Histoire de l'université de Paris au XVII* et au XVIII* siècles* (2 vols., Paris, 1862–1866). In spite of the indifference and hostility of some of the universities, science — at centers like the Universities of Leyden and Cambridge and among scientists who enjoyed state patronage — made great advances in the seventeenth century. "Physics before the seventeenth century," says Rosenberger, "knew only the methods of 'natural philosophy'; . . . experiment was used in special instances to measure relations of magnitude of phenomena; an individual inventor might try to win from nature her secrets through experiments, but a systematic questioning of nature — observation as a method in physics — was not known . . . There was still in 'natural philosophy' something of Platonic revery, of the 'idea,' and of scorn of matter. The student of 'natural philosophy' thought it beneath his dignity to busy himself like an artisan, outside of his study, and was proud to live in the realm of the spirit. Thus it happened that although experiments were made and cleverly made, yet science was little affected by them. It was the task of the seventeenth century to introduce experiment into science." F. Rosenberger, *Die Geschichte der Physik* (2 vols., Brunswick, 1882–1890), Vol. 1, p. 3.

Journal des savants was founded with state aid. The state employed some of the Academy members to study industrial processes and to recommend changes. The *Académie des sciences,* like the Royal Society in London, was a great clearing house for ideas, and in the course of time furnished a series of important books and teachers in all the fields of science. While not primarily concerned with technical education nor always with the practical applications of science, it proved to exert ever since a first-rate influence on both.

The *Jardin du roi,* reorganized in 1671, besides conducting research and giving courses in botany and pharmacy, also offered instruction in drawing and in designing for fabrics. Two great art collections were opened to the public, one of painting and sculpture in the Louvre and one of prints and engravings in Colbert's own house on the Rue Vivienne. A collection of machines and models of machines—an idea earlier suggested by Descartes and by Sully and put into practice by a number of private individuals — was set up in association with the king's library. Colbert does not seem to have conceived the idea of giving courses in connection with these museums of art and of industry. He did, however, have printed at state expense a number of treatises on painting (by Lebrun and Perrault), on cloth and furniture making, on silk manufacture (Isnard), on dyeing (Albo and Perrot), an excellent study by Desargues on methods of stonecutting, and a series of works on architecture. Colbert's own instructions on certain processes, especially on dyeing, were in themselves technical treatises. Bruant brought out, with state help, a manual on land surveying and his *Architecture pratique;* Davilez published his *Cours d'architecture classique,* and Blondell his *Cours d'architecture;* Mignard translated the work of the Italian architect Scamozzi, and Perrault published his translation of Vitruvius, as well as his own work on the *Ordonnance des colonnes.* Three state-supported chemical laboratories were set up — in the king's library, in the Louvre, and at the Observatoire. At the same time the newly founded *Académie des sciences* sponsored the publication of several books on mechanics, in which were "described all the machines in use in France and elsewhere." This eventuated in the publication in 1699 of the first volume of the *Recueil des machines*. In the meantime the members continued to publish works of practical application in chemistry and mechanics, notably Blondell's *Traité de l'art de jeter des bombes*. The *Journal des savants* had as one of its objects the publication of the new processes useful to industry.[47]

[47] Colbert gave help to the experiments of Varignon and de la Hire on applied mechanics, of Du Clos on the analysis of mineral water, of d'Auzout and of Picard on leveling, of Mariotte on air and water pumps, of Huygens on the pendulum, on the movements of clocks, on the force of wind and of powder explosion, of Papin on steam power, and of a number of men working on the improvement of artillery equipment. Colbert sent agents abroad to study and to buy foreign machines. Boissonnade's *Colbert,* ref. 34, pp. 33–36. Cf. Bigourdan, *Les premières sociétés savantes de Paris au XVII*^e *siècle* (Paris, 1918); H. Brown, *Scientific Organizations in Seventeenth Century France* (Baltimore, 1935); M. Ornstein, *The Rôle of Scientific Societies in the Seventeenth Century* (Chicago, 1928); H. Lyons, *The Royal Society, 1660–1940* (Cambridge, 1944); H. C. Brugmans, *Le séjour de Christian Huyghens à Paris* (Paris, 1935); Académie royale des sciences, *Les membres et les correspondants 1666–1793* (Paris, 1931).

The great significance of the scientific societies for the advancement of sciences is summed up in Ornstein, *op. cit.,* pp. 260–62: "The societies concentrated groups of scientists in one place, performed experiments and investigations impossible to individual effort, encouraged individual scientists and gave them both opportunity and leisure, often through financial support, for scientific work. They became centers of scientific information, published and translated scientific books, promulgated periodically scientific discoveries, and thus coördinated the scientific efforts of the various progressive European countries. They concerned themselves about matters of homely interest such as trade, commerce, tools, and machinery, and tried to improve everyday life by the light of science. They contributed to the general enlightenment by dispelling popular errors. . . . But first and foremost they developed the scientific laboratory, created the national observatory, devised, perfected and standardized instruments, originated and insisted on exact methods of experimentation, and thus established permanently the laboratory as the only true means of scientific study. These societies were the *Kulturträger* of the second half of the seventeenth century. . . . They typify this age drunk with the fullness of new knowledge, busy in the uprooting of

The worlds of science and industry drew closer together than they had ever been before, though both remained full of self-contained units which often jealousy guarded their secrets from one another. After studying the general relations of science and industry in the seventeenth century, a recent writer concludes that "few of the inventions . . . owed anything to scientific inquiries for which the century is famous. The one outstanding example of an invention by a great scientist is the improvement of watches and clocks. In the metallurgic industries [and, he might have added, in the dyeing and weaving industries] science made some contributions." — "But," he continues, "inventions were for the most part made by artists and craftsmen, not by men of science."[48] The progress of

superannuated superstitions, breaking loose from traditions of the past, embracing most extravagant hopes for the future. In their midst the spirit of minute scientific inquiry is developed; here the charlatanry and curiosity of the alchemist and magician are transformed into methodical investigation; here the critical faculty is developed so that the disclosure of an error is as important as the discovery of new truth; here the minute fact is put as high — nay higher — than generalization; here the individual scientist learned to be contented and proud to have added an infinitesimal part to the sum of knowledge; here, in short, the modern scientist was evolved."

[48] G. N. Clark, ref. 17, pp. 63–64. The scientists were keenly interested in applying their discoveries; they were interested in improving technology and in promoting national prosperity — the idea of "pure science" pursued apart from all practical purposes is a recent ideal — but the worlds of scientific investigation and of industry were so widely separated and the crafts were so used to getting on with traditional rule-of-thumb methods that it was not until the eighteenth or even the nineteenth century that the great scientific syntheses and inventions began to affect industry appreciably. The relations of science and invention show that most important inventions before the nineteenth century were made with little or no help from "pure science," and that pre-existing technical methods sometimes supplied the data and the apparatus for scientific discoveries. In practice the scientists learned more from technology — their experiments were often made possible by processes borrowed from the arts and crafts — than the scientists contributed to technology. The matter is discussed in Wolf, ref. 11, pp. 450–53. Also in A. J. George, "Genesis of the Académie des Sciences," *Annals of Science,* 1938, esp. pp. 378–80; H. Brown, "Utilitarian Motive in the Age of Descartes," *ibid.,* 1936, G. N. Clark, *Science and Social Welfare in the Age of Newton* (Oxford, 1937), esp. pp. 13, 64–65, 71, 76.

pure science and the development of invention, while difficult to trace in detail, were more related than the author admits. Although the scientists and the inventors did not work in collaboration, the discoveries of science slowly filtered down to those who were next to the machines and the practical processes of industry, and science gradually improved these devices. At the same time, as has often been pointed out by the critics of mercantilism, the guild regulations and the stupidity of state inspectors were often by the end of the seventeenth century a serious hindrance to the introduction of new processes. After Colbert's death this situation worsened. During the first half of the eighteenth century the government succeeded in surrounding industry with a network of legislative regulations, sometimes wise, often foolish and always annoying, which gradually hardened into immobility.[49]

Efforts to put paupers to work and to teach them trades had been made since the sixteenth century both by the municipalities and by a number of religious orders.[50] Colbert tried to

---

Cf. also W. E. Houghton, Jr., "The History of Trades; Its Relation to Seventeenth Century Thought," *Journal of the History of Ideas,* 1941, and two articles by R. K. Merton, "Science, Technology, and Society in Seventeenth Century England," *Osiris,* 1938, and "Science and the Economy of Seventeenth century England," *Science and Society,* 1939. On the history of early modern inventions, cf. A. P. Usher, *History of Mechanical Inventions* (New York, 1929); E. Eude; *Histoire documentaire de la mécanique française* (Paris, 1902); and C. Fremont, *Les outils, leur origine, leur évolution* (Paris, 1928). The proceedings of the *Académie des sciences* down to the Revolution are basic: *Histoire et mémoires de l'Académie des sciences* (114 vols., Paris, 1733–1797); on relation to inventions, cf. also *Machines et inventions approuvées par l'Académie royale des sciences, 1666–1701* (Paris, 1735).

[49] The whole matter is well summed up in G. Renard and G. Weulersse, *Life and Work in Modern Europe* (New York, 1926), pp. 182–185.

[50] Cf. P. E. Griselle, "Une école catholique d'arts et métiers en 1599," *Revue de Lille* (1898), and A. Guettier, *Histoire des écoles nationales d'arts et métiers* (new ed., Paris, 1880), pp. xxii–xxiv, for work of St. François de Sales. For parallel efforts in England, cf. Foster Watson, ref. 27, pp. xliii–xlix.

push these enterprises, but they were never sufficiently extensive to include more than a small percentage of the indigent classes. The regular craftsmen were very jealous of these activities, fearing the competition from the articles produced. Boissonnade and Cole, who have studied this and other aspects of Colbert's policy in great detail, find that these efforts of Colbert and of those who had preceded him were not entirely lost. The workshops of the *hôpitaux* furnished to industry a certain number of skilled workers. They helped the success of certain great enterprises like those of woolen serge, of hat, and of lace making. The system of Colbert had the merit of trying to deal with the rising tide of pauperism.[51] The state administration during the eighteenth century and into the Napoleonic period followed the same methods in its fight against unemployment; it was continually creating workshops in connection with the poorhouses.

In all his enterprises,[52] Colbert attempted to continue the work of earlier governments in strengthening France by raising her industries to the level of the best that was then being done in Italy and the Low Countries. He understood more clearly than anyone up to his time the importance of practical artistic and technical education as a means of improving taste and of perfecting processes. To accomplish his ends he sketched vast plans, some of which were never carried out. But the result of his whole effort was to make France the dictator of Europe in dress and all the luxury trades, and the leader in many of the staple industries. France was thus prepared to take the position of the leading manufacturing nation on the continent. Some of his ideas about technical education were later to bear fruit.

[51] Boissonnade, *Colbert* (ref. 34), pp. 129–31 and bibliography, pp. 381–82.

[52] The standard edition of Colbert's writings, P. Clément, *Lettres, instructions et mémoires de Colbert* (10 vols., Paris, 1861–1882) contains much interesting material not available elsewhere; it is unfortunately not adequately indexed.

5. *Technical Training for the Army and Navy*

Important strides toward a modern type of technical training were made in the army and navy. The rise of a modern type of state and the whole balance-of-power system had greatly increased the importance of state armaments. In sixteenth-century Italy great improvements were made in fortifications, a change which for some centuries now turned warfare largely to siege operations. These changes demanded new technical military services in artillery and fortifications, services for which knowledge of mathematics and mechanics was very important. Moreover, there were only four years in the seventeenth century when war was not going on somewhere in Europe. Yet when Louis XIV came to power, a regular army was still to be created. As Lavisse says, speaking of the situation in 1661, "the king of France, though he had made war almost continually for centuries, did not have an organized army. . . . There was no regularly constituted administration for war, no methodic service of munitions, of food, or of hospitals. The armament and the tactics were a century out of date, the infantry was neglected, the cavalry remained the noble branch. The artillery and the engineering services were subordinate. . . . The creation of the royal army was the work of three men, Le Tellier, his son, Louvois, and the King." [53]

By 1678 Louis XIV had an army of 300,000, which was not only the largest and best equipped in Europe but in both respects superior to any military force in western Europe since the Roman Empire.[54] Much of this army had come to be a

[53] E. Lavisse, *Histoire de la France* (Paris, 1911), Vol. 7, pt. ii, pp. 230–32. C. Oman, *The History of the Art of War in the Sixteenth Century* (London, 1937). Cf. L. André, *Michelle Tellier et l'organisation de l'arnée monarchique* (Paris, 1906).

[54] The population of France in the first half of the seventeenth century has been estimated to be ca. 14,000,000; this was larger than that of the Holy Roman Empire and three times as large as that of England and Scotland combined. E. Levasseur, *La population française* (3 vols., Paris, 1889–1892), Vol. I, pp. 191–92, 206.

standing army which served the monarch the whole year through and which was gradually being organized into infantry, cavalry, and artillery, with a hierarchy of officers and a regular system of promotion. Back of these changes in France lay the military experience and theorizing of the Italian Renaissance. The modern arts of fortification and siegecraft and the modern theoretical study of warfare were begun by the Italian *condottieri;* the intense intellectual life of the fifteenth and early sixteenth centuries, combined with the bitter rivalry of a number of crowded and competing states, prepared the way for fostering these new branches of learning. With the extension of inquiry into the mechanical forces controlling the use of firearms and the building of defenses, there began in Italy the separation between the learned and the less technical branches of soldiering. Moreover, the *condottieri* founded small military schools at which they analyzed strategic and tactical problems, emphasizing the relationship of the different operations of a campaign. They also helped to stimulate the writing of treatises on warfare which combine shrewd observations on contemporary conditions with arguments and illustrations culled from the Greek and Latin classics.[55]

The idea of giving a new type of training to army officers, which as in the case of industrial training would raise France to the level of Italy, was first seriously considered by de la Noue in his *Discours militaires* (1587). "The education of boys," he says, "is now given in the infantry regiments. . . . They enter at fifteen, sixteen, or seventeen years of age; . . .

---

[55] F. L. Taylor, *The Art of War in Italy, 1494–1529* (Cambridge, 1921), pp. 7, 128, 157. For Italian treatises on war, cf. Taylor, *op. cit.,* Chap. 8; for further details on schools of *condottieri,* cf. E. Ricotti, *Storia della Compagnia di Ventura* (4 vols., Turin, 1845), pt. IV, Vol. 3. On warfare in the sixteenth century, cf. C. Oman, *A History of the Art of War in the Sixteenth Century* (London, 1937) and I. Gilbert, "Machiavelli, the Renaissance of the Art of War," in E. M. Earle, ed., *Makers of Modern Strategy* (Princeton, 1943). Galileo clearly saw the need for a new type of military education. *Le Opere di Galileo Galilei* (20 vols., Florence, 1890–1909), Vol. 2, pp. 606–08.

it is a perilous institution for youth, for often having as teachers only debauched men . . . they are led to dissipation." There should be, de La Noue thought, regular schools for the training of officers, and he advised Henry IV to establish four military academies, in Paris, Lyons, Bordeaux, and Angers. If places could not be prepared at these cities, four royal châteaux rarely occupied by the king could be used: Fontainebleau, Moulins, Plessis-les-Tours, and Cognac. The instruction given should be both physical and theoretical. Physical exercises should include handling a horse, use of all sorts of firearms, swimming, and dancing. "As to exercises for the mind . . . they will do reading in our own language of the best books of the ancients" on war and history. "They should likewise be taught mathematics, geography, fortifications, and several vernacular languages." Finally, their instruction might well be completed by some training in music, drawing, and painting.[56] Until Frenchmen could be trained, instructors should be brought from Italy. The religious wars had seriously impoverished many of the nobles, who were now unable to educate their sons. This problem Henry IV had in mind when he aided in the foundation of a *collège* at La Flèche (1604), which he turned over to the Jesuits and for which he established a large number of scholarships for the sons of nobles. By 1626 La Flèche had over two thousand pupils, but the military features of its instruction were relatively unimportant. Henry IV, though unable to undertake the elaborate program of de La Noue, did establish a small military academy in connection with the royal court. Sully described it as an institution "very useful for individuals and very advantageous

---

[56] F. Funck-Brentano, "L'éducation des officiers dans l'ancienne France," *Réforme sociale 6*, 1918, pp. 18–20, and C. de Montzey, *Institutions d'éducation militaire jusqu'en 1789* (Paris, 1866), pp. 65–66. The best bibliography of the French army in the seventeenth century is in L. André, *Les sources de l'histoire de la France, XVIIe siècle* (Paris, 1934), Vol. 7, pp. 309–340; cf. also de Favitski de Probobysz, *Répertoire bibliographique de la littérature militaire et coloniale française depuis cent ans* (Paris, 1935), invaluable.

for the king if it becomes a nursery for true men of war."
Instruction was given in fencing, horsemanship, and music.
Its importance lies not in anything it accomplished, for it
seems to have been on a small scale and to have lasted only a
few years, but it stands as an early state attempt to meet the
new problem of military education.[57]

Richelieu was greatly concerned about the military weakness of France. The Assembly of Notables in 1626 proposed
the creation of a military school for the instruction of young
nobles, and Richelieu drew up one project for an academy
for a thousand students, four hundred to be trained for the
church and six hundred for the army.[58] Three years later,
Louis XIII founded the *Académie des exercises militaires* for
twenty noble youths. Of it Richelieu wrote, "Letters and arms
. . . are both equally required for the establishment and maintenance of great empires, the former for regulating and civilizing within the state, the latter for extending and protecting
it. Nevertheless the endowments of colleges and seminaries
seem only to be destined for young men who are studying
letters . . . without thought . . . of those who carry arms. So
to . . . remedy this notable deficiency, and to excite the emu-
lation of those who will come after us, . . . we have given to
the new academy . . . the sum of 20,000 *livres* annually . . .
for the . . . instruction of twenty gentlemen . . . for two years
. . . in all military exercises." Paying students were also to be
taken. All students were to be admitted at the age of fourteen
or fifteen years, and all must be healthy, Catholic, and of
French birth. They were to be taught "to manage a horse, to
handle arms, and to be instructed thoroughly in morals, mathematics, fortification, logic and physics, more superficially in

[57] L. Mention, *L'armée de l'ancien régime* (Paris, 1910), p. 70, and E. Boutaric, *Institutions militaires de la France avant les armées permanentes* (Paris,
1863), p. 393. Richelieu's ideas on the army are discussed in Hanotaux et de
La Force, ref. 27, Vol. 4, pp. 377ff.

[58] Richelieu, *Lettres, instructions diplomatiques et papiers d'état,* ed. by
J. Avenel (Paris, 1863), Vol. 5, p. 421.

the French language, geography, and history." At the end of two years of such instruction, the students were to serve in units of the royal army. The academy lasted only a few years and was closed after Richelieu's death, but to him belongs the credit of establishing the first military school in France. Mazarin wanted to open a new military academy but failed because of the opposition of the University.[59]

It was not commonly believed in France that army officers need be overburdened with book learning. As one seventeenth-century French noble wrote, "It will suffice if the young man studies until the age of fifteen or sixteen years so that he may learn philosophy, ancient and modern history, and the principal maxims of politics so that he may regulate his conduct in the society of the nobility. After this he should be placed in an academy so as to learn to manage a horse, to handle firearms, . . . and to dance. Those exercises will strengthen him and make him adroit . . . so that he will walk with grace and a noble air. . . . In the academy he will also learn mathematics, so as to know how to fortify places, how to attack and defend them . . . all this to be learned in two or three years. . . . On leaving the academy he should take a trip to foreign countries to learn languages, . . . and how different peoples are governed."[60] Another noble wrote to his son, "If you have an inclination for the army, you must first consider whether you are strong enough. . . . When you are not on duty, use your time to learn history, and all the rules of arithmetic, and to draw plans of fortified places and methods of attacking them, also the plans of battle formations and camps."[61]

[59] Mention, ref. 57, p. 70; Funck-Brentano, ref. 56, pp. 20–22; and J. Isambert, ed., *Recueil général des anciennes lois françaises depuis l'an 420 jusqu'à la révolution de 1789* (Paris, 1833ff.), Vol. 16, pp. 468–69. This school was situated in Paris, rue Veille-du-Temple, and was opened with twenty-two pupils.

[60] J. Roy, *Turenne* (Paris, 1884), pp. 2–3, and Hanotaux et de La Force, ref. 27, Vol. 4, p. 391.

[61] For the riding academies, cf. ref. 27. A pamphlet advocating the founding of similar academies for training infantry officers was S. d'Aubarède and

The ideas of de La Noue and of Richelieu were taken up in the time of Louis XIV by Le Tellier and Louvois, who made it their object to create a well-equipped standing army on regular pay and regular rations. In 1682 Louvois established first two and finally nine special companies for the training of officers. Young gentlemen from fourteen to twenty-five were to be recommended by the *intendants* for the *compagnies de cadets-gentilshommes*.[62] Four thousand applied, and the *intendants* seem to have turned few away; indeed, by 1684 there were 4,275 *cadets-gentilshommes*.[63] They were clothed and paid by the state. Many who entered could neither read nor write, and in age they ranged from fourteen to forty-five years. Most of them were from families of the lesser nobility; the sons of the higher nobility who wished to follow a military career served an apprenticeship in the *Maison du Roi*. A few bourgeois were also admitted to the corps.

The youths were taught mathematics, drawing, fortification, the use of arms, military drill, and, in addition, German and dancing. As many were illiterate, the instruction must have come to little. The cadets were put into barracks; at certain hours they were allowed to go about the town, though they

---

P. Laboureur, *L'académie militaire pour l'infanterie établie à Paris* (Paris, 1614); a full course of study, including mostly exercises in gunnery and military drill, is outlined.

[62] Funck-Brentano, ref. 56, pp. 22–26. The origin of the *cadets-gentilshommes* lies in the system of taking pages into *compagnies d'ordonnance* and into *gardes du corps* beginning in the fifteenth century: De Montzey, ref. 56, pp. 18–21, 24–25. Cf. L. Hennet, *Les compagnies des cadets-gentilshommes et les écoles militaires* (Paris, 1889), pp. 14–21. The king's orders spoke only of gentlemen, but Louvois told the *intendants* to admit also bourgeois candidates, which they did. The *cadets-gentilshommes* were revived in the first quarter of the eighteenth century: P. de Briquet, *Code militaire* (2 vols., Paris, 1728), Vol. 2, pp. 252–257. Two orders of noblemen, the *Chevaliers de Notre-Dame du Mont-Carmel* and those of *Saint-Lazare,* co-operated in conducting, during the years 1671 to 1720 a number of small schools for noblemen who wanted to enter the army or navy: De Montzey, *op. cit.,* pp. 98–99, 294, 323–29.

[63] C. F. Rousset, *Histoire de Louvois* (new ed., 4 vols., Paris, 1864), Vol. 3, p. 314.

were not permitted to attend the theater. They were to have two lessons of mathematics a day, each two hours and a half in length. The enterprise seems to have been hardly more than a scheme for recruiting officers for the army, though it was later copied in Holland, Prussia, Poland, and Russia. Vauban thought the whole thing absurd, and said of the cadets that "they brought nothing to the service, they have seen nothing, thought about nothing, and know nothing but fencing, dancing and quarrelling." [64] In 1683 many were given temporary appointments as *sous-lieutenants* because of the war with Spain, and the next year some were sent from the companies at Sarrelouis and Longwy to the siege of Luxembourg. The companies were neglected following Louvois' death (1691); by 1696 only two survived and these were dissolved in April, 1696. The system failed partly because of the poor quality of the young men recruited, though the instruction and the discipline were also poor. It got no backing from the officers of the army regiments who preferred to fill vacancies by bringing in their sons or relatives and training them up to be officers. The government was not strong enough to curb this nepotism. After Louvois' system was given up, the government reverted to an older system of *volontaires,* young men who elected to serve a military apprenticeship without pay in various army units; the same system existed for the navy. Only a small number, mostly sons of officers, availed themselves of this privilege. Except for the artillery school, mentioned later, this was the only attempt of the government

[64] Mention, ref. 57, p. 73; P. Lazard, *Vauban* (Paris, 1934), pp. 74–75 *note;* R. Blomfield, *Vauban* (London, 1938), pp. 96–98, 159–160; H. E. Guerlac, "Vauban," in E. M. Earle, ed., *Makers of Modern Strategy* (Princeton, 1943). On Vauban, cf. also F. Gazin, *Essai de bibliographie, oeuvres concernant Vauban; écrits personnels du Maréchal* (Paris, 1933). For the influence of the *cadets-gentilshommes* in the armies of the German states, cf. B. Poten, *Geschichte des Militär-Erziehungs- und Bildungswesens in den Landen deutscher Zunge* (5 vols., Berlin, 1889–1897).

to provide professional training for the army that survived the reign of Louis XIV.

Until the beginning of the sixteenth century the construction of the innumerable fortifications which covered the soil of France — town walls, castles, and manor houses — was not subject to any rules beyond those applied to all constructions of masonry. The upkeep of the important defenses was left to the town officials; the attack on fortified places and their defense were undertaken by the national government. This demanded the use of military machines (*engins*) whence comes the word *ingénieur,* applicable to those who looked to their construction and use. The first government inspectors of fortifications were appointed by Charles VII about 1445. From this time on the central government paid more attention to its fortresses. A new style of bastion fortification designed to resist gunfire was introduced from Italy, and until the time of Henry IV many of the *ingénieurs* were Italians. Henry IV was the first to employ only French *ingénieurs.*[65] The *corps du génie* was first organized in 1676; until then the artillery and the engineers were not separated from the infantry. Such

[65] Lazard, ref. 64, pp. 3–10. Lazard gives a list of the first Italian and French *ingénieurs* in France and discusses the careers of a number of them. He also analyzes the contents of a number of the early treatises on military engineering and gives a fairly complete list of such works down to the Revolution. After the middle of the seventeenth century many of these treatises were written by ecclesiastics. (Lazard, *op. cit.,* pp. 10–34, and bibliography, pp. 635–42.) A. d'Augoyat, *Aperçu historique sur les fortifications, les ingénieurs et sur le corps du génie en France,* 2nd ed. (3 vols., Paris, 1860–1864) contains many interesting details about the early history of French military engineering; cf. also C. Lecomte, *Les ingénieurs militaires en France sous le règne de Louis XIV* (Paris, 1904); E. Crouzet, "Travaux des typographes du génie militaire en France," *Revue du génie militaire* (1908); H. M. Berthaut, *La carte de France* (2 vols., Paris, 1898–99), and, by the same author, *Les ingénieurs géographes militaires* (2 vols., Paris, 1902); the good brief survey of the history of the French army engineers by E. Legrand-Girade: "Étude historique sur le corps du génie," *Revue du génie militaire* (1897–98), and P. Lazard, "Quelques ingénieurs militaires au XVIIᵉ siècle," *ibid.* (1936).

officers, detailed to do engineering work, directed military and civil constructions for the royal service with the aid of companies of workmen enlisted for a time and later discharged. In 1683 there were 132 military engineers in the part of the army commanded by Louvois; they were scattered in the frontier provinces from the North Sea to Switzerland and along the Pyrenees.[66] Vauban's *corps du génie,* which contained the ablest group of officers, soon attained a European reputation for its unusual achievements in military constructions. No school of engineers was opened before the eighteenth century. The officers got their training merely by learning their profession in the service and by reading the treatises on engineering which were either printed or circulated in manuscript. Some had studied mathematics and fortification with private teachers or in secondary schools. Such instruction was almost exclusively confined to drawing ground plans of fortresses and entrenchments. It was a sort of descriptive geometry, far too theoretical; the instruction was especially defective in fitting fortifications to different sites. An artillery school was opened at Douai in 1679; it was later transferred to Metz and then to Strasbourg.[67] The principles of artillery instruction were given in drawing, history, mathematics, and fortification. None of these schools amounted to much before the eighteenth century, chiefly because the wars of Louis XIV continually interfered with the instruction.

The seventeenth century in France saw not only the beginnings of a modern type of army and of military education but also of a modern navy and of naval education. Naval experience was showing that the naval battle was increasingly an affair of fighting ships, that the pressed and hired merchant

[66] For the location of all military engineers in 1683 and later, cf. d'Augoyat, *op. cit.,* Vol. 1, pp. 117, 230–31.

[67] De Montzey, ref. 56, p. 104, and T. Le Puillon de Boblaye, *Esquisse historique sur les écoles d'artillerie* (Metz, 1838), p. 36. The program of studies is outlined in P. Surirey de Saint-Rémi, *Mémoires d'artillerie* (3rd ed., 2 vols., Paris, 1745), Vol. 1, pp. 40–72.

vessel was disappearing from the line of battle, and that a settled personnel was necessary. The methods of fighting were brought under regular tactical principles, as in the army; a regular corps of officers was slowly organized, and increased efforts were made to bring all pilots under a system of state licensing. Observing the rapid extension of these changes in the English and Dutch navies, Richelieu worked to further similar improvements in the French navy. Ideas of naval reform were in the air. In 1626 Le Clerc presented to Louis XIII a memoir urging him to establish naval instruction in each maritime province of France, and to turn over to teachers of hydrography the right to license pilots. Later Le Clerc outlined a course of study which included map making, knowledge of tides, currents, and winds, and the use of the astrolabe and compass; such instruction was to be given on shipboard. Some of these proposals were embodied in the *Code Michaud* of 1629, which proposed that schools be opened both for the royal navy and for the merchant marine; these reforms were slow in taking shape. The chief improvements in navigation before 1680 were due to seamen and to scholars who, without state support, gave private instruction to small groups of seamen; in this, Dieppe was the most important center.[68] Riche-

[68] For these proposals and improvements, cf. A. Anthiaume, *L'Abbé Guillaume Denys de Dieppe 1624–1689, premier professeur royale d'hydrographie en France* (Paris, 1927); A. Anthiaume, *Évolution et enseignement de la science nautique en France* (2 vols., Paris, 1920), Vol. I, pp. 245ff.; and C. de la Roncière, *Histoire de la marine française* (6 vols., Paris, 1899–1922), Vol. I, pp. 365–92; F. Marguet, *Histoire générale de la navigation du XVe au XXe siècle* (Paris, 1931); and A. Anthiaume, *Le navire, sa construction en France* (Paris, 1922). The *Code Michaud* is quite specific in its proposals. It deplores the lack of trained navigators, suggests that organized instruction be given three times a week in every port for those serving in the state navy, and calls on the local authorities to establish similar instruction of the merchant marine. On the bibliography of the navy, cf. André, ref. 56, pp. 340–55. There is an interesting description in the autobiography of a seventeenth-century corsair, Jean Doublet, who studied hydrography with a priest of Dieppe: "He started me off with the principles of the sphere, tides, elevations, the handling of the quadrant, the English scale . . . as well as sines, tangents and logarithms. Whereupon

lieu, after he became sole head of the navy, instituted some naval reforms, chiefly in ship construction and in the establishment of new arsenals, and in 1642 he made a move toward establishing a training corps for officers by ordering the payment of four hundred *livres* to three instructors for the men in charge of recruiting officers for the royal navy.[69]

The neglect of the sea forces after Richelieu's death, because of the disturbances of the *Fronde,* left Louis XIV and Colbert to make a practically new start in the improvement of the navy. Colbert found twenty royal vessels in 1661, but he left two hundred and fifty-eight, with 53,200 men and 1,200 officers in 1683. He organized a kind of general staff for the navy and proposed to reform the method of recruiting by replacing the odious press-gang system with one that registered the men in seaboard towns and automatically ensured a supply of crews.[70] Prizes were given for excellence in

---

he asked me what I wanted to do, since I was taking so much theory and practice with him. I told him that I wanted to perfect myself with a capable master, and so would he be good enough not to spare any pains on me. He taught me the spherical triangles and the elements of Euclid and calculation." When Doublet received a good offer to go away on a ship, the priest persuaded him to stay three months longer. At the end of the six-month period the priest urged Doublet to take a pilot's examination. Doublet says he was examined "by four former captains and four pilots who questioned me on all subjects, and with their approval I was registered with naval authorities." J. Doublet, *Journal,* ed. by C. Bréard (Paris, 1883), pp. 58–60.

[69] Anon., *Histoire de l'école navale* (Paris, 1889), p. 8; and de Crisenoy, "Les écoles navales et les officiers de vaisseaux depuis Richelieu," *Revue maritime et coloniale 10,* 1864, p. 764. In an attempt to improve the navy, all power was put in the hands of the "Grand Master and Superintendent of the Navigation and Trade of France," and this position was given to Richelieu.

[70] "The systematic recruiting of men for the naval service dates from 1665. Previous to this time when a fleet was fitted for sea the ports were closed and a general press of all the seamen needed took place. This brutal and clumsy method was . . . in 1665 . . . set aside by a decree, ordering the enrollment of all sea-faring men who were divided into three classes, each class being obliged to serve one year at a time in the ships of the fleet; during the other two years the men of this class were free to take service in any other capacity." F. E. Chadwick, *Report on the Training*

naval construction, the arsenals were reorganized, and new developments were made in the science of navigation by the *Académie des sciences,* the state *Observatoire,* and by an improved system of ship and port inspection, the *Service hydrographique.* Experience showed that it was much more difficult to get officers for the navy than for the army.

In the case of industry, Colbert wished, by improving the training of skilled workers, to raise the quality of French products to the level of those of Italy and Flanders; for the navy, he desired, by means of organized instruction, to raise both the royal navy and the merchant marine to the level of those of Holland and England.[71] In 1671 Colbert wrote, "The king wants pilot schools established in all the ports," and in a report of 1678 he insisted that "it is not sufficient that they

Systems for the Navy and Mercantile Marine, England and France (Washington, 1880), p. 165. Theoretically, this system of registering seamen and allotting them for service in the navy and in the merchant ships was the most enlightened in Europe, but in practice it was stupidly and harshly administered. Moreover, the system was abandoned and impressment was resorted to every time war broke out. On the subject of recruitment, cf. R. Mémain, *Matelots et soldats de vaisseaux du roi* (Paris, 1932).

[71] A manuscript memoir of 1681 says, "Being always close to land in the Mediterranean, pilots in that sea have neglected to study navigation, and merely follow a routine. The Dutch on the contrary have schools for training pilots and do not let anyone embark who is not properly trained. Pilots are obliged to keep journals and to report so that maps can be corrected. In France, pilots who collect information keep it secret and sell it. . . . The most experienced pilots in France have no ability to learn much from their experience and they are incapable of teaching others. They spread the notion that one can only learn navigation by practice." (*Arch. Nat. Marine* G 86.) A manuscript memoir of 1687 outlines the instruction given at Toulon, "The teacher of hydrography gives two hours of instruction each morning from eight to ten, which he divides into four classes of a half hour each. In the first the most elementary pupils will learn the use of the compass, tides, map reading, etc., the second class will learn the method of construction and use of instruments for observing the stars. In the third, the quadrant and its use in laying courses, variation and correction of the compass, etc. The fourth, plane and spherical trigonometry and calculation of courses. Those who had the preparation might study astronomy, etc., at special hours. Dated, Toulon 14 May 1687." Similar documents exist for Rochefort, Havre, Brest (*Arch. Nat. Marine* G 86).

[prospective pilots and ships' officers] have practical experience, but they must also have theory." He complained that navigation was mostly carried on by outworn and routine methods, that new instruments of navigation and new scientific discoveries had little influence on naval practice, that map makers were often ignorant, and that such private instruction as was given in the port towns was too haphazard. By 1682 a number of state schools of navigation had been added to the unorganized instruction given for over a century by ecclesiastics, private scholars, and retired seamen. In the state schools — the principal ones were a *Collège de marine* at Saint-Malo and two *écoles flottantes* at Rochefort and Brest — the equipment of maps, compasses, and other instruments was supplied by the government. The courses were given by a professor, assisted by two pilots, and included drawing, mathematics, methods of map making and of determining time, latitude, and longitude. The regulations demanded that the journals of pilots using a port should be deposited for a month for the teachers to study. These *écoles d'hydrographie,* whose chief work was in training men for the merchant marine, lasted down to the Revolution, but they never realized the hopes of Colbert.

For the royal navy, the *gardes de la marine* were founded in 1670 with two schools, in Toulon and Rochefort, each of a hundred students. Like the system of the *gardes-gentils-hommes* for the army, this organization was primarily a method of recruiting officers. The students at Toulon were not quartered in barracks but were lodged with private families and assigned an inadequate number of teachers; consequently the port authorities had so much difficulty in maintaining discipline that Colbert dismissed the companies the following year and sent a few of the students directly into the royal navy to be trained as officer apprentices. From 1681 to 1689 Colbert, with the help of the *états* of Brittany, maintained on the island of Indret in the Loire a small school for twenty young nobles who were preparing to enter the navy. In 1683 new companies of *gardes* were formed, and by 1696 there were seven hundred and six men, sixteen years of age or older, training in the ports of Brest, Rochefort, and Toulon. The teaching included mathematics and the general principles of navigation, artillery, and ship construction. The instruction at Toulon was in the hands of the Jesuits; at the other ports the teaching was done by ecclesiastics and civilians. A letter of the intendant of the navy at Rochefort (1682) says that classes were held three times a week, from one to four o'clock, in arithmetic, geometry, trigonometry, and the use of maps and navigation instruments, all with definite application to practical problems of navigation. The other three afternoons were devoted to the study of ship construction in the shipyards and to methods of attacking and defending forts. He complains that the majority do not know how to read and write and that the problems of instruction are nearly insurmountable.

Beginning in 1682, three frigates of eighteen to twenty cannon were supplied to the three training ports as practice ships; every student had the experience of at least one month's cruise. Students in these special courses were from sixteen to twenty-five years of age and were selected by the king partly from lists sent by the *intendants* and partly from candidates proposed by the nobles at court. As in the case of the army, the continual changes in all regulations for the navy, and the calling of the students to service undid most of the practical benefits.[72] An example of the incessant doing and undoing of

---

[72] *Histoire de l'école navale* (ref. 69), pp. 21–33. Anthiaume, *Évolution* . . . , ref. 68, Vol. 1, pp. 117–21. Some statistics on the men trained in the *gardes* are given in de Montzey, ref. 56, p. 297. A number of interesting documents can be found in A. Jal, *Glossaire nautique* (Paris, 1848), pp. 769–70. Cf. also de Crisenoy, ref. 69, pp. 766–67; Anthiaume, *op. cit.*, Vol. 1, pp. 432–33. There is an excellent series of articles on early teachers, textbooks, and schools of navigation by A. Didier-Neuville, "Les établissements scientifiques de l'ancienne marine" (Paris, 1882) and "Cosmographie et hydrographie avant Colbert," *Revue maritime et coloniale,* Vols. 1–4 incl. (1878–1879); cf. also Villaret, "Notions historiques sur les services des constructions navales,"

everything is shown in the fact that the *gardes de la marine* were founded in 1670, with two schools organized for them; these companies were disbanded in 1671 and new ones organized with better arrangements for discipline and for instruction. In 1683 a second corps of three companies, the *nouvelles gardes de la marine,* was founded, and then, in 1686, the remains of the old and the new *gardes* were combined.[73] At the same time their numbers were fixed at two hundred for Brest, the same for Toulon, and a hundred and fifty for Rochefort. Barracks were arranged for them; most of the theoretical instruction was turned over to the Jesuits. As time went on, the recruits were somewhat more carefully selected, and thus were capable of doing more substantial work. An ordinance of 15 April 1689 codified the regulations for the *gardes* — regulations which, with few changes, were followed until the Revolution. The ordinance speaks of instruction in dancing,

---

Memorial du génie maritime, 1902, and P. D. Dislère, "Notice historique sur le corps du génie maritime," *Revue maritime,* 1921. In these articles, and in the two volumes of Anthiaume, are given many details about the various schools of hydrography in the seventeenth and eighteenth centuries, details mostly concerned with changes in personnel in such school, and the efforts to improve the construction of ships and the training of officers. Efforts were also made to improve gunnery in the navy. An ordinance of 1629 orders that 150 sailors between the ages of sixteen and twenty who have served five or six years at sea and who wish to become cannoneers be taught in each of the larger ports three times a week, during periods when they are not at sea. This ordinance seems to have come to little, for in 1676 orders were given for the establishment of a regular *École des canonniers.* Isambert, ref. 59, Vol. 16, p. 331. An ordinance of 15 April 1689 provided that young men who wanted to learn shipbuilding might be employed at a port for two years. After two years they were sent to a school of ship construction in the Louvre in Paris. Dislère, *op. cit.,* pp. 433–38.

[73] Anon., *Histoire de l'école navale* (Paris, 1889), pp. 35–71, essential documents quoted. Cf. de Crisenoy, ref. 69, p. 765 *note,* for numbers appointed in the *gardes de la marine* for each year between 1672 and 1686. Another small corps of about forty men was that of the *gardes de l'étandard réal,* founded by Louis XIV as a guard for the admiral and vice-admiral of France. The men received lessons in mathematics and the sciences of navigation, and were later given positions in the navy. The corps was dissolved in 1743. De Montzey, ref. 56, pp. 299–304.

fencing, drawing, mathematics, fortification, and hydrography; also of the use of nautical instruments, gunnery practice, military drill, field maneuvers, and shopwork in ship construction. Colbert deserves the credit for having had some excellent ideas, which unfortunately he was never able to carry through; they included a plan to change the *Collège de Guyenne* at Bordeaux into a central naval school. The *gardes de la marine* continued to train officers for the state navy until the Revolution.

In the later seventeenth century and during the eighteenth there was often a confusion between the instruction given in the chief ports for the royal navy and that for the merchant marine. Sometimes they existed separately, in other cases they were united. Also some of the instruction for service in the merchant marine was state supported, some was not. The best instruction was that given for the merchant marine. In both the naval services young men showed little interest in seeking naval instruction. Government agents complained that even the officers of the royal navy, who might presumably have taken some interest in urging youths to receive better training, were indifferent or hostile. In licensing pilots and in appointing officers in the navy the government in the later seventeenth century began the practice of consulting teachers of navigation in the ports. In spite of this practice there were frequent complaints that some state officials gave pilot's licenses and appointed men to positions in the navy for as little as "three or four bottles of Spanish wine." It is interesting to note, however, that these abuses were worse in ports where there were no teachers of navigation.[74]

6. Conclusion

The practical attempts of the sixteenth and seventeenth centuries to plan and then to set up various types of technical instruction were both tentative and haphazard. Older types of

[74] Anthiaume, *Évolution* . . . , ref. 68, Vol. 2, pp. 76–128.

general education, as well as apprentice training for industry, the army, or the navy, were already well organized, and new ideas and methods had to grow not in an open plain of ignorance but in a jungle of old ideals, institutions, and usages. Tremendous inertia and great resistance had to be overcome everywhere.

Throughout the seventeenth century the efforts to imitate and to reform technical education were based on the theories of mercantilism. To make the state strong in a military and naval way, to improve the quality and amount of its manufactures so that they would command both domestic and foreign markets were the steady aims of statesmen. Unless this is clearly grasped, the efforts to improve technical education cannot be understood.

The whole regime of formal education was still dominated by the study of theology or the classics, and by the ideals of training for character and for the life of a gentleman. The new proposals for education "through the senses," and of proceeding from the known to the unknown and from the concrete to the general were still in the process of formulation and were largely without practical programs for their realization. They continued to remain mostly on paper until the nineteenth century. Industrial processes and even the technics of the army and navy continued to be learned by some sort of apprentice system. The master worked at all the various processes of his handicraft, and, with such an organization of industry, it was easy for the apprentice to learn the trade completely. It was to the interest of the master to make his apprentices skillful, as all the profits went to the master; the more skilled his apprentices, the greater his gains. The apprentice system in training for the army and the navy lacked even this stimulus. At the same time the great advances in science were as yet largely without influence on the schools and had no consistent influence on industry or on the army and navy. The one important influence of science on education was seen in some of the secondary schools.

Certain advances toward a modern type of technical training were due to the active intervention of government. The founding of the art and science academies, and earlier the establishment and extension of state industries and industries under royal patronage, enlisting the best artistic talent and the most skilled workers to improve processes, pointed the way to the industrial schools of the nineteenth century. Herein lay Colbert's greatest contribution toward creating a situation in which a modern type of technical education was later to develop. Even in these fields he was seriously hampered by lack of funds and by the indifference or hostility of other forces in the state. Nevertheless, the academies and the state industries continued to play important roles down to the Revolution. But they lacked organization; still worse, they failed to bridge the gap between what the ablest artists and scientists knew and what was taught to the skilled artisans of France — even to those who worked directly under the scientists and artists in the state industries. Everywhere there is evidence that there was still too much faith in the rule-of-thumb method of the older types of apprentice training and too little attention to theoretical education for industry, especially in mathematics, mechanics, and even in such chemistry as was known in France before Lavoisier. Still, some substantial results were achieved despite the fact that the plans were only partly realized.

In its efforts to improve the training for the army and the navy, the government encountered somewhat similar difficulties. Most of the army and navy schools, *corps,* and *gardes* were charitable organizations to which impoverished nobles might send their sons. Frequently such nobles had been able to afford no previous schooling, and the youths were illiterate. In such a social system, the most elementary educational requirements were often out of the question. The boys and their families usually saw little value in these schools and *corps* and were merely waiting for a chance to secure a commission and get into service. Dancing, riding, fencing, and even writing they needed, but the regiment or the ship was *the* place to learn the *métier;* of course, the officers of the line who had come up that way agreed, for officers in the army and the navy, including the ablest, had learned little of their profession in any school. They were usually skeptical or even contemptuous of organized instruction. Little wonder that young men, anxious to rise in the service, saw no need for theoretical studies. There was also great difficulty finding teachers; they seem to have been either clerics who did not seem to the boys very close to warfare, disabled old "salts" who knew a little navigation, or down-and-out or crippled army officers who turned a penny by teaching fortification and gunnery. It was obvious that if ill luck had not cast them aside they would have been in active service. Just as the apprentice system had the economic stimulus of producing good wares, so the merchant marine had the economic interest in competent navigation and therefore was more inclined to stress the training of pilots and their licensing.

Military and naval science, moreover, were only beginning to have much practical value, and they still did not command the respect of the best minds. Wars on land and sea were constant, and active military and naval careers had a vivid and immediate appeal to youths who would far rather go out to service directly than spend first a tedious term in some *corps* or *garde*. Even in cases where provision for training officers was made, the tremendous pressure to get men into service — because of the wars of Louis XIV — undid the best plans for training them. By the end of the reign of Louis XIV the state had neither solved the problem of organizing substantial courses in military and naval science nor had it geared technical training into the whole organization of the military and naval establishments. The first higher technical schools for the army were those organized for the engineers and for the artillery in the eighteenth century. By that time the higher positions in the learned branches of soldiering began to go preferentially to those who had received such special types of training.

Everywhere and in all types of schools, before the eighteenth century, reforms met an almost insurmountable obstacle in the absence of qualified teachers. Thus it remained for periods after 1700 to organize technical education and to convince the state and the public that, in matters technical, "knowledge is power." It was, however, a great accomplishment to have progressed so far in defining the problems and in laying the broad foundations. In no other country in Europe had so much been done.

The Age of the Enlightenment
1700–1789

The eighteenth century teems with publications on the subject of education. "Every week appear new writings on education," wrote Melchior von Grimm in 1758. In his *Correspondance* for 1762 he again remarked, "the rage of this year is to write on education." "Everywhere," declared Mme. d'Épinay, "in Germany, in England, as in France, there was nothing considered of more importance, no question oftener discussed than how to bring up the ideal man and the perfect citizen."[1] Even works that aimed at other types of reform devoted much space and attention to educational problems.

The ideals of rationalism and of science, and those of democracy and humanitarianism all played a larger role than in the preceding century; this led to every manner of attack on older educational systems which were denounced as unscientific and undemocratic, fit only for the education of priests and of such nobles as never intended to be of use in the world.

[1] G. Compayré, *Histoire critique des doctrines de l'éducation en France,* 5th ed. (2 vols., Paris, 1885), Vol. 2, p. 112; cf. also H. M. Pollard, *Pioneers of Popular Education 1760–1850* (Cambridge, Mass., 1957).

Stupid conventions in school discipline and in the courses of study and the influence of the church in education were peculiarly detested. Schools should be made civil institutions; it was a menace to the state to allow the priest to control the training of youth. Rousseau, La Chalotais, Rolland, Diderot, and Helvétius — to mention only the more widely read of the French educational theorists — were all insistent on the idea that education is an affair of the government. The first purpose of instruction should be to promote the practical interests of society by training men for the varied activities of the state.[2] Grimm wrote in 1762 that the teaching in French schools "unfitted young people for every state of society," and the next year, in a speech at Tours, La Chalotais declared that "at twenty years of age the student falls into the world as a newborn babe."[3] Most of these ideas were hardly new except in emphasis. In fact, the educational theorizing of the eighteenth century is less original than that of the seventeenth, and the Enlightenment, at least down to the Revolution, produced nothing so new as the *collèges* of the religious orders. Not until the nineteenth century did most of the pedagogical notions of the *Philosophes* begin to bear fruit.

In the field of elementary technical education Rousseau in his *Émile* came nearer than any previous writer to estimating the manual arts at their true educational value. At the same time more schoolmasters took manual work into the school and, for both economic and pedagogic reasons, gave it an important place in elementary instruction. The state-supported and state-patronized industries established in earlier centuries

[2] "The pedagogy of the eighteenth century is dominated by the idea of the necessity of secularizing education. Resolute Gallicans, like La Chalotais or Rolland, and intrepid freethinkers, like Diderot or Helvétius, believed and proclaimed that public instruction is a civil matter, a 'work for the government,' as Voltaire said. All wish to substitute lay for ecclesiastical teachers, and to open state schools on the ruins of monkish schools." Compayré, *op. cit.,* Vol. 2, p. 203.

[3] L. R. La Chalotais: *Essay on National Education,* ed. by H. R. Clark (London, 1934), intro., p. 17.

continued to give practical instruction in improved industrial processes, and just before the French Revolution the Duc de La Rochefoucauld-Liancourt opened the first good trade school in France.

The greatest strides in technical education were made in the higher schools which prepared students for careers in state services, especially in mining and civil engineering, the army, and the navy; before the outbreak of the Revolution many positions in the state technical services were filled by young men who had gone through a theoretical technical training. The services of bridges and highways, of military, mining, and geographical engineering, of naval construction, and of military and naval artillery, all showed improvements due to better educational opportunities. Special *corps* and schools were well organized, admitting only those who were able to complete the course of study required. Out of such instruction came, after 1789, the *École polytechnique*. In these fields of higher technical training the French were in advance of the rest of Europe.

1. Technical Education in the Elementary and Secondary Schools

The greatest influence in the educational theorizing of eighteenth-century France was the Englishman John Locke. In his *Essay on Human Understanding* (1690), he elaborated the doctrine that the mental development of the child is conditioned almost entirely by his experience; the mind at birth is a blank sheet; experience, especially that part acquired through the sense organs, changes this blank into the intelligence and character. "I imagine," he says, "the minds of children as easily turned this or that way as water itself." In *Some Thoughts Concerning Education* (1693), Locke advocates the idea that education should fit a boy for practical life in a trade or profession. "Since it cannot be hoped [that the pupil] should have time and strength to learn all things, most pains should be taken about that which is most necessary; and that principally looked after which will be of most and frequentest use to him in the world."[4] Several trades should be learned; Locke especially approved of gardening and woodworking.[5] Training in the manual arts not only increases dexterity and skill but "contributes to our health too, especially such as employ us in the open air."[6] Locke emphasized the value of instruction in drawing to teach the child to observe the relation of objects in space. In teaching science, books which are concerned with observations and experiments, like those of Boyle and Newton, are preferable to those containing merely speculative systems.

Locke considered primarily the education of a gentleman, and the manual arts are discussed partly as a means of learning and partly as recreation. In 1697, when he held a state administrative position, he suggested a system of working schools for pauper children between the ages of three and fourteen, a system long advocated in England, France, and Germany, and first successfully organized by the *Frères des écoles chrétiennes* in France and by Francke's schools in Halle. Here

[4] J. W. Adamson, ed., *The Educational Writings of John Locke* (London, 1912), p. 76.

[5] Rousseau said of woodworking, "The trade I should choose for my pupil . . . is that of a carpenter. It is clean and useful; it may be carried on at home; it gives enough exercise; it calls for skill and industry, . . . there is scope for elegance and taste." J.-J. Rousseau, *Émile* (Everyman ed., London, 1933), p. 163. An earlier statement of this idea is that of the Englishman, Sir William Petty: "All children, though of the highest rank, [should] be taught some genteel manufacture," and Petty then gives a list of suitable crafts: wood turning, watchmaking, painting, engraving, carving, and the making of architectural and ship models. J. W. Adamson, *Pioneers of Modern Education 1600–1700* (Cambridge, 1905), pp. 133–34; Foster Watson, *The Beginning of the Teaching of Modern Subjects in England* (London, 1909), pp. 225–29.

[6] Adamson, ref. 4, p. 169.

they could be taught spinning, knitting, or some other manual employment.[7] A French translation of Locke's *Some Thoughts Concerning Education,* by Coste, appeared in 1695, and the work soon began to exercise a significant influence on French thought.[8] This influence increased as the century progressed. Rousseau, La Chalotais, and Condillac all followed Locke's theory that human knowledge has its source in sensations which are the bases for reflective thinking, and that firsthand experience and reason must replace authority in education.

In 1728, the Abbé de Saint-Pierre, a prolific and somewhat naïve author of all sorts of reform projects, published his *Projet de perfectionnement de l'éducation.* His first interest was in teaching morality but, after that, the rest of education must be practical. He envisaged a type of elementary school surrounded by shops and grounds, where agriculture and all kinds of trades would be taught. "My advice," he wrote, "is that children should be instructed, in all the eight or nine classes . . . in all the arts and sciences." [9] He is quite positive in his rejection of everything that is not directly useful and has no possibility of direct application — the first educational theorist in France of whom this may be said.[10]

---

[7] Preserved Smith, *History of Modern Culture* (2 vols., New York, 1930–1934), Vol. 2, p. 434.

[8] On the influence of Locke on French educational theory, cf. Compayré, ref. 7, Vol. 2, pp. 21–28. Helvétius carried to greater lengths than any other theorist Locke's belief that children are born without any inherent ideas, that all ideas are due to sensations, and that individuals enter the world as equals and differ only in their experience. By his oversimplification of Locke's ideas he gave them a greater vogue. In emphasizing the importance of social factors in education, his *De l'homme, de ses facultés intellectuelles et de son éducation* (1772) was a valuable corrective to Rousseau's *Émile.* Cf. M. Grossman, *The Philosophy of Helvétius, with Special Emphasis on the Educational Implications of Sensationalism* (New York, 1926).

[9] E. Bertrand, *L'enseignement technique en Allemagne et en France* (Montpellier, 1913), p. 213.

[10] Compayré, ref. 1, Vol. 2, p. 13. On Abbé de Saint-Pierre, cf. J. Drouet, *L'Abbé de Saint-Pierre* (Paris, 1912).

Many of the ideas of Comenius, Locke, and the Abbé de Saint-Pierre reached a wider public through Rousseau's *Émile* of 1762, a work characterized by Preserved Smith as "the most celebrated and influential treatise on education ever written, and the worst." [11] Rousseau, throughout his treatise, insists on the value of learning through doing. "I hate books," he declares; "they only teach us to talk about things we know nothing about. . . . The boy will learn more by one hour of manual work than he will retain from a whole day's verbal instructions." [12] Rousseau's theories of manual training, like those of Comenius and Locke, form merely a part — and a subordinate one — of a general scheme of education. With Locke, instruction in a craft was to cultivate the senses of the child, to develop his physical powers, and to offer him an agreeable distraction. Rousseau accepted these aims but added a utilitarian motive: The society of western Europe is approaching great changes, even revolution, and the youth should be prepared to earn his living, come what may. A trade, he believes, is a more certain means of making a living than are the leading professions. A youth taught to use his hands "is ready for anything. He can handle the spade and hoe, he can use the lathe, hammer, plane or file; he is already familiar with these tools which are common to many trades. He needs only to acquire sufficient skill in the use of any one of them to rival the speed, the familiarity, and the diligence of good workmen." [13] Being of democratic views Rousseau, moreover, wished by glorifying work to bridge the gap between the upper classes and the workers. "Though Rousseau's enthusiasm," writes Cubberley, "took the form of theory run mad, and the educational plan he proposed was largely impossible,

[11] Smith, ref. 7, Vol. 2, p. 442.
[12] Rousseau, ref. 5, p. 147.
[13] Rousseau, *op. cit.*, pp. 157, 162–63. Rousseau rejects for his pupil the crafts of weaver and stonecutter as stupid crafts, mason and shoemaker as dirty crafts, and perfumer as a craft overcivilized, and proposes carpentry and woodwork.

he nevertheless popularized education, not only in France, but among the reading public of the progressive European states."[14] His ideas of manual education had their greatest influence in the elementary schools of the later eighteenth and early nineteenth centuries in Germany; he especially influenced Basedow, Pestalozzi, and Fröbel.[15]

In 1761 the Jesuit order was expelled from France, and the question of what was to be done to take the place of their secondary schools became one of the great questions of public discussion. The curriculum in the schools of the teaching orders had been severely criticized ever since the beginning of the eighteenth century; too much emphasis, it was said, was given to discipline and to religious instruction, scholastic philosophy, and Latin studies; the French language, history, and science were neglected. The stress placed on Latin rhetoric seemed to the critics peculiarly absurd. Ridiculous subjects for composition were given to young boys: "A young man explains his reasons for wishing to die"; "The remorse of Nero after murdering his mother"; or "The speech made by the Serpent to Eve when he seduced her."[16] Such exercises called only for memory, and demanded merely a rehash of phrases used by Cicero or Virgil, or, in the cases where the

[14] E. P. Cubberley, *The History of Education* (Boston, 1920), p. 509.

[15] On the influence of Rousseau's ideas of manual instruction on education, cf. C. A. Bennett, *History of Manual and Industrial Education up to 1870* (Peoria, Ill., 1926), Chaps. 3–6 incl.; P. Natorp, *Pestalozzi,* 5th ed. (Leipzig, 1927); A. Basedow, "Basedow 1724–1790," *Friedrich Manns pädagogisches Magazin,* 1924; H. Hecker und M. Muchow, *Fröbel und Montessori,* 2nd ed. (Leipzig, 1931); and B. Bendokat, *Industriepädagogik bei den Philanthropen und bei Pestalozzi* (Halle a. d. Saale, 1933). Rousseau's influence, in the matter of manual training is shown in the constitution of 1793, which states that young Frenchmen could be inscribed on the civil register only if they exercised "a mechanical profession." F. Dubief: *L'apprentissage et l'enseignement technique* (Paris, 1910), p. 45 *note.*

[16] As Preserved Smith writes, "Few boys, even in Jesuit schools, wished to die; still fewer, even under the tuition of the casuists, had murdered their mothers; none of them had much experience with talking serpents or with naked women in Paradise." Smith, ref. 7, Vol. 2, pp. 430–31.

instruction was given in French, of Boileau, Bossuet, or Racine.

The expulsion of the Jesuits suddenly brought these questions to an issue. The *Parlements* proposed new schemes of education, and the royal government in 1763 founded *Bureaux d'administration* to take over the hundred Jesuit schools which were closed. The same year La Chalotais, a magistrate of Rennes and a bitter opponent of the Jesuits, published his remarkable *Plan d'éducation nationale*. Herein he advanced — without Rousseau's paradox or sentimentality — the idea that the state must control the schools and that their curricula should be reconstructed to promote the everyday interests of society rather than the welfare of the church.[17]

"The public welfare, the honor of the nation," he declares, "require that we substitute a civil education which will prepare each coming generation to follow successfully the different occupations. . . . I claim the right to demand for the nation an education that will depend upon the state alone, because education belongs essentially to it, because every nation has an inalienable . . . right to instruct its members, and finally because the children of the state should be educated by members of the state." Moreover, as a result of the existing system of education, "most young people know neither the world in which they live, nor the earth which nourishes them, nor the men who supply their needs, . . . nor the artisans whom they employ. They have not even the beginnings of knowledge concerning them." Reforms in education should be made to bring young students into first-hand contact with the world about them: One should begin to study nature by observing nature, manufactures by visiting workshops and by studying the actual working of machines, so as to notice

---

[17] Voltaire wrote of the work of La Chalotais, "It is a terrible attack on the Jesuits, made even stronger by its moderation." Compayré, ref. 1. Vol. 2, p. 216. Suggestions of secularizing the schools were fairly common at the time; for others, cf. H. C. Barnard: *The French Tradition in Education* (Cambridge, 1922), p. 232; also the article "Collèges" by d'Alembert in the *Encyclopédie*.

"the effects of the lever, of wheels, of pulleys, of the screw, of the wedge, and of balances; . . . it would be desirable that children should early be made familiar with globes, maps, spheres, thermometers, and barometers, that they should know how to use the rule and compass; . . . they should handle the air pump; . . . they should see the phenomena of electricity." He had the common eighteenth-century belief that more mathematics ought to be taught in the schools not only because mathematics is in itself useful in many of the occupations but also because it teaches students to reason. "It is very possible and very common to reason badly in theology, in politics; it is impossible in arithmetic and in geometry; if accuracy of mind is lacking, the rules will supply accuracy and intelligence for those who follow them." [18] The directness and clarity of

[18] Besides the edition by H. R. Clark (ref. 3) there is also a convenient edition of La Chalotais by F. de La Fontainerie, *French Liberalism and Education in the Eighteenth Century, La Chalotais, Turgot, Diderot, and Condorcet* (New York, 1932); the quotations are from this edition, pp. 40, 53, 56, 90, 93, 95. Cf. J. Delvaille, *La Chalotais, éducateur* (Paris, 1911) and E. Künoldt, *La Chalotais und sein Verhältnis zu Basedow* (Oldenburg, 1897); another treatise, much like that of La Chalotais, is that of Guyton de Morveau, *Mémoire sur l'éducation publique* (Paris, 1764). The attacks on the church schools made by anticlerical writers should not obscure the fact that the ecclesiastical system of education was extensive. Even after the Jesuit *collèges* were closed, there were still 562 *collèges* for a population of 25,000,-000. In 1843, when the population had increased to a third more, the number of *collèges* had sunk to 368, though the loss was offset by a large number of private secondary schools. In 1789 there was one pupil for each 382 inhabitants; in 1843 there was one for each 413 inhabitants. Just before the outbreak of the Revolution in 1789 there were 40,000 pupils who received their instruction either entirely or in part gratuitously. The eighteenth-century reformers were unreasonably severe in their criticism of the church schools, and the Revolutionary regimes, though they created plans aplenty, never succeeded in creating any educational order that was as good. Villemain, "Rapport au roi," *Moniteur,* 8 March 1843. The best work on primary education before the Revolution is E. Allain: *Instruction primaire en France avant la Révolution,* 2nd ed. (Paris, 1881); cf., also S. T. McCloy, *Government Assistance in 18th Century France* (Durham, 1946), pp. 411–412, 424–29; on secondary education, cf. A. Sicard, *Les études classiques avant la Révolution* (Paris, 1887); there is a useful bibliography of French primary and secondary education in the eighteenth century in D. Mornet, *Les origines intellectuelles*

La Chalotais's argument and his very practical suggestions to meet the needs of the time gave the work a great vogue; its influence on the public-school system of modern France is fundamental. Although he is not specifically interested in the problems of technical education, his influence helped greatly to create a general educational regime of a type in which technical education might develop.

Roland, president of the *Parlement de Paris,* published in 1768 a report on national education in which he went even further than La Chalotais. His scheme included plans for a hierarchy of educational institutions from a central university down to primary schools. He was extraordinarily forward-looking in proposing the extension of education to everyone and in offering young men different types of education. It is a mistake, he insisted, to have all the students in the higher schools studying the same subjects in exactly the same number of years. The training necessary for some is quite useless for others. Rolland clearly saw the need for improvement in scientific instruction; he praised the success of the instruction in experimental physics at the *Collège de Navarre,* and demanded the creation in all *collèges* of special professorships

de la Révolution française (Paris, 1933), pp. 518–22. The author has found the following useful: E. Allain, *L'instruction primaire dans la Gironde avant la Révolution* (Paris, 1895); G. Carré, *L'enseignement secondaire à Troyes du moyen-âge à la Révolution* (Paris, 1888); V. Chauvin, *Histoire des lycées et collèges de Paris* (Paris, 1866); F. J. Demange, *Les écoles d'un village Toulois au commencement du XVIIIe siècle* (Paris, 1892); Destandau, *L'Enseignement aux Baux avant 1789* (Avignon, 1904); E. Fontaine de Rebecq, *L'Enseignement primaire avant 1789 dans le département du Nord* (Paris, 1878); L. Maître, *L'Instruction publique dans les villes et les campagnes du Comté Nantais avant 1789* (Nantes, 1882); C. Muteau, *Les écoles et collèges en province depuis les temps les plus reculés jusqu'en 1789* (Dijon 1882); F. N. Nicollet, *L'Enseignement primaire dans le département des Hautes Alpes en 1789* (Gap, 1894); B. Paumès, *Le collège royale et les origines du lycée de Cahors* (Cahors, 1907); E. Poupé, *L'Instruction publique à Correns sous l'ancien régime* (Paris, 1900); C. de Robillard de Beaurepaire, *L'Instruction publique dans le diocèse de Rouen avant 1789* (3 vols., Evreux, 1872); and M. Soulice, *L'Instruction primaire dans les Basses Pyrenées 1385–1880* (Pau, 1881).

of mathematics and physics, which were still taught as parts of philosophy. He believed, too, that the more skilled crafts, business methods, military tactics, and navigation should have a place in public instruction.[19]

In the second half of the eighteenth century popular works on science, like the Abbé Pluche's *Spectacle de la nature* and the Abbé Nollet's *Leçons de physique expérimentale,* were studied in some of the *collèges* and helped to popularize experimental methods. A few of the *collèges* had models of machines and conducted experiments — at the *Collège de Navarre* Nollet gave an excellent course in experimental physics — though, in general, the remark of Diderot remained true, that "almost everywhere, under the name of physics, one got no further than discussions about the elements of matter and the system of the world." The critics of the schools found them hopelessly behindhand in training their pupils for all sorts of later scientific work, and beyond that inadequate in preparing young men to understand the world in which they would live. Such attacks on the older types of schools became common after the first quarter of the eighteenth century. In a manuscript, *Plan détaillé d'un établissement maritime,* of 1757 by the Abbé Vatan, the author says, "All our cities are full of *collèges,* founded at great expense, wherein ignorant pedants teach very badly a few words of a useless language. . . . There

---

[19] P. Pompée: *Études sur l'éducation professionnelle en France* (Paris, 1863), pp. 38–39. Bossuet in the later seventeenth century wrote of the physics lessons given to the Dauphin, "These experiments teach the Dauphin the activity of the human spirit, the inventions of the arts for discovering the secrets of nature . . . but most important, they are to make the prince admire the marvels of nature herself . . . and the providence of God." H. Druon, *Histoire de l'éducation des princes dans la maison des Bourbons de France* (2 vols., Paris, 1897), Vol. 1, Chap. LXVII, p. 309. Nevertheless, Girault de Koudon, fifty years later, wrote to the *Académie des sciences,* "Arbitrary and metaphysical questions so easy to dispute and so useless for the knowledge of the real world, remained . . . those treated with care in the *collèges;* young men . . . have more taste for this sort of discussion . . . and know nothing of real physics." F. Vial, *Trois siècles d'histoire de l'enseignement secondaire* (Paris, 1936), pp. 16–17.

are no schools which interest themselves in teaching agriculture, navigation, commerce, and manufacturing." The Abbé then proposes schools where "the present form and functioning of each government, the condition of its agriculture, of its population, of its manufactures, and of its domestic and foreign commerce; and . . . methods for increasing . . . the products of the soil and of industry should be taught." [20]

Diderot, in his *Plan d'une université russe,* drawn up for Catherine the Great of Russia about 1775, repeats many of the criticisms of contemporary French education made shortly before by Rousseau, La Chalotais, Roland, and others. He believes that education should be free and obligatory for all, and he gives a larger place to science than had any of the earlier writers; indeed, the foundations of higher education, he believes, should be laid in the study of mathematics, physics, astronomy, natural history, and chemistry. "I begin the course," he writes, "with arithmetic, algebra, and geometry, because in all conditions of life, from the highest to the last of the mechanical arts, the knowledge of them is needed. Everything is counted, everything is measured." He has great interest in geometry, "the best and simplest of all logics, and it is the most suitable for fortifying the judgment and the reason." Throughout his discussion of the teaching of science, Diderot emphasizes its practical applications.[21]

---

[20] *Arch. nat. marine* G 86. Cf. Diderot's attack on the use of the classics in secondary education. De La Fontainerie, ref. 18, pp. 214–15, 240–54; and Sicard, ref. 18, Vol. 1, Chap. 4. Some idea of the scientific teaching in French eighteenth-century secondary schools is shown in the list of mathematical theses defended by a student at the *Collége Louis-le-Grand* in 1746; these included advanced geometry, trigonometry, and fortification. C. de Rochemontieux, *Un collège des Jésuites au XVIIe et XVIIIe siècle, le collège Henri IV de la Flèche* (4 vols., Le Mans 1889), Vol. 1, pp. 368–86.

[21] De La Fontainerie, ref. 18, pp. 229–36. Typical of Diderot's point of view is the following: "Experimental physics enters into almost all the arts and crafts. . . . No machines can be made without calculating solidity and fragility, heaviness and lightness, softness and hardness, rigidity and flexibility, humidity and dryness, friction and elasticity." De La Fontainerie, *op. cit.,* p. 235. On the *Encyclopédie* and education, cf. L. Thorndike, "L'Encyclopédie and the History of Science" in *Isis* (1924) and P. Albien, *Das Pädago-*

In editing the *Encyclopédie* (1751–1772), Diderot showed his great interest in science and in all sorts of technological processes; under his general direction a series of over fifty volumes, describing all the fundamental processes of industry, was published as a supplement to the *Encyclopédie*. A more substantial series of over seventy volumes was published by the *Académie des sciences* between 1761 and 1788. The extraordinary collection, with about thirteen thousand pages of text and approximately eighteen hundred plates, presents a marvelous and unrivaled survey of the technical processes in use in western Europe just before the Industrial Revolution.

In their writings, the Physiocrat economists emphasized the importance of state education. Turgot made one of the strongest appeals of the whole eighteenth century for state-supported and state-controlled education. But their interest in developing agriculture led them to neglect the problems of technical education; furthermore, they were not in agreement as to whether such education is always useful.[22] In their periodical, *Ephémérides du citoyen,* the Hapsburgs are praised for establishing a school of commerce in which mathematics, drawing, geography, and modern languages are taught.[23] On

---

gische in der Encyclopédie von Diderot (Magdeburg, 1908). On the teaching of science in French secondary schools, cf. Sicard, ref. 18, Vol. 4, Chap. 1, and Mornet, ref. 18, pp. 324–26.

[22] The best works on the *Physiocrates* are those of G. Weulersse, *Le mouvement physiocratique en France* (2 vols., Paris, 1910), *Les physiocrates sous le ministère Turgot* (Paris, 1924), a briefer compend, *Les physiocrates,* 2nd ed. (Paris, 1931), and *La physiocratie sous les ministères de Turgot et Necker* (Paris, 1950). A good introduction in English is H. Higgs, *The Physiocrats* (London, 1897). "The Physiocrats were the first scientific school of political economy. . . . In the Physiocrats we see an alliance of persons, a community of ideas, an acknowledged authority, and a combination of purposes, which banded them into a society apart." Higgs, *op. cit.,* p. 3. The clearest connected contemporary account of their doctrines is Mercier de la Rivière, *Ordre naturel et essentiel des sociétés politiques* (London, 1767); cf. also H. Gourdon, "Les physiocrates et l'éducation nationale au XVIIIe siècle," *Revue pédagogique* (1901).

[23] *Ephémérides du citoyen,* year 1770, pp. 168–69.

the other hand, Cantillon, one of the leading Physiocrat theorists, believed that "the charity schools in England and the projects in France for increasing the number of artisans are quite useless . . . There can never be lack of artisans in a state, when there is enough work to give them regular employment."[24]

The *cahiers*, the list of grievances composed by groups throughout France in anticipation of the meeting of the States-General in 1789, show the general influence of both the *Philosophes* and the *Physiocrates*. In the matter of technical education they made a number of specific requests: the nobility of Lyons asked that a course in applied chemistry be given in their city, the third estate in Corsica requested a school of architecture, that of Riom petitioned to have schools with teachers of mathematics and drawing established in all cities where they did not then exist, a request repeated by Caen and other cities.[25] In considering the theorizing on education in eighteenth-century France it is surprising that few followed Roland in pointing out what Bacon, Leibniz, Comenius, and others had suggested much earlier, namely the great need for different types of schools for different classes and different careers in society.[26]

[24] A. E. Monroe, ed., *Early Economic Thought* (Cambridge, 1924), p. 248.

[25] E. Allain, *La question d'enseignement en 1789* (Paris, 1886), pp. 131–32, 231, 285, 295–97; cf. also L. Bourrilly, *Les cahiers de l'instruction publique en 1789* (Paris, 1901), and A. Duméril, *Des voeux des cahiers de 1789 relatifs à l'instruction publique* (Toulouse, 1880). There is now an admirable guide to the *cahiers* by B. F. Hyslop: *A Guide to the General Cahiers of 1789* (New York, 1936); cf. also, by the same author, *Supplément au répertoire critique des cahiers de 1789* (Paris, 1953).

[26] As John Dury wrote in England in the later seventeenth century, ". . . the vulgar should be equipped with those [arts and sciences] necessary for trades and servile work; the learned for the increase of science and the training up of others; the nobles should be fitted for public charges in peace and war." Similar statements were made in the theoretical writings of Sir William Petty and Cowley. L. F. Anderson, *History of Manual and Industrial School Education* (New York, 1926), pp. 24–27. The idea that different types of training were necessary was growing in the eighteenth century. Sicard, ref. 18, pp. 219–24.

Such ideas were being put into effective practice in some of the primary and secondary schools of the German states. Finding the ordinary schools closed to the teaching of applied science, the Pietist philanthropists Francke and Semler in Halle had, about 1700, established a series of elementary schools which embodied many of the ideas of Bacon, Comenius, and other early theorists. Francke's work was to introduce industrial crafts into the ordinary grammar schools. Semler created an industrial school which combined the teaching of industrial subjects with the typical shop experience of the apprentice. Semler's enterprise was the more original. Its purpose he described in a report to the *Society of Sciences* at Berlin: "Just as the advanced and elementary schools, as well as the academies for the nobility, have been established in order that the young might be trained in them to serve the commonweal in ecclesiastical, civil, and military offices, so it is advisable and practicable that those who are to take up a trade and who have hitherto received instruction for the most part only in reading, writing, and arithmetic . . . should in the future receive in a certain Mechanical School such training and instruction as is suited to their purposes and future condition in life, in order that their sense and understanding might be developed, and in particular that they might know the different materials and objects . . . and . . . useful instruments and tools, and might utilize this knowledge in a better understanding and practice of their handicraft." [27]

[27] Anderson, *op. cit.,* p. 22. The Berlin Society of Sciences stated in 1706 that some boys should "be instructed in an actual mechanical school, so that their understandings and senses might become acquainted with common materials and subjects, their value and price, with the common proportions of circles, lines, angles, and weight, as well as with different sizes and their measurement, with weighing, and upon opportunity with the simple microscope, for the better understanding of the constituents of bodies; and with the use of other useful instruments, together with tools and levers; to the end that this knowledge might serve them for improved understanding and practices, and to the invention of new and useful modes of using them. Thus it can be seen that there would be attained by such

In 1747 Hecker, another German, founded the first permanent *Realschule,* a secondary school intended for those who would not go on to the university but were expecting to enter commerce and industry. Its curriculum included, besides Latin, modern languages, history, drawing, mathematics, and science, combined with shopwork. Although there seems to have been no mutual influence, this curriculum parallels that of the French Oratorian *collèges,* though the Germans went much further in teaching pupils from models and from nature and in emphasizing the practical applications of science.[28]

---

scholars, good proportions in their work, a steady hand, and the like advantages, such as are derived from a more intelligent use of the outward senses, which are the foundation of all the skill which nature can offer and practice can perfect." H. Barnard, *Memoirs of Eminent Teachers* (rev. ed., Hartford, 1878), p. 434.

[28] The background of these German movements is discussed in E. Friedrich. *Die Entwicklung des Realienunterrichtes bis zu den ersten Realschulgründungen* (Weida, 1913). Cf. also ref. 15. Francke and his followers in Germany wanted to teach children practical things. In teaching composition, boys were shown how to write business forms, and in arithmetic and accounting practical problems were used; as Francke said, ". . . children should be taught to see arithmetic." Algebra, geometry, and trigonometry were to be taught in connection with surveying and building problems. Cf. J. W. Adamson, *Pioneers of Modern Education 1600–1700,* ref. 5, pp. 241–57. Late in the eighteenth century there were also some efforts made to introduce technical education into the German universities by the teaching of applied chemistry and mechanics, under the Latin name *cameralia.* This movement, most marked at the Universities of Halle, Heidelberg, and Göttingen, met the strong opposition of the professors of theology and the humanities, and the new subjects were thrown out. The same opposition had prevented the teaching of applied science in the German secondary schools. To supply elementary and secondary technical and commercial education in the German states had been the purpose of reformers like Francke, Semler, and Hecker; to furnish adequate advanced technical training, a number of the German princes founded institutions like the mining schools in Freiberg in Saxony, opened in 1765, and some military schools. In 1799 a *Bauakademie* was established in Berlin for the theoretical and practical training of civil and hydraulic engineers. Its success, like that of most of the early higher technical schools in Germany, was limited by the fact that it took students at fourteen years of age. A similar school was opened at Prague in 1806, and in 1815 a better one was established at Vienna. The first good higher technical school, chiefly for civil

These types of German schools — together with those instituted at the end of the eighteenth century by educators like Pestalozzi — met the specific problem of elementary and secondary technical education better than anything undertaken by the French state or by the French teaching orders, both in the training of poor children to trades and in technical instruction for the middle class. In these fields the French, during the eighteenth century, did little more than continue the undertakings of the seventeenth century. The influence of German and Swiss philanthropists and reformers seems to have had no significant effect in France until after 1800; its effects were found not in higher technical education but in primary schools, in popular trade schools, and in the general field of "manual training," especially in Germany, Switzerland, Holland, the Scandinavian countries, and the United States.

Some of the French municipalities opened schools of drawing and design. One founded in 1741 at Rouen was intended to improve designs used in printing cotton cloth; others were at Nancy (1702), Toulouse (1726), Bordeaux (1744), Rheims (1751), Marseilles (1753), Lille (1755), Lyons (1756), Amiens (1758), Grenoble (1762), Dijon (1765), St. Omer (1780), Calais (1787), Nantes (1789).[29] An *École royale gratuite de dessin,* established in Paris by the government in 1767, was the best of its kind in France. The letters patent establishing it speak of the importance of design and quality in French manufactures and the necessity of maintaining high standards,

---

engineering, in the Germanies was the one founded in Karlsruhe in Baden in 1825. W. E. Wickenden, *A Comparative Study of Engineering Education in the United States and in Europe* (Lancaster, Pa., 1929), pp. 44–47. Some English parallels are discussed in D. M. Turner, *History of Science Teaching in England* (London, 1927).

[29] A. Audiganne, "L'Enseignement industriel en France," *Revue des deux mondes,* 1851, pp. 877–82, and C. Schneegaus, "L'Enseignement des arts en Alsace, des écoles de dessin de Strasbourg au XVIIIe siècle," *Archives alsaciennes* (6e année), pp. 185–224. Cf. Père M. Ferry: *Plan des écoles des mathématiques pratiques et de dessin qui s'ouvriront à Reims* (Rheims, 1774).

and they provide for instruction in mathematics and all types of designing.[30]

The Paris *École de dessin* — which after the Revolution became the *École des arts décoratifs* — was largely the creation of Bachelier, a professor at the *Académie royale de peinture* and an important pioneer in the development of modern technical education. The schoolmen of eighteenth-century France had already begun to realize the importance of teaching drawing. They even exaggerated its value: "Drawing is the basis of all mechanical work," says a minor report preserved in the naval archives,[31] "and skilled workers are only superior in so far as they excel in this art." Bachelier went further and proposed that the *École de dessin* should become a sort of general technical school for industrial workers: "We propose to open a complete course in the mechanical arts in which will be demonstrated the working of machines, the materials used and all the operations relative to manufacturing."[32] Bachelier's project called for instruction for fifteen hundred students in three groups of five hundred each; on Mondays and Thursdays instruction was given in architecture and geometry, on Tuesdays and Fridays in figure drawing, and on Wednesdays and Saturdays in ornament and the designing of fabrics. Such training would be gratuitous for boys from eight years of age, though most of the students would be older. Such a system, if extended, would bring into society not a lot of useless young men educated only in Greek and Latin but youths trained in both the theory and practice of industry, and industry and en-

---

[30] J. Isambert, ed., *Recueil général des anciennes lois françaises* (Paris, 1833ff.), Vol. 22, p. 469; Vol. 23, pp. 562–563; Vol. 24, pp. 276–277. Cf. McCloy, ref. 18, pp. 418–419; also J. J. Bachelier: *Mémoire concernant l'école royale gratuite de dessin* (Paris, 1774).

[31] *Arch. Nat. Marine* G 86.

[32] J. J. Bachelier, *Projet d'un cours public des arts et métiers* (Paris, ed. of 1789), pp. 14–18; cf. F. Buisson, *Nouveau dictionnaire de pédagogie* (Paris, 1911), Vol. 1, p. 691.

gineering, in turn, would no longer be bound down by a stupid and blind routine.[33] The letters patent of 1767 establishing the Paris *École de dessin* embodied Bachelier's ideas, and the school perfomed a useful service down to the Revolution.[34]

A number of private manufactures, imitating the older state industries, instituted practical training in machine processes, especially in the cloth industries.[35] Some experiments in agricultural education were also undertaken. Proposals for such training go back to Palissy, Olivier de Serres, Sully, and Le Nôtre.[36] Before 1700 the only action taken by the government had been the establishment by Henry IV of two chairs of botany with experimental gardens at the universities of Montpellier and Paris, the collections of which were the richest in Europe. Such instruction was almost entirely limited to pure science and had little effect on agricultural methods.[37] In the

[33] J. J. Bachelier, *Discours sur l'utilité des écoles élémentaires en faveur des arts mécaniques* (Paris, ed. of 1789), pp. 7, 16–17; Anon., *Mémoire sur l'origine, le progrès et la situation de l'école royale gratuite de dessin* (Paris, 1790), pp. 6–7. Cf. also M. J. B. Deschamps, *Sur l'utilité des établissements des écoles gratuites de dessin en faveur des métiers, 1767* (Paris, 1789).

[34] The letters patent of 1767 and a number of the early regulations are preserved. *Arch. Nat.* A.D. VII, 4.

[35] C. Ballot, *L'introduction du mécanisme dans l'industrie française* (Paris, 1923), pp. 14, 44; cf. also, A. H. Cole and G. B. Watts, *The Handicrafts of France as recorded in the 'Description des arts et métiers,' 1761–88* (Boston, 1952).

[36] On Sully, cf. C. Turgeon, "Les idées économiques de Sully," *Revue d'histoire économique et sociale* (1923).

[37] H. Barnard, *Systems, Institutions, and Statistics of Scientific Instruction* (New York, 1872), 545; on *Jardin du roi*, cf. P. A. Cap, *Le muséum d'histoire naturelle* (Paris, 1854). The state poorhouses opposed the attempts of the agricultural societies to open farms for training foundlings. The poorhouses had manufactures of their own and wanted to use foundlings and orphans themselves. E. Justin, *Les sociétés royales d'agriculture au XVIIIe siècle* (Saint-Lô, 1935), pp. 134–35, 233. In the course of the eighteenth century, many of the German universities introduced courses in agricultural management. These were taken chiefly by men preparing to become administrators for the royal and other large estates. T. von der Goltz, *Geschichte der deutschen Landwirtschaft* (2 vols., Berlin, 1902–1903), Vol. 1,

eighteenth century proposals for agricultural education be-came more numerous. One of the most interesting was that made by the Abbé Rosier in a report submitted to Turgot in 1775, which outlined the program for a national school of agriculture to be set up in the park of the Château de Cham-bord. Nothing came of it at the time, and he submitted it, again without success, to the National Assembly. In 1761 the *Société d'agriculture,* made up largely of gentlemen farmers, advocated the appointment of teachers of agriculture to explain the improved methods used on model farms to anyone who might be interested. In 1763 a small school was organized at La Rochette, near Melun; another was started in 1771 near Com-piègne, and in 1786 Louis XVI provided for some instruction in connection with his model farm at Rambouillet.[38] However, no really effective agricultural education was established in France until after 1800.

Several proposals for schools of commerce were made. The most significant school opened was that at Mulhouse. The pupils were admitted between the ages of eleven and fifteen; besides instruction in German, French, English, and Italian, courses were given in religion, history, geography, writing, drawing, arithmetic, geometry, trigonometry, physics, and commerce. The last was "practical," consisting of practice in writing commercial letters, in bookkeeping, in calculating foreign and domestic weights and measures, and in handling all types of commercial transactions. The school was opened in 1781 with funds collected from the merchants of Mul-house.[39] Although the Revolution a few years later ended its

---

pp. 317–89. The beginning of modern elementary agricultural education is usually dated from Fellenberg's school at Hofwyl in Switzerland after 1802.

[38] A. H. Leake, *The Means and Methods of Agricultural Education* (Boston, 1915), p. 4.

[39] A. Engel, *Création d'une école de commerce à Mulhouse à la fin du 18ème siècle* (Mulhouse, 1875), pp. 6–8, 12–17. Cf. J. Vernier, ed., *Cahiers*

existence, the Mulhouse *École de commerce* seems to have been an important pioneer enterprise. Such instruction in France had earlier been gleaned from books of the type of Savary's *Parfait négociant* or from practical experience with a merchant house or a bank. Toward the end of the eighteenth century there is evidence of a growing belief that such instruction could be better handled in a school. After 1800 the number of proposals for this type of education increased, though wars and continual changes of regime prevented their realization until after 1815.

The one important undertaking in elementary technical education parallel to the work of the German *Philanthropen* that was made in France was the school opened by the Duc de La Rochefoucauld-Liancourt. This able and enlightened nobleman first won fame for his interest in scientific agriculture; his model farm at Liancourt was the finest on the Continent. Here in 1780 he founded an elementary trade school for twenty orphans of former soldiers of his regiments; in nine years the number in his school had increased to a hundred and sixty. The teachers were mostly army officers — a captain, a lieutenant, and fourteen noncommissioned officers — though there were also a master metalworker, a tailor, a shoemaker, and other craftsmen to direct the work in wool and cotton weaving.[40]

---

de Troyes (Troyes, 1909), Vol. 1, p. 90. The best commercial schools of the eighteenth century were in Germany. Cf. Bendokat, ref. 15; A. von Geusau, *Geschichte der Stiftungen, Erziehungs- und Unterrichts-Anstalten in Wien* (Vienna, 1803), pp. 403–04; H. Gilow, *Das Berliner Handelsschulwesen des 18. Jahrhunderts* (Berlin, 1906); B. Penndorf, *Geschichte der Buchhaltung in Deutschland* (Leipzig, 1913).

[40] F. Dreyfus, *La Rochefoucauld-Liancourt* (Paris, 1903), pp. 32–38; and Isambert, ref. 30, Vol. 28, pp. 223–24. Cf. P. Crouzet, *Observations . . . sur l'école . . . de Liancourt* (Paris, n.d.). A similar school was started near Paris in 1788 by a philanthropic Irish noble who received some help from the state. The two hundred children were to be taught trades, and at sixteen years of age they were either to enlist in the army for eight years, or to be apprenticed to some trade for five years. The school lasted only a short time. C. de Montzey, *Institutions d'éducation militaire jusqu'en 1789* (Paris, 1866), pp. 264–66. For elementary and secondary industrial schools

Out of this school the Revolutionary governments organized the first *école des arts et métiers*.

An important contribution to the spread of scientific ideas — though not directly connected with organized schools — were the science lectures given at the *Collège de France* and at the *Jardin du roi*. Especially at the *Jardin du roi* one could hear public lectures, often with demonstrations, given by the best mathematicians, physicists, chemists, botanists, and anatomists of the eighteenth century. In one form or another much of this material was published.[41]

2. *The Rise of Civil-Engineering Schools*

The new types of instruction advocated by the educational theorists and those introduced into the schools affected the elementary and secondary schools only. The real beginnings of higher technical education in France (and for that matter in Europe) were due not to the educational theorists but to scientists and mathematicians trained in the ecclesiastical *collèges* of the *Ancien Régime*. In spite of the criticism of their traditional curricula, these *collèges* gave excellent training in mathematics and physics, and they were to be found in every part of France. When new educational needs were felt, men trained in the old *collèges* were prepared to meet these needs.

Higher types of technical instruction arose through the development of the mechanical apparatus of the army, navy, transportation, and manufacture, and thus there arose the need of better engineering. The word *ingénieur* had come into common usage through the army. Only in the later eighteenth

in Germany, cf. K. Iven, *Die Industriepädagogik des 18. Jahrhunderts* (Langensalza, 1929) and works cited in footnote 15.

[41] Cf. J. P. F. Deleuze, *Histoire et description du Muséum royale d'histoire naturelle* (2 vols., Paris, 1823). The *Société Apollonienne,* organized by one of the Masonic lodges, sponsored similar scientific lectures. McCloy, ref. 18, p. 410. Cf., also, by the same author, *French Inventions of the Eighteenth Century* (Lexington, Ky., 1956).

century, however, did it begin to be applied commonly to builders of roads, canals, bridges, and nonmilitary constructions; then the term "civil engineer" was invented to distinguish them from the military engineers. The rapid development of mathematics in the seventeenth century had made possible much more thorough calculations and plans for all types of construction in both military and civil engineering. By the eighteenth century, in the field which was coming to be known as that of civil engineering, some of the work, formerly done by men trained as stone masons, carpenters, and practical mechanics, demanded a knowledge of mathematics and physics that could best be learned through an advanced type of instruction.

The government of the regent, the Duc d'Orléans, in 1716 instituted the *corps des ponts et chaussées* to supervise certain state construction projects. In 1720 further regulations established for the new corps a general inspector, an architect-engineer, three subordinate inspectors, and twenty-one engineers for the *généralités* and *pays d'éléction;* the *pays d'état* like Brittany and Languedoc continued to look after their own bridges and roads. The corps soon proved very useful, but it was found difficult to obtain the services of men adequately trained in both the theoretical and the practical aspects of engineering. This problem of personnel became more acute when the government of Louis XV decided, soon after 1740, to make maps and plans of all the great highways of the kingdom. Perronnet, who was in charge of the corps, found a lack of uniformity in standards and practices. To train more men for the service and to improve their effectiveness (1744) the number employed was increased, and the members of the corps when not otherwise occupied were ordered to work in the central offices on maps and plans, the teaching being done by the most outstanding man present at the time. For some years Perronnet spoke sometimes of his "office" and sometimes of the *École des ponts et chaussées*. Up to 1750 the men recruited for the *corps des ponts et chaussées* were known for their practical ability and experience in architecture and engineering. They had been prepared in various ways, though few had had much theoretical training in mathematics or other sciences. Gradually the corps came to be made up of men who had received some scientific instruction in a *collège* and were now, in addition, given more advanced training in the corps itself. Perronnet "may be called the father of modern civil engineering, and he was certainly the father of engineering education."[42]

The whole system was regularized by Turgot in 1775, in which year the *École des ponts et chaussées* was given its official name. At the same time the personnel of the whole corps of seventy men was divided into three classes: the first of *sous-ingénieurs* or *inspecteurs,* the second of *employés élèves,* and the third and lowest of *auxiliaires.* There were no entrance examinations, but the simplest subject taught was geometry, so that even the lowest rank of students had to have some preliminary training. Besides the instruction given in the central offices in Paris, the students were all sent out to work on projects during the summer. By 1788 there were a hundred and twelve students.[43]

The instruction given in the *École des ponts et chaussées* down to the Revolution was never of a very high order judged by modern standards, nor was it to be compared with that given in the later eighteenth century in a few of the army schools. The school had no regular staff of professors; such instruction as was offered was given by practicing engineers in

---

[42] P. Mantoux, *The Industrial Revolution in the Eighteenth Century* (New York, 1928), p. 221. M. d'Ocagne, *Les grandes écoles de France* (new ed., Paris, 1887), pp. 370–371, and Wickenden, ref. 28, pp. 9–10. Cf. also, P. Mousnier, *Progrès scientifique et technique au XVIIIe siècle* (Paris, 1958).

[43] J. Guillaume, *Procès verbaux du comité d'instruction publique de la convention* (5 vols., Paris, 1891–1907), Vol. 5, p. 632.

the state service or by older students. This use of advanced students to aid in the teaching was later developed in the system of *répétiteurs* used by the *École polytechnique*. Many of the abler students studied architecture, mathematics, physics, chemistry, and even mineralogy with private teachers outside the school.[44] But the whole enterprise is interesting because it is an early example of a government service tied up with a system of advanced technical training. During the Revolution the *École des ponts et chaussées* became one of the more advanced technical schools (*écoles d'application*) to which students went after completing the course in the *École polytechnique*.

An important branch of engineering, that of mining, had made advances during the early modern period. A number of elaborate treatises on mining methods had appeared since Georgius Agricola published his remarkable *De re metallica* in 1553.[45] The earliest schools of mining were founded in Germany: 1745 in Brunswick, 1765 in Freiburg, and 1775 in Clausthal.[46] During the first half of the eighteenth century there was much criticism of French mining methods both by government officials and by mine owners. The methods were condemned for their clumsiness and their wastefulness. After

[44] Ministère des travaux publiques, *Notice sur l'école des ponts et chaussées* (Paris, 1873), pp. 3–5; and A. Fourcy, *Histoire de l'école polytechnique* (Paris, 1828), p. 8. Cf. F. P. Tarbé de St. Hardouin, *Notices biographiques sur les ingénieurs des ponts et chaussées depuis la création du corps* (Paris, 1884); E. J. Vignon, *Études historiques sur l'administration des voies publiques en France an XVIIe et XVIIIe siècles* (4 vols., Paris, 1862–1880); Lucas, *Études historiques sur les voies de communication en France* (Paris, 1873); D. des Cilleuls, *Origines et développement du régime des travaux publics en France* (Paris, 1895); and A. Debauve, *Les travaux publics et les ingénieurs des ponts et chaussées depuis le XVIIe siècle* (Paris, 1893).

[45] English translation, with facsimiles of all original woodcuts, by H. C. and L. H. Hoover (London, 1912). The main ideas and a selection of the illustrations are given in A. Wolf, *A History of Science, Technology and Philosophy in the 16th and 17th Centuries* (London, 1935), pp. 505–24.

[46] For the German mining schools, whose curricula influenced the *École des Mines,* cf. Ludwig Beck, *Geschichte des Eisens in technischer und kulturgeschichtlicher Beziehung* (4 vols., Brunswick, 1884–1903), Vol. 3, pp. 57–63.

the establishment of the *École des ponts et chaussées* some of the state mining inspectors and some private mining engineers were trained there, and the advantages of training became more evident. About the middle of the century it was proposed to Bertin, head of the state mining-inspection service, that two mining schools be established, one at Forez for coal mining and one at Sainte-Marie-aux-Mines for the mining of metals. Bertin was not interested; the best way to learn mining, he declared, was to work in a mine. All he had to suggest was that the state give subsidies to certain students to follow courses of lectures in mathematics, chemistry, metallurgy, and mineralogy at the *Jardin du roi*. Nothing came of this proposal.

In 1769 the government of Louis XV, when issuing concessions for mines, began to demand payment of from 200 to 800 *livres* a year, the income to be set aside for establishing a school of mines. The school, however, was not authorized until 1778 and not given its name until 1783, when the *corps des ingénieurs des mines* was organized. An order of the government of Louis XVI stated its purposes: "The king advised that the arts of discovering and of exploiting mines have not in his kingdom made the progress of which they are capable. . . . His Majesty has considered various means by which to stimulate a kind of industry from which neighboring states have derived great advantages, and he has recognized that it is not sufficient merely to give concessions, but that it is also necessary to train men to carry on such work with both safety and economy. . . . It is these motives that have led His Majesty to establish a *school* of mines, like the *École des ponts et chaussées* established with so much success in the previous reign."[47]

The leading spirit in the founding of the *École des mines* and its first teacher was the chemist B. G. Sage, a member of

[47] Isambert, ref. 30, Vol. 27, p. 260. The *École des mines* was suppressed in 1802 and restored in 1816. A bureau of tests for mineral substances, the forerunner of industrial research laboratories in engineering schools, was established in 1845. Wickenden, ref. 28, p. 11.

the *Académie des sciences* and on the staff of the mint. The school was established in the Hôtel des Monnaies, though it was not formally organized till 1783. Sage taught chemistry, mineralogy, and the assaying of metals, and a short time later a second teacher, Duhamel,[48] added courses in physics, underground structures, hydraulics, and practical methods of mining and of mine ventilation. The students admitted had to be at least sixteen years old and were required to pass examinations in German, geometry, and drawing. Twelve scholarships for sons of mine directors and of skilled workers were established. The course was three years in length; in the winter and spring, instruction was given in Paris, and during summer and fall the best students were sent to accompany government mining inspectors or were placed in mining camps. On finishing the course, the students who passed the examinations were made *sous-ingénieurs des mines;* within a few years most of the positions as mine inspectors were filled by graduates of the *École des mines*. The *École des mines* was closed by the Revolution in 1790 and reopened with a much improved organization in 1794.[49]

At the outbreak of the Revolution, the *École des mines* was no better than several mining schools in Germany, but the *École des ponts et chaussées* was without a peer as a general school of civil engineering.

---

[48] In 1787 L. H. Duhamel de Monceau, who had written the articles on mining in the *Encyclopédie,* published a two-volume work, *Géométrie souterraine.*

[49] M. Rouff, *Les mines de charbon en France au XVIIIe siècle* (Paris, 1922), pp. 480–87; cf. also L. Aguillon, ed., *Législation des mines françaises et étrangères* (3 vols., Paris, 1886), and, by the same author, *Exposition universelle de 1889 — Historique de l'École des mines de Paris* (Paris, 1889); this sketch is reprinted in the *Annales des mines* (1889). On the science of mineralogy, cf. M. Caullery, *La science française depuis le XVIIe siècle* (Paris, 1933), pp. 58–59. Many important documents are in L. Fleury, *Recueil des lois, décrets, ordonnances . . . concernant le service des ingénieurs des mines* (2 vols., Paris, 1856–1857).

3. Military Education

The victories of the French armies in the wars of the Revolution and the Empire were due to no sudden changes that followed the downfall of the old monarchy; their roots lay deep in the improvement in organization and training which the royal military forces had received during the later eighteenth century. Because of financial difficulties and the opposition of many who had influence at the royal court the reforms in organization were less thoroughgoing than those in military tactics and military education.[50] The interest in all aspects of military science was enormous; in the writings in this field the French outdistanced all other European peoples both in originality and in influence. The taste for the study of military questions came to pervade all ranks of the French army.[51]

These changes affected the whole range of military education; older types of training were revitalized and extended, and new ones were created. The simplest type of military instruc-

[50] The reforms in the organization of the French army during the eighteenth century are summarized in A. Tilley, ed., *Modern France* (Cambridge, 1922), pp. 193–96; in E. Lavisse, ed., *Histoire de France* (14 Vols., Paris, 1900–1911), Vol. 8, Pt. 2, pp. 369–75 and Vol. 9, pp. 65–70; and in E. Boutaric, *Institutions militaires de la France* (Paris, 1863), Book VI, Chap. 3. Cf. also, A. Latreille, *L'armée et la nation à la fin de l'ancien régime* (Paris, 1914); L. Mention, *L'armée de l'ancien régime* (Paris, 1900); L. Tutey, *Les officiers sous l'ancien régime* (Paris, 1908); A. Babeau, *La vie militaire sous l'anciens régime* (2 vols., Paris, 1889–1890); A. Duruy, *L'armée royale en 1789* (Paris, 1888); R. Laulan, "Pourquoi et comment on entrait à l'école royale militaire de Paris," *Revue d'histoire moderne,* 1957; and R. Laulan, *L'École militaire de Paris 1751–88* (Paris, 1945). The standard bibliography for the history of the French army is de Favitski de Probobysz, *Répertoire bibliographique de la littérature militaire et coloniale française depuis cent ans* (Paris, 1935).

[51] The development of military thought in eighteenth-century France is discussed by R. Villate, "Le mouvement des idées militaires en France au XVIIIᵉ siècle," *Revue d'histoire moderne,* 1935, pp. 226–60. The library of the Prince de Ligne in the Austrian Netherlands contained, toward the end of the eighteenth century, 123 French military works written in the eighteenth century, as against 116 German, Dutch, Italian, Spanish, and English works. Villate, *op. cit.,* p. 259.

tion, the special training camp, usually of only a short duration, had been instituted by Louis XIV as early as 1666. By 1727 half of the army went through at least a month of this training. Here new military methods of all sorts were tried out; the officers organized discussions and made elaborate reports to the Secretary of State for War. As the training camps rarely lasted longer than a month, their value lay not in providing any real military education but in disseminating new ideas among soldiers already trained either in schools or through regimental experience.[52]

A simple type of military education, the old *cadets-gentils-hommes,* was revived in 1716, because of the insistence of a number of higher officers that the officers trained in the corps of *cadets-gentilshommes* under Louis XIV were superior to those trained in the regiments. The recruits must still have been poorly prepared, for the regulations contained stipulations for the teaching of reading and writing to such members of the corps as needed it. Repeating the conditions of the reign of Louis XIV, the regulations for the *cadets-gentilshommes* were continually being changed.[53] Of a similar elementary nature were the new cavalry schools started in 1764 at Metz, Douai, Angers, and Besançon, which lasted only three or four years; in 1771 a new school was opened at Saumur.[54] The only good

[52] Villate, *op. cit.,* pp. 237–44.

[53] The companies of *cadets-gentilshommes* were reduced to six in 1720, to two in 1728, and to one (at Metz) in 1732; this last one was disbanded in 1733. For the history of the *cadets-gentilshommes* in the eighteenth century, cf. P. de Briquet, *Code militaire* (3 vols., Paris, 1728), Vol. 2, pp. 254–55; L. Hennet, *Les compagnies de cadets-gentilshommes et les écoles militaires* (Paris, 1889), pp. 6–9, 22–24; L. Mention, *Le comte de Saint-Germain et ses réformes* (Paris, 1884); and F. Funck-Brentano, "L'éducation des officiers dans l'ancienne France," *Réforme sociale* (1918), pp. 24–26. The French system of *cadets-gentilshommes* was copied with some modifications, in connection with the Jesuit *collège* in Madrid, in cadet corps in some of the German states, and in one in St. Petersburg, founded in 1732. Mention, ref. 50, p. 74; de Montzey, ref. 40, pp. 115–116, 120–21.

[54] The whole early history of cavalry training in France is exhaustively treated in L. A. Picard, *Origines de l'école de cavalerie et de ses traditions équestres* (2 vols., Saumur, 1889). Cf. also E. Desbrière and M. Sautai, *La*

military schools in France before 1750 were the artillery schools.

The idea of a permanent military school which should give instruction useful to all branches of the army had been discussed since the opening of the seventeenth century, though no such institution had been founded before the death of Louis XIV in 1715. The great interest in applying scientific discoveries to military engineering and to the uses of artillery, shown in the military treaties of the first half of the eighteenth century,[55] increased the demands for better methods of military instruction. This need particularly impressed a wealthy merchant, Antoine Pâris, who began popularizing the idea in court circles. His brother, Pâris-Duverney, interested Mme de Pompadour and she in turn won over the King. Pâris-Duverney was anxious to strengthen the influence of Mme de Pompadour, and to buy off some of the animosity of the army and the court aristocracy toward the financiers. Mme de Pompadour was chiefly interested in sponsoring a foundation from which she could derive prestige, as Mme de Maintenon had earlier won fame from her school for girls at Saint-Cyr. Louis XV was at the time (about 1750) interested in strengthening the army, which had suffered serious defeats at the hands of the British and the Austrians, and in meeting the problem of educating the sons of impoverished aristocrats. Like his mistress he, too, wanted to build himself a monument; he would create an institution comparable to the *Hôtel des Invalides* founded by Louis XIV. Finally, he wished to win favor with the nobility in certain quarrels he was running with the Church and with *Parlement*.[56] All these motives — few of

---

cavalerie de 1740 et 1789 (Paris, 1906). Villate (ref. 51, p. 251) believes that cavalry training in the eighteenth century was inferior in quality to that of the seventeenth century.

[55] Villate, ref. 51, pp. 252–56.

[56] *Encyclopédie,* Vol. 5, pp. 307–08; de Montzey, ref. 40, pp. 108–83. The correspondence relating to the foundation of the *École royale militaire* and the official regulations concerning its organization reveal the influence of various small military academies established in the early eighteenth century

which were scientific — went into the edict of January 1751, which ordered the foundation of the *École royale militaire*.

The regulations organizing the new institution provided for the education of five hundred nobles, preference being given to those without fortunes; the purposes of the school were charitable as well as educational. Boys might enter between the ages of eight and thirteen and might stay on until the age of twenty. Besides having to prove their nobility for four generations on the father's side, applicants had only to know how to read and write. In selecting students, preference was usually given to sons of officers, and actually some sons of the *bourgeoisie* were admitted. The course of studies was quite comprehensive and included French, Latin, Italian, German, English for those who wanted to enter the navy, as well as history, geography, drawing, elementary and advanced mathematics and physics — including mechanics, hydraulics, and the principles of fortification — and, finally, horsemanship, fencing, and dancing. With the work in mathematics, mechanics, and physics, practical exercises were to be given; military tactics was taught only during the first few years after the school was opened. When the courses were organized, the students were divided for purposes of instruction into two groups, one more advanced than the other.[57]

---

by the monarchs of Spain, Russia, and some of the German states; the early organization of the French *École militaire* shows especially the influence of the St. Petersburg school. *Arch. Nat.* Mm 656. All the regulations for the *École militaire* are printed in *Recueil des édits, déclarations, ordonnances, arrêts, et règlements concernant l'école royale militaire* (2 vols., Paris, 1782); de Montzey's full account cites most of the relevant documents. The best account of life at the *École royale militaire* is in de Vaublanc, *Mémoires* (Paris, 1883) and an anonymous English manuscript, of about 1770, obtained by Dr. Henry E. Guerlac for the Harvard Library, *General Establishment of the Officers Military and Civil . . . Belonging to the École royale militaire at Paris*. The Royal Military Academy in England, founded in 1741, is described in Francis Duncan's *History of the Royal Regiment of Artillery,* 3d ed. (2 vols., London, 1879), Vol. 1, Chap. 10.

[57] Hennet, ref. 53, pp. 40–79. Hennet discusses not only the course of study but also the disciplinary regulations, teaching personnel, and methods

In 1753 the *École royale militaire* was opened at the Château de Vincennes with eigthy-four pupils. Gradually the number was increased, and by 1756 the school was moved to temporary quarters in Paris and later to the sumptuous building designed by Gabriel and erected on the flat plain of Grenelle along the Seine and near the edge of Paris.

The new school in Paris met all sorts of difficulties. Many of the pupils proved to be unfitted for study, and the curriculum was being continually changed. Much of the instruction had to be quite elementary. The higher nobility and all those with sufficient influence continued to place their sons in the *Maison du roi* where they presently received commissions establishing them in their careers in the army. Thus the higher branches of engineering and artillery — *les armes savantes* — were considered socially inferior, and it was hard to interest the students of the *École militaire* in these important subjects.[58]

The *École royale militaire* passed through three periods: In the first period, 1753 to 1764, all the pupils were in the one central establishment. In the second period, 1764 to 1776, in order to raise the quality of the instruction, two hundred and fifty of the younger pupils — from eight to fourteen — were sent to do preparatory work at the *Collège de La Flèche*. Here the courses were of an elementary character, and no purely military subjects were taught. At the same time some of the students at the *École militaire* who showed unusual aptitude in mathematics were sent to the *École du génie* at *Mézières* or to the advanced artillery school at La Fère.[59] In the third pe-

of financing the *École militaire* through taxes on playing cards and lotteries. Most of the accounts of the *École militaire* are in the National Archives in Paris. The regulations of the *École militaire* were influenced by those of the *Hôtel des gentilshommes de Bretagne,* a small military school for the education of the sons of impoverished nobles run by the *états* of the province of Brittany. Hennet, *op. cit.,* p. 35.

[58] Mention, ref. 50, pp. 84–86; M. Caullery, ref. 49, pp. 40–45.

[59] Latreille, ref. 50, p. 90 *note.* For continual changes in regulations at both the *École militaire* and the *Collège de la Flèche,* cf. de Montzey, ref. 40,

riod, 1777 to 1787, the younger pupils were scattered about in a number of schools and were then sent to Paris. After the *École royale militaire* was finally closed in 1787, the provincial elementary military schools continued to 1793. Napoleon's experience is typical of the middle period of the school: he started at the preparatory school at Brienne, then went to the *École royale militaire* at Paris, and finished in a regimental artillery school at Auxonne. His experience shows how the whole system of military education had come to be arranged in a hierarchy.

The history of the *École militaire,* like that of other army reforms of the eighteenth century, shows a conflict between two purposes, one of aiding the poorer noble families to maintain themselves and the other of increasing military efficiency by better training of the corps of officers.[60] Though the *École militaire* was intended for 500 pupils, only about 250 ever attended it at any one time. The students in the *École royale militaire* were much waited on; the establishment swarmed with servants. There were about thirty teachers for the instruction in Latin, Italian, German, French, history, geography, drawing, mathematics, fortifications, dancing, horsemanship and the handling of arms. After 1771 Latin was dropped, and the teachers of mathematics and physics were increased. The emphasis on teaching abstract science to men who were to go into practical activities — so marked later in the *École polytechnique* — is evident here. The school was run by a governing council of school officials; the studies were directed by one member of this board, an inspector of studies. Monthly reports were made on all the students. Examinations were held at the beginning of each year and prizes were given. The setting of the school was luxurious and elegant, but the discipline was severe, the food plain, and the routine exacting.

Livre II, Chaps. 3–6, incl., and Mention, *op. cit.,* pp. 57–59; also the *Recueil* cited in ref. 56.

[60] Lavisse, ref. 50, Vol. 9, p. 70.

In 1776, to save money for the government and for the families of the students and at the same time to educate a larger number of young nobles, Saint-Germain — then Minister of War — closed the *École royale militaire* and distributed the students among ten (later twelve) *écoles militaires* in the provinces. These provincial schools were under the direction of ecclesiastics, though some of the teachers were laymen and some army officers were to be on the grounds. Each school was to have fifty to sixty noble students supported by the state; for each pupil the state was to pay the religious order 700 *livres*. The young nobles were to be taught writing, French, Latin, German, history, geography, mathematics, drawing, and the usual music, dancing, and fencing. The main emphasis in the scientific studies was on mathematics and fortification, with some physics. They were to wear a uniform and to be lodged together in one part of the school; otherwise they shared the life of the other pupils. The Secretary of State for War was to prescribe standard textbooks, and each school had to maintain a library and a physics laboratory. The teachers were to be chosen by the religious orders that controlled the schools, though on complaint of the royal government these could be changed. Each year an examination was to be held at the *Collège de Brienne* in Champagne for students who wanted to continue their training in the army. The best of those who passed the examinations in mathematics and drawing were to be urged to enter the *École royale militaire* in Paris which had been reopened, and some were distributed in infantry and cavalry regiments.[61] After studying in these *écoles militaires* until the age of fourteen, those who entered the army directly were to finish their training in the regiments. A certain number returned to their families or entered schools

[61] Hennet, ref. 53, pp. 76–77; Isambert, ref. 30, Vol. 23, pp. 307–310, 505–19. The schools were at Auxerre, Beaumont, Brienne, Dôle, Effiat, Pont-à-Mousson (the best one), Pontleroy, Rebais, Sorèze, Tiron, Tournon, Vendôme. The religious orders to which these various *collèges* belonged are given in R. Laulan, *L'École militaire de Paris 1751–88* (Paris, 1945), p. 42.

for training priests and magistrates. From 1776 to 1787 the *écoles militaires* educated 2,381 youths, including 603 young nobles supported by the state; one of these was the young Napoleon Bonaparte.[62]

For a year after the government closed the *École royale militaire* in Paris (1776) it tried to sell the building. Unable to do so it reopened the school in 1777 for the ablest students in the provincial *écoles militaires* between the ages of thirteen and fifteen and for other young nobles for whose education their parents had to pay 2,000 *livres* a year.[63] It was, at this time, that Latin was dropped from the curriculum. The students in the reopened *École militaire* were organized into a *corps des cadets-gentilshommes* somewhat on the model of the army corps of the same name, though in this case the members received most of their training in school rather than with the regiments.[64] As a further inducement to get and to hold students, who knew they could get positions in the army

[62] Of the 1592 supported by their families, 14 went into the engineers, 72 into the artillery, 169 into the navy, 537 entered directly into regiments, 320 went to the corps of *cadets-gentilshommes* in the *École militaire* at Paris, 25 became *pages du roi,* and 17 went into the church; none entered the magistracy; the rest died, failed, or withdrew while students. At the time of their suppression there were 661 pupils in eleven schools. De Montzey, ref. 40, pp. 240–45, 286. These provincial *écoles militaires* were not closed until May 1793. Mention, ref. 50, p. 90. For lists of teachers in all military schools in France, 1753–1790 and the students in the *École militaire* of Paris, cf. de Montzey, *op. cit.,* pp. 331–59. The principal regulations for the *écoles militaires* are given in Hennet, ref. 53, pp. 74–76. The courses are discussed in Mornet, ref. 18, pp. 175–76, 181, 325, 330, 333; A. Chuquet, *La jeunesse de Napoléon* (3 vols., Paris, 1897–1899), Vol. 1; J. Colin, *L'éducation militaire de Napoléon* (Paris, 1900); and Sicard, ref. 18, pp. 430–39. A number of the general *cahiers* of 1789 ask that more military schools be established in the provinces, both to help the sons of indigent nobles and for the benefit of the middle class. *Archives parlementaires de 1787 à 1799,* Vol. 2, p. 142, art. 6; Vol. 3, p. 606, art. 2; Vol. 5, p. 414, col. 1, and pp. 566–567, sec. 8, art. 1; Vol. 6, p. 169, art. 59; also L. Porée, ed., *Cahiers de Sens* (Auxerre, 1908), p. 816.

[63] Isambert, ref. 30, Vol. 25, p. 144.

[64] *Arch. nat.* C 818. For life in the *École militaire,* 1777–1787, cf. de Montzey, ref. 40, pp. 253–57, and de Vaublanc, ref. 56.

through favoritism and experience in the regiments, the government in 1778 agreed to make all students in the *École militaire* in Paris second lieutenants at the age of sixteen.[65] The *École militaire* as reorganized in 1777 remained open for ten years. During this period it became an advanced military school; the number of students rose from thirty-four in 1777 to one hundred and fifty in 1782. Finally, in 1787, the government found it too expensive and closed it again, sent its eighty-seven pupils into the army or back to their homes and turned over the great building to the city of Paris.[66]

The *École militaire* of Paris and the provincial *écoles militaires* never fulfilled the hopes of their founders, largely because in their administration the government tried to combine the two conflicting ideas, that of educating a large number of poor nobles and that of advancing technical education. Another hindrance lay in the fact that there were other and easier ways to gain positions in the army. However, the work of these schools was by no means negligible. The pupils in the twelve *écoles militaires* received a good elementary education, though the purely military features hardly went beyond wearing a uniform, living a sort of barrack life and taking more mathematics than was usually taught in the *collèges*. As in the seventeenth century, some army officers continued to be trained in the *Maison du roi;* the majority were formed in the regiments. The best periods of the *École militaire* of Paris were in the years 1764 to 1776, between the removal of the elementary pupils to La Flèche and the first closing of the school, and the decade 1777 to 1787 when it became an advanced military school. An examination of the organization of the institution and of the type of work done during these

<hr>

[65] De Montzey, *op. cit.,* p. 236.

[66] Latreille, ref. 50, pp. 241–42. Napoleon Bonaparte later wrote of his experiences at the *École militaire* in 1784–85, "At this school we were looked after and waited on in magnificent style, in a manner quite beyond that of most of our families and also above that which most of us will know in the future." Laulan, ref. 50, p. 47.

periods makes it evident that the *École royale militaire* takes rank as one of the earliest good army schools giving general military training.

The *École des ponts et chaussées* laid the foundation for most of the modern higher schools of civil engineering. Much the same was done for higher military education the world over when the government of Louis XV organized the first advanced schools of artillery and engineering. There was, of course, much borrowing back and forth of the technological achievements in different fields, and the same borrowing went on between the higher schools for civil and military education. After 1750, specialization marked the growth of technical education, but this should not obscure certain general advances common to all its fields.

The first artillery schools in Europe had been temporary affairs organized by the *condottieri* of Renaissance Italy. The earliest artillery school in France, started at Douai in 1689, was shortly divided into two sections and transferred to Metz and Strasbourg. In the artillery schools instruction was given in artillery theory and practice, in mathematics, fortification, methods of siege, drawing, and in fencing and dancing. In the course of the eighteenth century striking improvements were made in the accuracy of artillery fire and in methods of attack and defense. New types of officers were needed; the regulations issued in 1720 describe the sort of artillery officer the times demanded: "There are officers who devote themselves entirely to mechanical details, others regard such details as beneath their notice. Both types are deficient. The latter must be made to realize that mechanics is an absolute necessity; the officer should know the language of the workman so as to make the workman understand, and on occasion to instruct him. On the other hand, those absorbed only in mechanical details must know that a knowledge of them alone, without a wider view, does not raise them above the level of a cannon founder, a powder maker or a workman. . . . The artillery officer who knows his profession must not be ignorant of details, but he must know them, as in building an architect must know more than a mere stone mason." [67] In order to recruit able men for the schools of artillery and military engineering, the regulation demanding that army officers have a number of generations of noble ancestors — a rule often waived in both the army and the navy of the *Ancien Régime* — had frequently to be relaxed.

After reforms instituted in 1720 there were good artillery schools at Metz, Strasbourg, La Fère, Perpignan, and Grenoble. All these were in army garrisons where on three days practical exercises were given in the uses of artillery, in fortification, bridge building, and mining. This alternated with three days a week of theoretical work in geometry, algebra, conic sections, trigonometry, mechanics, fortification, the methods of defense and attack, and especially in the use of artillery pieces; for all the courses there was a good deal of work in freehand and mechanical drawing. In 1756 an advanced artillery school was opened at La Fère; it was transferred to Bapaume in 1766 but later returned to La Fère; it offered the first comprehensive training in artillery practice in Europe.[68] The courses at La Fère were given by men of good training, and some of the best students were sent there from the *écoles militaires,* though after 1720 the instruction was improved in all the artillery schools. The theoretical training was restricted to officers and

[67] De Briquet, ref. 53, Vol. 2, pp. 37–38. Cf. Ernest Picard, *L'artillerie française au XVIII*^e *siècle* (Paris, 1906); J. Apffel, "L'artillerie lourde de campagne au XVIIIe siècle," *Revue d'artillerie* (1935); Villate, ref. 51, pp. 252–56; A. Basset, *Essais sur l'historique des fabrications d'armement en France jusqu'au milieu du XVIIIe siècle* (Paris, 1935), and "Deux siècles d'histoire de l'artillerie française," *Revue historique de l'armée,* 1954–55.

[68] The regulations for the artillery school of Douai and the regulations for the new schools established in 1720 are given in full in P. Surirey de Saint-Remi, *Mémoires d'artillerie* (3d ed., 3 vols., Paris, 1745), Vol. 1, pp. 40–72. Cf. also, B. de Bélidor, *Nouveau cours de mathématique, etc.* (Paris, 1725), Introduction. The best history of the *écoles d'artillerie* is that of T. Le Puillon de Boblaye, *Esquisse historique sur les écoles d'artillerie* (Metz, 1858).

those preparing to become officers, and was given in a *Salle de mathématique,* a classroom supplied with models but without any real laboratory equipment for work in chemistry and physics.[69]

Some excellent textbooks were provided for the artillery schools; most outstanding were the manuals published by de Bélidor, who in 1720 became a teacher at La Fère: *Nouveau cours de mathématiques à l'usage de l'artillerie et du génie* (1725, new ed. 1757), *La science des ingénieurs* (1728), *Bombardier français* (1731), and *Architecture hydraulique* (1737–1753). Another admirable textbook that came out of the artillery schools was Bezout's famous *Cours des mathématiques* (1772). The combination of theoretical work at certain times with practical exercises at others, which has been one of the dominant traits of modern technical education, had its real beginnings in these French artillery schools of the seventeenth and eighteenth centuries. From the artillery schools, this method of instruction passed into the advanced technical schools of the later eighteenth century, and thence into the *École polytechnique.*

The most advanced type of technical education offered in France and indeed in the whole of Europe was that given by the famous *École du corps royal du génie* at Mézières.[70]

---

[69] De Montzey, ref. 40, p. 108, and *Encyclopédie,* Vol. 5, p. 313.

[70] For the engineering corps in the French army of the eighteenth century, cf. d'Augoyat, *Aperçu historique sur les fortifications, les ingénieurs et sur le corps du génie en France* (3 vols., Paris, 1860–64), esp. Vol. 2. At the outbreak of the Revolution in 1789, the French army engineers were regarded as the best in Europe. *L'École polytechnique: Livre du centenaire* (3 vols., Paris, 1894–97), Vol. 2, pp. 1–3. The army engineers were originally officers assigned, somewhat arbitrarily, to services of fortifications and siege. Their assignments were usually temporary, except when they showed particular aptitude or special interest, in which cases they stayed in engineering work. Louvois, Vauban, and their successors wanted to raise the standards of the service by getting men of better qualifications. This is the background of the moves made by d'Argenson in 1748 and 1749 to institute the school at Mézières. A. Dorbeau, "L'École de Mézières," *Revue du génie militaire,* 1937, pp. 311–17.

Established in 1749 for twenty students — largely through the efforts of the Comte d'Argenson — it had from 1751 very severe entrance examinations in arithmetic, geometry, and drawing, given by a member of the *Académie des sciences*. Each student admitted received 720 *livres* from the state and the family had to pay 200 *livres*. Some students got a part of their elementary training in the *écoles militaires* or in the artillery school at La Fère. Some bourgeois youths were admitted along with noble youths, though after 1777 their number was reduced. On entering the school the students were grouped according to their ability; as in the artillery schools, certain times were devoted to theoretical work and other times to practical exercises. The theoretical work was taught in three one-hour sessions from eight to eleven in the morning: first hour, a lecture, second hour, questioning of the students by the teacher, and third hour, questions by the students and discussion. From two to five in the afternoon practical exercises both inside and outside the school occupied the students. Much time was spent in drawing plans and in working out engineering problems. According to the regulations of 1777, the students at the end of the first year had to pass examinations on stereotomy, all types of wood construction, on "the science of shadow and perspective," and on the drawing of plans and maps; at the end of the second year the examinations included physics, chemistry, natural history, machine design, map making, and fortification design. There were well-equipped laboratories for chemistry and physics, the best in Europe.[71] The summers were spent in field work, and the

[71] D'Augoyat, *op. cit.*, Vol. 2, pp. 440–48, 476–470, 552, 596–606, 648. The École du génie had thirty students from 1740 to 1763, fifty from 1763 to 1770, and thirty from 1770 to 1794, when the school was transferred to Metz. Between 1750 and 1789 the school trained about three hundred engineers. L. de Launay, *Un grand français, Monge* (Paris, 1933), p. 19. Cf. also, R. Tatou, *L'Œuvre scientifique de Monge* (Paris, 1951), and P. Aubry, *Monge* (Paris, 1954). On the school at Mézières, cf. also Dorbeau, *op. cit.;* F. Lambert-Hettier, "L'École du génie et la préfecture de Mézières" in *Almanach-Annuaire Matot-Braine* (Reims, 1913), a study of the building in

students were required, among other things, to report on the industrial plants in the Ardennes. The course lasted two years; the school never graduated more than fifty-one students a year, oftener the number was under twenty-five. For six years after they left the school the graduates were required to send in periodic reports of the work they had been doing.

The teaching at Mézières was entrusted to a professor of mathematics and physics, a professor of chemistry, a teacher of drawing who not only taught drawing but also made working models, and a corps of assistants. The school had an excellent collection of models in metal, wood, and plaster, and a carefully selected library of between five and six thousand volumes[72] — in 1789 it moved into a new building specially designed and built for its use. The more advanced students assisted in the instruction, especially in the handling of the practical courses. From this practice was derived the system of *répétiteurs* of the *École polytechnique*.

It was at the school of Mézières that the great mathematician

---

which the school was held, and the article "Génie" in "Dictionnaire de l'art militaire" of *Encyclopédie méthodique* (1785), the best contemporary account.

[72] Fourcy, ref. 44, pp. 4–5. In the German states, the developments of French military education are closely paralleled. In some cases the German schools show the influence of French experience. The earliest military school in the Holy Roman Empire was one founded at Siegen in 1617. During the eighteenth century the *cadets-gentilshommes* of Louis XIV were widely copied; these were followed by a great number of schools whose work was on the level of that offered in France in Louis XV's *École militaire*. The first of these were established by the Hapsburgs in 1717 at Brussels and in 1718 at Vienna. The first advanced military school was the *Ingenieur-Akademie* founded in Saxony in 1743, improved in 1763. A school similar to this was the *Militär-Akademie zu Wiener-Neustadt* founded by Maria Theresa in 1752 and giving advanced instruction after 1775. The best of all the German schools seems to have been the *Artillerie-Schule* of Hannover, in which Scharnhorst taught, founded in 1782. These last three institutions approached the excellence of the *écoles d'artillerie* and the *École du génie*. B. Poten, *Geschichte des Militär-Erziehungs- und Bildungswesens in den Landen deutscher Zunge* (5 vols., Berlin, 1889–1897), especially Vol. 2, pp. 26–45, 325–46, Vol. 3, pp. 23–77, and Vol. 5, pp. 165–70, 220–26.

Gaspard Monge invented, in the 1780's, his system of teaching descriptive geometry, perhaps the most significant contribution ever made by a single man to the teaching of engineering. Herein he developed a graphic method of working out on paper, through precise diagrams made with rule and compass, a whole series of practical problems dealing with spatial relations: solids, other figures in three dimensions, the intersection of surfaces, and the shaping of vaults. In describing his method, Monge wrote, ". . . this art has two objects, the first is to represent exactly in drawings of two dimensions objects that exist in three, and the second is to deduce from exact description of objects all that follows necessarily from their forms and their respective positions." Monge's descriptive geometry has ever since been the root of all mechanical drawing and of the graphic methods used in engineering. It was not an entirely new idea, but Monge reduced earlier practice to clarity and worked it out as the basis for a system of teaching engineering. The officers trained in Monge's method were forbidden to communicate it even to those engaged in other branches of government service, and it was not until 1795 that the method was published.[73] Among the teachers were both Louis and Gaspard Monge, the Abbé Bossut and the Abbé Nollet. Among the graduates of the school were Lazare Carnot, Saint-Simon, the early Socialist, Borda, the naval engineer, Poncelet, the mathematician who continued the work of Monge in projective geometry, Cugnot, the inventor, Coulomb, one of the pioneers in the development of modern mechanics and of modern electrical theory, and Rouget de l'Isle, author of the *Marseillaise*.

[73] De Launay, ref. 71, pp. 28–29. It is interesting to note that, although Monge was taken into the *École du génie* as a draftsman and later as a teacher, his birth was so low that he could never have been admitted as a student. The best edition of G. Monge's *Géométrie descriptive* is the seventh, published in 1847. Cf. F. G. Higbee, "A Short History of Descriptive Geometry," *Journal of Engineering Education*, 1929.

4. Naval Education

The promising improvements furthered by Colbert in the merchant marine and in the royal navy lapsed before the close of the reign of Louis XIV, and during the first half of the eighteenth century the French navy was in decline. This was somewhat offset by the great interest in nautical science which permeated all ranks in the navy,[74] and by some definite improvements in naval education. The system of apprenticeship for naval officers, established under Louis XIV, with the organization of companies of *gardes de l'amiral* and *gardes de la marine,* paralleling the *cadets-gentilshommes* in the army, was continued.[75] In 1716 the Regent organized an additional group of apprentice officers, the *gardes du pavillon,* made up of twenty-four young men who, unlike those recruited for the earlier companies, were not to be fixed in one of the ports

[74] On the French navy in the eighteenth century, cf. R. Jouan, *Histoire de la marine française* (2 vols., Paris, 1932), Vol. 1, Chaps. 5–8 incl.; G. Lacour-Gayet, *La marine militaire de la France sous le règne de Louis XV,* 2nd ed. (Paris, 1910), and by the same author, *La marine militaire de la France sous le règne de Louis XVI* (Paris, 1905). On the improvement of nautical science, cf. R. Castex, *Les idées militaires de la marine au XVIIIᵉ siècle* (Paris, 1911); A. Anthiaume, *Évolution et enseignement de la science nautique en France* (2 vols., Paris, 1920); F. Marguet, *Histoire générale de la navigation du XVᵉ au XXᵉ siècle* (Paris, 1931); A. Doneaud, "La marine française du XVIIIᵉ siècle au point de vue de l'administration et des progrès scientifiques," *Revue maritime et coloniale 21,* 1867; and in the same periodical (1878–1879), A. Didier-Neuville, "Les établissements scientifiques de l'ancienne marine." There is a very useful collection of laws concerning all branches of the navy: M. Blanchard, *Répertoire général des lois, décrets, ordonnances, règlements et instructions sur la marine* (3 vols., Paris, 1848–1859); the standard guide to the naval archives is A. Didier-Neuville, ed., *État sommaire des archives de la marine antérieures à la Révolution* (Paris, 1898). For British naval history, cf. G. E. Manwaring: *Bibliography of British Naval History* (London, 1930).

[75] An ordinance of 15 April 1689 had summarized and codified the earlier regulations for the *gardes de la marine;* it remained the fundamental basis of all regulations for these gardes until the Revolution. Anon., *Histoire de l'école navale* (Paris, 1889), pp. 8–65.

but were to serve wherever they were sent. At the same time, the *gardes de la marine,* whose membership had risen to 700, were reduced to three companies of eighty each, stationed in the ports of Brest, Toulon, and Rochefort. All the members of these groups were supposed to be nobles, preference being given to men who had already seen some service in the army; however, some youths who were not noble were accepted.

The young men were taught mathematics, drawing, the elements of naval construction, navigation with practical exercises in ship piloting, and also the usual fencing and dancing. After three years of such training, at about the age of seventeen, the abler students were to continue as *gardes du pavillon.* The type of instruction continued to be that given in the companies of naval apprenticeship under Louis XIV, though the work was better organized. The instruction on land ran from 7:30 A.M. in the summer and 8:30 in the winter to 11, and in the afternoon from 1 to 5 in summer and 1 to 4 in winter. The course was interrupted from time to time to take the students on practice cruises, during which each student was obliged to keep a detailed journal on which he had to pass an examination.

In 1771 de Boynes, the Minister of Marine, prepared a long report on the *gardes;* he found the teaching good but the students dissolute and lazy. De Boynes attributed this to the fact that many students, in spite of the rules, were admitted under fourteen years of age and thus many of them were too ill prepared to take any professional interest in their studies, abuses similar to those in the apprentice corps in the army. As a result of his investigation de Boynes, in 1771, closed the school at Rochefort, transferred the students to Brest and Toulon, and then organized a new advanced naval school at Le Havre.[76] The regulations for these companies of naval ap-

---

[76] Anon., *Histoire de l'école navale,* pp. 66–122; A. Jal: *Glossaire nautique* (Paris, 1848), pp. 770–771; Lavisse, ref. 50, Vol. 9, pp. 68–69; *Encyclopédie méthodique* (Paris, 1784), Vol. 2, pp. 474–80.

prentices were continually changed down to the Revolution. Reports in the archives complain that too many youths were admitted, that they were inadequately prepared, that there were too many officers to look after the students, that government inspection was lax, that there were too few positions in the navy for those trained, and that the expenses of the companies were out of proportion to the results.[77]

De Boynes' advanced *École de marine* at Le Havre was opened in 1773 for eighty students who must be fourteen years of age, be able to read and write, and know the four rules of arithmetic; students paid 600 *livres* a year. Classes opened in December 1773 with thirty-two students, some of whom were not nobles. The courses ran until 1 May, when the students went on a four months' practical cruise; the earlier training of the *gardes* had been much condemned for being too theoretical. The courses at Le Havre were carefully planned following the six-volume *Cours des mathématiques* of Bezout. This work included practical exercises in calculating the specific gravity of woods, metals, and liquids, the science of gunnery, problems of naval construction, and navigation; the drawing included sketching of fortifications, and laying out ground plans of forts and arsenals, ship and machine designing, and map making. At sea the students were taught how to use the compass, how to determine latitude and longitude, the rigging and piloting of ships, and all the uses of artillery. The school reopened at the end of 1774 but was closed by royal ordinance 2 March 1775, and the students were sent to the companies of *gardes* at Brest and Toulon and to a reconstituted company of *gardes* at Rochefort. Thus ended the most notable attempt of the *Ancien Régime* to improve advanced naval training by

[77] For changes in regulations, cf. references cited in note 76. There are two reports on the *gardes* in the *Arch. nat. Marine* G 86 and C 818; for a study of textbooks used 1764–1800, cf. *Arch. nat. Marine* G 88.

raising the standards of admission and improving the quality of instruction.[78] Its history is typical of the backing and filling of the seventeenth and eighteenth centuries in nearly all fields of technical education.

Various types of *gardes* continued to offer apprentice training for the state navy until 1786. In that year the *gardes* were disbanded and their place in training officers for the state navy turned over to two *collèges,* one at Vannes and one at Alais. To these schools, each under the local bishop, sons of nobles and some others were admitted, as *élèves de la marine,* between the ages of 11 and 13. The state paid 500 *livres* a year for each pupil and his family paid 600 *livres;* the teachers were appointed by the state. The courses were of an elementary nature and included arithmetic, geometry, mechanics, physics, hydrography, and navigation. Part of the year was spent on training ships at Brest, Rochefort, and Toulon. When the classes opened in March 1787, the school at Vannes had 58 pupils, that at Alais had 25. After a two-year course, in mathematics, physics, geography, drawing, navigation, French, and English, those who passed were to be advanced to the status of *élèves de la marine de deuxième classe* and to do service with the navy; finally they might be advanced to the status of *première classe* by passing examinations in navigation, ship construction, and artillery practice — in all a six-year course, only the first few years of which were devoted to school instruction, the rest being spent on regular ships of the state navy. It was the best system of elementary naval training the *Ancien Régime* had devised, but it was just getting well under way when in 1791 the Revolution pulled it to pieces.[79]

---

[78] There is an elaborate study of the Havre school by A. Anthiaume, *L'école royale de marine 1773–1775* (Paris, 1920); Chap. 5 discusses the curriculum in detail.

[79] *Histoire de l'école navale,* pp. 134–43, gives details of both the theoretical and practical work offered. There are extended reports of the work of

A number of minor special naval schools continued from the seventeenth century. The *École de la marine,* a small school for training ten or twelve ship designers, offered theoretical instruction in the Louvre and practical work in the shipyards. The examinations for entrance, consisting largely of tests in mathematics, were difficult; hence, the instruction given during the two-year course could be of an advanced nature. The first year's work consisted of theoretical and applied algebra and geometry, including conic sections, the elements of calculus, mechanics, and hydraulics, with exercises in estimating the displacement and stability of different kinds of ships. Some of the students were also given special work in calculating problems of wood and stone construction, though without the use of Monge's descriptive geometry, which the army kept a secret. The second year's work continued these courses, with special emphasis on ship design and the working out of practical problems. In the ports the students actually took part in the work of shipbuilding and repairing and any other tasks of construction. After 1765 new regulations required that the students have two years of practical experience in the navy yards before entering the *École de la marine* in Paris.[80]

The *écoles des apprentis-cannoniers* were founded in 1766 to train officers for the naval artillery. Three companies of these *apprentis-cannoniers* with provisions for their instruction

---

the students in *Arch. nat. Marine* G 86, and a description of the courses given at Vannes in a manuscript report of the Bishop of Vannes in *Arch. nat. Marine* G 86.

[80] Fourcy, ref. 44, p. 9. For changes in regulations of school and reports of its work, cf. *Arch. nat.* A.D. VII, 4; *Arch. nat. Marine* G 89, this series contains a number of reports of Duhamel de Monceau, the director and reorganizer at the school in the middle of the eighteenth century; *Arch. nat. Marine* C 818; A. Villaret, "Notions historiques sur le service des constructions navales dans les ports maritimes," *Mémorial du génie maritime,* 1902, p. 53; *Encyclopédie méthodique, ref.* 76, Vol. 2, p. 138. Other changes were made in 1786: cf. *Recueil des ordonnances et règlements de Castries* (Paris, 1786): "*Ordonnance: avril 1786.*"

were founded at Brest, Toulon, and Rochefort, 120 in each company except at Toulon where there were 96. Youths entered from the age of 18 to 25; the course lasted two years and contained the usual theoretical work and practical exercises.[81] Naval map makers were trained after 1720 in a centralized *Dépôt des cartes et plans de la marine* in the Place des Victoires in Paris.[82] In the reports on these schools, preserved in the *Archives nationales,* some critics insist that the courses should be extended and the quality of the students raised; others, on the contrary, complain that the instruction is too theoretical and is mostly a waste of time for the students. A report of 1765 says, "it's not in a classroom that a man learns seamanship. Some geometry and the general theories of navigation may be taught in school, but seamanship is learned only on the sea, as our jealous neighbors [the English] know." [83]

In 1752 the *Académie de la marine* was formed at Brest. Purely a learned society that offered no courses, its purposes were to prepare a naval dictionary and to help the publication of naval studies. It received royal protection in 1769, and it greatly helped stimulate the already widely extended interest in all types of naval theory.[84]

The schools of hydrography, founded in the seventeenth century for the training of men for the merchant marine, declined during the first half of the eighteenth century because the schools did not receive sufficient funds from the state and from the municipal treasuries. After 1760 the royal government made efforts to improve matters; in 1764 the Duc de Choiseul organized schools of navigation for training for the merchant

---

[81] *Encyclopédie méthodique,* ref. 76, Vol. 2, pp. 135–38.

[82] L'École polytechnique Livre du centenaire, ref. 70, Vol. 2, pp. 249–53.

[83] *Arch. nat. Marine* G 86.

[84] Doneaud, ref. 74, pp. 481–84, 493, 584–90; E. de Crisenoy, "Les écoles navales et les officiers de vaisseau depuis Richelieu," *Revue maritime et coloniale 10,* 1864, pp. 782ff., and Castex, ref. 74, Chap. 5.

marine at Brest, Rochefort, and Toulon, alongside those already existing for the corps of *gardes* for the state navy. To stimulate interest the professors were instructed to open their courses each year with a lecture on the advantages of a theoretical study of navigation. Other regulations ordered professors to be more assiduous in the performance of their duties, and to collect information from all the pilots who entered their ports. Not until 1786 were there any adequate regulations for government inspection of the teaching or for anything like uniformity in the courses and the examinations in these schools.[85] In nearly all the principal ports there were small schools of hydrography with one or two teachers and from fifteen to twenty students. These schools might or might not receive funds from the local municipality; the best ones were at Dieppe, Le Havre, Honfleur, and Rouen.[86] The teachers in the schools for training men for the merchant marine included the most celebrated of the scholars interested in the science of navigation; for this reason the teaching was better than in the schools offering instruction for the state navy.[87]

In spite of the excellent work done in some of the naval schools there were, in the later eighteenth century, many proposals for improvement; some of these have been preserved in the French archives. They complain that most pilots use stupid, routine methods, that pilots should be recruited from men trained in naval schools, that more funds should be given the naval schools, particularly those training for the merchant marine, that the courses need standardization and improvement, and finally that government inspection should be ex-

---

[85] Anthiaume, ref. 74, Vol. 1, pp. 122–126.

[86] Anthiaume, *op. cit.,* Vol. 1, pp. 147–64, 181, 428; Vol. 2, pp. 76–84. Volume 2, Book III, contains an elaborate study of the state of nautical science in the France of the *Ancien Régime.*

[87] Anthiaume, *op. cit.,* Vol. 1, p. 181; Didier-Neuville: ref. 74 (1878), Vol. 1, pp. 706–07 gives a list of the twenty-four schools of hydrography that existed in France in 1785; cf. the same work, Vol. 2, pp. 333-46, for an analysis of textbooks and courses.

tended.[88] The *cahiers* of 1789 contain occasional demands for improving or establishing naval schools.[89]

5. *Conclusion*

Modern technical education arose in a most haphazard fashion. Its origins lie principally in two quite different currents: First, there was the idea of teaching children through direct contact with things and situations; this the educational reformers often called learning by doing. Second, it proceeded from the practical needs of a system of scientific training — one more effective than the apprentice system — to enable men to handle the new mechanical equipment of the army, the navy, engineering construction, and manufactures. Both these currents had already become clearly marked by the end of the seventeenth century.

In the eighteenth century these distinct currents continued, meeting many of the same obstacles, though in the end arriving at some marked achievements. The religious orders, as in the seventeenth century, held their monopoly of primary and secondary education in spite of the closing of the Jesuit

[88] *Arch. nat. Marine* G 86, G 87, G 88, G 89. One report says, "The sailor should be not a routine machine, but a man capable of thinking and reasoning. . . . A sailor returns from a voyage and drinks and eats up all his wages, then embarks to start the same round over. How can this system bring improvement? . . . Teach these men to know the principles of their work. . . . Soon the sailor of today will pass . . . he will become industrious and sober and capable." *Arch. nat Marine* G 88, *Projet d'écoles pour les matelots.* Another proposal criticizes the teaching as being too abstract and too brief, and lays out a course including the theories of navigation, practical geometry, drawing, ship design, elements of geography, laws of the sea and of commerce, commercial arithmetic, the writing of business letters, and bookkeeping. *Arch. nat. Marine* G 89.

[89] The principal references are: *Archives parlementaires,* Vol. 4, p. 99; Vol. 3, p. 275; Vol. 4, p. 104; Vol. 5, p. 632, art. 4; J. Savina and D. Bernard, eds., *Cahiers de Quimper* (Rennes, 1927), p. 276; and J. Fournier, ed., *Cahiers de . . . Marseille* (Marseille, 1908), p. 184; two of these are from Brittany and one from Provence; Bordeaux, Le Havre, Marseille, and Toulon were already supplied with schools of hydrography.

collèges and in spite of the many proposals made by writers like La Chalotais and Rousseau, for the establishment of a system of state schools. In the Church schools the teaching of mathematics and elementary physics continued the high standards attained in the later seventeenth century, a movement not paralleled in the universities, where everything stagnated. The state manufactories and those under state patronage carried on their earlier work of giving both theoretical and practical training to craftsmen in some of the luxury industries. At the end of the period, the Duc de La Rochefoucauld-Liancourt laid the foundations of a new type of elementary trade school, but in this field France was distinctly behind in what was being done in a number of the German states and, at the end of the century, in Switzerland. In 1789 most of the workers in French industries were still trained by rule-of-thumb methods passed on by the guilds.

It was in the field of higher technical education that the substantial advances of the eighteenth century were made. Two state services, that of highways and bridges and that of mines, were connected with school training, and the *École des mines* and the *École des ponts et chaussées* take rank as the first well-organized school of civil engineering in the modern world. In the army and in the navy, earlier types of apprenticeship training continued, though in some of the work at the *École militaire,* in the instruction in the *écoles d'artillerie,* in the short-lived *École de marine* at Le Havre, and above all in the training given in the *École du génie* at Mézières, the advanced types of military and naval education that have spread everywhere since 1800 were first clearly anticipated in France. The progress of these enterprises, however, met a multitude of obstacles. The military and naval corps and schools were used by the government as charitable institutions to provide for the education of the sons of indigent nobles, many of whom were unfit subjects for training. Many of the higher aristocracy resented the whole idea that their sons needed more than noble birth to qualify them for commissions, and through their influence men with training were held back from attaining high army and navy positions. This seriously interfered with giving higher technical education the status it might have acquired. The extreme youth of the students in some of these schools, and their utter lack of adequate preparatory training meant that, no matter what the purposes and the equipment of the school, the instruction had to be very elementary, and thus cannot in any proper sense be called higher technical training. To make matters worse, the army and navy schools were badly handicapped by irregularities in the granting of funds. Also, the bitter rivalry between various branches of the service seriously interfered with the free circulation of new ideas — Monge's descriptive geometry, for example, was kept a close secret by some of the engineering corps and was not published until 1795. Above all, the schools were hampered by the endless backing and filling in the matter of government regulations. In this the military schools represented the most scandalous example. In spite of all these shortcomings, however, the conviction was growing that progress in engineering could only come through combining theoretical training in the sciences with practical training in a highly skilled métier.

The French continued to be the leaders in all this; schools like the *École des ponts et chaussées* and the *École du génie* stood first in Europe. In the higher French technical school of the eighteenth century is prefigured most of the accomplishment of the nineteenth and twentieth centuries in advanced technical education.

The Era of the French Revolution
1789–1815

1. Scientific and Technical Instruction
in Primary and Secondary Schools

The central idea of the French eighteenth-century thinkers had been the belief that man could improve his lot by modifying the social organism.[1] For this great work of human amelioration a number of writers had insisted that a new education must be created. In the eyes of these reformers, the older types of schools, though numerous enough, were badly co-ordinated, and, worse, they encouraged superstitious beliefs and reactionary political and social views. A new pedagogy must be founded on reason rather than on religious faith and ecclesiastical authority. It must be adequate for the needs of a reconstructed society and conducted by a body of teachers in sympathy with the philosophy of the age. So, with the meeting of the revolutionary assemblies, all types of education that were to create a better type of citizen, and through him a better society, were bound to receive extended consideration.

[1] A. Mathiez, *Les origines des cultes révolutionnaires* (Paris, 1904), p. 15.

The first two revolutionary assemblies produced a number of projects of reform, and then, after 1792, so extensive and so doctrinaire became this educational discussion — one improvisation succeeding another — that Marat likened those who led it to generals who would amuse themselves by planting and transplanting trees that might bear fruit for the future nourishment of soldiers already perishing of starvation.[2] Later, Taine[3] found in all this discussion only "miles of abstract babbling" — certainly a biased, though understandable, judgment.

The first important projects of educational reform are found in a number of Mirabeau's speeches.[4] Herein, along with his fundamental proposals for improving the existing schools, are scattered suggestions for reforms in scientific and technical

[2] *Moniteur,* 20 Dec. 1792.

[3] H. Taine, Preface to *Correspondance de Mallet du Pan,* ed. by A. Michel (Paris, 1884), Vol. 9.

[4] G. Compayré, *Histoire critique des doctrines de l'éducation en France* (5th ed., 2 vols., Paris, 1885), Vol. 2, pp. 250ff. Cf., on the educational discussions of the revolutionary assemblies, various articles in F. Buisson, *Dictionnaire de pédagogie* (4 vols. in 2, Paris, 1887-8), especially articles under the names of leading educational reformers and those on *Assemblées nationales* and *Convention;* also J. Ruttenberg, *An Examination of the Important Educational Projects Presented in the French Revolutionary Assemblies* (Ithaca, 1927) and S. T. McCloy, Government Assistance in 18th Century France (Durham, 1946), pp. 433–46. The following collections of documents are useful: *Recueil des lois et règlements concernant l'instruction publique depuis l'édit d'Henri IV en 1598* (Vols. 1–4, Paris, 1814; Vols. 5–9, Paris, 1820–28); of this series Vol. 9 is an index. The series is fairly complete down to 1800; after this the documents are scattered. It stops in 1815. This collection is continued in *Bulletin universitaire* (18 vols., Paris, 1828–1849). For the years 1802–1830 there is material in Vol. 1 of *Circulaires et instructions de l'administration relatives à l'instruction publique* (Paris, 1863); in Vol. 1 of O. Gréard, ed., *La législation de l'enseignement primaire (1789–1833)* (2nd ed., Paris, 1890); in L. Dion, ed., *Recueil complet de la législation de l'enseignement secondaire* (3rd ed., Paris, 1935); and in Vol. 1 of A. de Beauchamp, *Recueil des lois et règlements sur l'enseignement supérieur, 1789–1849* (Paris, 1880). These should be used together; no single one can be depended on, and it is also useful to check them with the *Bulletin des lois.* Cf., also, J. Godechot, *Les institutions de la France 1789–1815* (Paris, 1952) and M. Gontard, *L'Enseignement primaire en France 1789–1833* (Paris, 1959).

education. Though Mirabeau considers the study of science inferior to that of letters, which "furnish us with the first models of poetry, oratory, philosophy, and politics," he nevertheless believes that those with scientific interests should be given opportunity to develop them. His most interesting proposal is for a great national *Lycée* for a hundred young men in which the best teachers available are to give courses in algebra, geometry, physics, chemistry, physiology, and natural history.[5]

Far more significant are the proposals of Talleyrand of 1791.[6] His plan outlines, first, a state system of primary schools for each canton, schools whose classes would be open to the children of workingmen and peasants; then, in turn, a series of secondary schools in the larger urban centers, special professional schools of theology, law, medicine, and war; and, finally, a national university in Paris. He plans a system to train citizens for a Liberal state, following the injunction of Montesquieu that "in a free society . . . each citizen must possess the necessary virtue to moderate his passions and to observe the limits of his rights."[7] Talleyrand proposes for his secondary schools, *écoles de district,* "geometry and the part of algebra necessary to understand mechanics, and the elements of chemistry and botany." In his national institute, advance instruction is to be given in higher mathematics, astronomy, physics, and mechanics, chemistry, mineralogy, and geology, botany, anatomy, medicine, agriculture, architecture, and civil, military, and naval engineering.[8] In the military schools Tal-

[5] Compayré, *op. cit.,* Vol. 2, pp. 254–256 and *Archives parlementaires,* Vol. 30, pp. 512–554. The article on "Mirabeau" in Buisson, *op. cit.,* is good.

[6] Talleyrand's report is in *Arch. parl.,* Vol. 30, pp. 447–512. Before preparing his report, Talleyrand says he consulted, among others, Lagrange, Laplace, Monge, and Condorcet. Talleyrand, *Mémoires* (5 vols., Paris, 1891–1892), Vol. 1, p. 134.

[7] Montesquieu, *Esprit des lois,* Book IV.

[8] Some details of the contents of these courses may be found in *Arch. parl.* Vol. 30, pp. 502–03, 507–11. In a separate edition of Talleyrand's report (1791) there is a series of large, folded tables that show the general layout of all his proposals.

leyrand proposes for students, who would enter at the ages of fourteen to sixteen, a two-year course in English, German, geography, history, mathematics, and theoretical and applied military science. Higher military schools should be established at Lille, Metz, Strasbourg, Besançon, Grenoble, and Perpignan. Other proposals include a series of lectureships in agriculture, each to be supplemented with scientific equipment and experimental farms and gardens lest they become like many of the useless lectureships in the *collèges,* in the *Jardin du roi* and other scientific establishments which had long been left inadequately supplied with libraries, laboratories, collections of models, and other scientific equipment. All these proposals are only broadly sketched; the details are not filled in.[9]

Talleyrand clearly saw the need of more scientific and technical education. "In the mechanical arts," he writes, "how many methods of improvement are demanded! Who does not regret to see a large number of our workers bound to a routine which is neither directed by any principle nor rectified by any? . . . We need to bring together skilled theorists and capable artisans; . . . this would raise our national industry to a degree of perfection . . . to which France has shown, even in her state of imperfection, that she is worthy of pretending."[10] Talleyrand's proposals represent no substantial advance over those made by a number of men in the eighteenth century, nor were they ever seriously discussed by the Legislative Assembly to which they were presented in September 1791. But they were widely read and received much notice in the press and in pamphlets; their chief interest now lies in their summarizing of Liberal educational opinion at the opening of the Revolution.[11]

[9] *Arch. parl.,* Vol. 30, pp. 461–62.

[10] C. Hippeau, ed., *Instruction publique en France pendant la Révolution* (2 vols., Paris, 1881–1883), Vol. 1, pp. 174–75. Cf. J. Helmreich, "Establishment of Primary Schools under the Directory," *Finch Historical Studies,* 1961.

[11] For a contemporary discussion of Talleyrand's educational proposals cf. *L'ami des patriotes,* Vol. 3, No. 48, pp. 499–516; *Révolutions de Paris,* Vol.

The third great educational program presented was that of Condorcet,[12] a project which is not only the most generally influential one of the revolutionary era but also the first to lay more emphasis on scientific studies than on the humanities. Condorcet's fundamental motive, like that of the other educational reformers of the Enlightenment, lies in his desire to build a democratic society. "A free constitution which is not paralleled with the universal education of the citizens will destroy itself after a few storms and degenerate into one of those forms of government which are able easily to impose order among an ignorant and corrupt people."[13] His belief is in a system of free state schools open to both sexes. His plan proposes five grades of schools: Talleyrand had proposed only four. Primary schools in all towns of four hundred or more are to be the basis of a complete system; then in every town of four thousand or more a secondary school is to be established. Above these are to be a hundred and ten *instituts,* at least one for each *département,* and nine *lycées* (universities) scattered over France. Condorcet sympathizes with the Girondists; hence he wishes to decentralize higher education. Finally, to direct the whole system of national education, he proposes a *Société nationale des arts et sciences* in Paris. The whole thing sounds like an early draft of Napoleon's *Université de France.*

Throughout his plan, Condorcet emphasizes science because, he says, science teaches the young to think clearly and is, besides, of high utility to society. "Sciences are a remedy against prejudice and against pettiness, . . . they are useful

---

9, No. 114, p. 467; *La feuille villageoise,* Vol. 4, No. 10; *Moniteur,* 27 Sept. 1791. Cf., also, the article on "Talleyrand" in Buisson, ref. 4.

[12] *Arch. parl.,* Vol. 55, pp. 197ff. and Marquis de Condorcet *Œuvres* (13 vols., Paris, 1848–1849), VII: 464–573. Cf. F. Vial, *Condorcet et l'éducation démocratique* (Paris, 1903). Condorcet's plan reached the largest number of its readers through a first sketch of it that appeared in five articles published in 1791 in the *Bibliothèque de l'homme public.*

[13] Compayré, ref. 4, Vol. 2, p. 276.

in all the professions. . . . There is approaching a time when the practical utility of their application is reaching an extent beyond all earlier hopes. . . . The progress of the physical sciences ought to produce a happy revolution in the arts, and the surest way of spreading this revolution is to spread scientific knowledge among all classes of society."[14] Had he lived, Condorcet would undoubtedly have had a hand in the founding of the *Conservatoire des arts et métiers* and the *École polytechnique,* and a few years later in the establishment of Napoleon's *écoles centrales.*

In the primary schools of Condorcet's project, emphasis is to be laid on arithmetic, on basic notions of agriculture and of manufacture, and on a knowledge of the products of the district. In the secondary schools, some of the important subjects to be taught are "the principles of the mechanical arts, the practical elements of commerce and drawing . . . with lessons in mathematics, physics, and natural history as they are related to agriculture and commerce." In the *instituts,* and, above them, in the *lycées,* the work in both theoretical and applied science is to be pushed with the use of the best library and laboratory facilities. Finally, the *Société nationale* is to devote one of its four sections to theoretical and applied science.[15] The teaching of science from the bottom to the top

---

[14] *Arch. parl.,* Vol. 55, p. 201.

[15] *Arch. parl.,* Vol. 55, p. 216–19 and Condorcet, ref. 12, vol. 7, pp. 536–38, 380–412. A few selected passages of Condorcet's educational writings will give a somewhat fuller idea of the kind of suggestions he makes about technical education: "Among the essential subjects in elementary education is drawing, indispensable in all the luxury trades when decoration is joined to utility, and also in all the crafts where are manufactured instruments and tools employed in other arts, . . . likewise the knowledge of chemistry is useful to all working in metals, leather, and glass." "In primary and secondary schools, there should be taught the first principles of mechanics, the commonplaces of physics, the elements of commercial arithmetic, of measurement, of estimating solids, and finally some parts of elementary geometry, which are not understood in ordinary instruction, such as the theory of cutting stones, and perspective . . . All these subjects are not necessary for every profession"; after elementary instruction, special classes

is to avoid separating theoretical and applied science, and to avoid separating one science from another, for the sciences grow, he believes, by cross-fertilization, an idea which reappears shortly in the organization of the *École polytechnique* as a nurse of all the sciences and of all types of engineering. Education is throughout to be a great organ of social utility.

Condorcet's great project, like that of Talleyrand, was presented near the end of a legislative session and was not immediately given the consideration it deserved. In a few years, however, this project and some of his other writings became the basis for the *Law of 1795,* and its influence may be seen in the educational reforms of Napoleon, Guizot, Duruy, Ferry, and Buisson. In the field of technical education, he touched on nearly every aspect of the subject, though he does not go further in practical suggestions than had some of the prerevolutionary theorists. His significance lies rather in bringing their suggestions together and presenting them clearly, succinctly, and forcibly.

With the meeting of the *Convention* in 1792, the number of educational plans increased; innumerable projects were presented by both corporations and individuals. A few concerned themselves with problems of technical education. In a plan prepared by Lakanal, he declared that children of both

---

for the training of special skills may be formed. Pupils "should reject instruction which does not offer them the idea of a direct and immediate utility. . . . One should avoid fatiguing the students both by fixing their attention too long on abstract ideas, and by degrading their reason through making them adopt, on authority, principles they do not understand . . . In spreading more knowledge of the practice of the arts, one will have more capable workers . . . and our riches will be augmented . . . men's liberty and self-respect will increase, and the dangers of tyranny and mob rule will be diminished." Schools should be supplied with "natural-history collections, collections of machinery, and samples of raw materials." . . . In every garrison, town, and naval station, military and naval instruction should be given, and for the artillery and army engineers special schools should be established. There are some interesting remarks on Condorcet's educational ideas in E. Durkheim, *L'évolution pédagogique de la France* (2 vols., Paris, 1938), Vol. 2, pp. 152–56.

sexes should be taught the fundamentals of manual work, such as "the use of the compass, the level, of weights and measures, and of the pulley," and they should observe farm work and the processes of craftsmen. Bourbou had proposed in 1792 to transform all the primary schools of Paris into *écoles d'apprentissage,* each with a series of workshops. Beauquier's plan of 1793 outlined, in very general terms, a scheme for the opening of a large number of elementary trade schools. After they had been established, anyone who had not learned a useful trade should be deprived of citizenship for ten years! Most of the educational projects brought into the *Convention* insist on the value of drawing, mathematics, physics, mechanics, and chemistry for the training of artisans and skilled workers.[16]

In the discussions of these educational projects in the years 1792–95 a number of the leading scientists, some of whom collaborated in the founding of the *École polytechnique* indicated in their criticisms of the general educational plans that they had infinitely greater insight into the real needs of technical education than had the Jacobin educational theorists who were elaborating the projects. They all had the general idea of making education socially useful; they were all more or less interested in the progress of society through improving science and technology, but the scientists were more acutely aware of just what should be done in the fields of scientific and technical training. The chemist Hassenfratz, ridiculing the proposals for national festivals, which nearly all the edu-

---

[16] Summaries of the more important of these projects will be found in J. Ruttenberg, ref. 4; in O. Gréard, ed., *La legislation de l'instruction primaire en France depuis 1789* (2nd ed., 7 vols., Paris, 1889–1902), Vol. I, pp. 24–127, and in Hippeau, ref. 10. Some of the reports are published in full in the *Arch. parl.,* for Lepelletier, Vol. 68, pp. 661–75; Vol. 72, pp. 124–27; for Romme, Vol. 77, pp. 25–26, 575–76, 709–11; Vol. 78, pp. 59–61. Cf. J. Guillaume, ed., *Procès-verbaux du comité d'instruction publique de la Convention nationale* (6 vols., Paris, 1891–1907, Vol. 3, pp. 567ff.; for Bourbou, cf. E. Bertrand, *L'enseignement technique en Allemagne et en France* (Montpellier, 1913), p. 214.

cational projects proposed, said "Let us be careful lest while we are busy organizing our festivals, our neighbors may organize their industry, and destroy our manufactures and commerce. It was not with festivals that the English have been able to acquire a great preponderance over the political balance of Europe. It was not with festivals that the United States of America became a flourishing people. . . . The most beautiful festival which we can give the French people is to organize education for arts and trades, and to give great stimulus to national industry."[17] Hassenfratz was also one of the signers of a petition sent to the *Convention* stating, with force, that there was no better way to improve French manufactures than to extend technical education.[18]

At the same time the great mathematician Monge proposed the opening of schools in each of the larger cities of France for the teaching of descriptive geometry.[19] The chemist Lavoisier outlined in 1793 a plan for two types of secondary education, one for state officials who should be trained in law and literature and another for those interested in science and the mechanical arts.[20] Fourcroy, another chemist, advocated the teaching of science and of mechanical skills in the secondary schools; "the professors should take care to consider in their demonstrations all the applications of science useful in the arts which have for their end the conserving, defending, protecting, dressing, and nourishing of men, and the creation of useful manufactures."[21] "We need," he said elsewhere,

[17] Guillaume, *op. cit.,* Vol. 1, pp. 578–580; *Arch. parl.* Vol. 68, pp. 210–11.

[18] Guillaume, *op. cit.,* Vol. 2, pp. 426–27. It is interesting to note that the statement of Hassenfratz contains little that one cannot find in other statements of the seventeenth and eighteenth centuries; one is always impressed with the continuity in the French tradition in all these matters.

[19] G. Monge, *Traité de géométrie descriptive* (Paris, 1789), preface.

[20] E. Grimaux, *Lavoisier* (Paris, 1888), pp. 248–53. Cf. also, D. McKil, *Antoine Lavoisier* (New York, 1952), J. Fayet, *La Révolution française et la science, 1789–95* (Paris, 1960) and L. P. Williams, "Science, Education, and the French Revolution," *Isis,* 1954.

[21] Guillaume, *op. cit.,* Vol. 3, p. 103.

"military engineers for the construction, and maintenance of fortifications, and for attack and defence, . . . engineers for bridges and roads, for the construction and upkeep of communications, . . . geographers to make maps, . . . mining engineers for the exploitation of mineral resources . . . and construction engineers for the navy."[22] Fortunately, though Lavoisier was dead, it was scientists of this type, rather than political reformers, who created great scientific institutions like the *École polytechnique* and the *Conservatoire des arts et métiers.*[23]

[22] *Moniteur,* 22 Sept. 1793.

[23] There were in the *Convention* some currents of equalitarian obscurantism. One member is said to have said to Lavoisier, "Keep still, the republic doesn't need scientists." Others attacked education as one of the causes of false distinctions in society; "the sciences detach from society all the individuals who cultivate them. "Compayré, ref. 4, Vol. 2, p. 305, and E. Allain, *L'œuvre scolaire de la Révolution 1789–1802* (Paris, 1891), pp. 32, 36. Certain scientists were persecuted during the Revolution, and Condorcet, Lavoisier, and Bailly lost their lives. The *Académie des sciences* was closed in 1793, and the *Journal des savants* was stopped. J. B. Biot, an admirer of Napoleon, in his *Essai sur l'histoire . . . des sciences . . . pendant la Révolution* (Paris, 1803) tried to show that the Jacobins hated science. But this has been shown to be untrue; the *Convention* created the *École polytechnique* and the *Conservatoire des arts et métiers,* reorganized other scientific institutions, and gave patronage to technological research. J. Guillaume, "Un mot légendaire," *La Révolution française,* 1900, 38: pp. 385–99; G. Pouchet, *Les sciences pendant la terreur,* ed. by J. Guillaume (Paris, 1896); Fayet, ref. 20; C. Ballot, *L'introduction du mécanisme dans l'industrie française* (Paris, 1923); T. S. Patterson, *Soda, Nicolas Leblanc and the French Revolution* (Glasgow, 1925); A. Labouchère, *Oberkampf (1738–1815)* (Paris, 1866); J. Pigeire, *La vie et l'œuvre de Chaptal* (Paris, 1932); A. Mathiez, *La victoire de l'an II* (Paris, 1916); and C. Richard, *Le Comité de salut public et les fabrications de guerre sous la terreur* (Paris, 1922). Moreover, a number of scientists were very active. Cf. L. de Launay, *Un grand français, Monge* (Paris, 1933), R. Tatou, *L'Œuvre scientifique de Monge* (Paris, 1951); P. Aubry, *Monge* (Paris, 1954); J. Mascart, *La vie et les travaux du Chevalier Jean-Charles de Borda* (Lyons, 1919); G. Darboux, *Notice historique sur le général Meusnier* (Paris, 1910); G. Bouchard, *Guyot-Morveau chimiste et Conventionnel 1737–1816* (Paris, 1938); and S. J. French, *Torch and Crucible, The Life and Death of Antoine Lavoisier* (Princeton, 1941). The work of these scientists and of others shows that despite many hardships and handicaps a thin but persistent line of scientific activity continued during the most troubled years of the Revolution. Private

When one turns from this brief survey of theories and proposals to what actually happened in the fields of primary and
secondary education in the years 1789 to 1815, one is inclined
to find nearly everything bad. The period began with an
almost wholesale destruction of existing schools. The suppression of tithes and of the town *octrois,* the confiscation of the
lands of the clergy, and the abolition of the monastic orders
deprived schools of their means of support. The *Civil Constitution of the Clergy,* to which most clerics refused to take an
oath, further deprived them of their teachers.[24] While this
work of destruction was proceeding in the years 1789 to
1795, its evil effects were obscured by the endless and very
flamboyant discussions of projects for new educational utopias,

----

initiative took over much that had been earlier fostered and directed by the
state. The *Lycée* of Paris, founded in 1780, continued — under different
names — to give excellent public lectures on science. C. Dejob, *De l'établissement connu sous le nom de Lycée et d'Athénée et de quelques établissements analogues* (Paris, 1889). The same was true of the *Société d'histoire
naturelle,* and — more important still — of the *Société philomatique,* which
included Vauquelin, Berthollet, Fourcroy, Monge, Lamarck, and Lavoisier.
In 1791, this group began to circulate a monthly bulletin in manuscript; a
few years later this bulletin was printed. M. Berthelot, "Origines et histoire
de la Société philomatique," *Mémoires publiés par la Société philomatique à
l'occasion du centenaire de sa fondation, 1788–1888* (Paris, 1888). All the
scientists of the Revolution were more or less Liberal in politics; none
emigrated. But their chief interest was not in politics but rather in theoretical and applied science and in building a modern society directed by an
intellectual elite. They were clearly the successors of a long line of
seventeenth- and eighteenth-century thinkers and at the same time the fore-
runners of Saint-Simon and Comte. Their great ideal was that of social
utility. Cf. H. Gouhier, *La jeunesse d'Auguste Comte et la formation du
positivisme* (2 vols., Paris, 1936), and J. Belin, *Les démarches de la pensée
sociale* (Paris, 1939). The lectureships in the various *Facultés des Sciences*
of the Napoleonic *Université de France* helped after 1808 to keep alive
scientific interests and to spread scientific ideas. A. Aulard, *Napoléon I et le
monopole universitaire* (Paris, 1911), pp. 325–29, 354. For some of the
material in this note, and for other suggestions I am indebted to an admirable
paper read at the American Historical Association meeting (in Chicago,
December 1941) by my friend Dr. Henry E. Guerlac, of Cornell University.

[24] The destructive work, especially of the years 1789 to 1793, is set forth
with a good deal of clerical acrimony in Allain, *op. cit.,* Chap. 1.

and by a series of unfulfilled laws ordering the opening of new schools. The most important of these new laws was that of 25 October 1795; as a summary of earlier projects and laws, it is often called "the academic testament of the *Convention*." One or more elementary schools were to be set up in each of the cantons, one secondary school (an *école centrale*) in each of the *départements,* and a normal school in the capital. To complete the system, a higher national institute was to be established. Private schools, under state supervision, were to be permitted. France possessed at least the blueprints of a complete system of national education.

The law of 1795 limited the work in primary schools to reading, writing, arithmetic, and Republican ethics. The state was to furnish the teachers with a house and garden; the pupils' fees were to supplement this income, though the state was to supply a certain number of free scholarships.[25] This system of state elementary schools remained largely on paper. Funds and teachers were not available, the nation was occupied with many internal problems and with foreign wars, and Catholic parents soon showed a strong opposition to sending their children to such new state schools as were opened. In 1797 in fifty-six state primary schools in the *département* of the Seine, there were only a thousand to twelve hundred pupils, although there were over twenty thousand children of school age.

After 1795 private schools (and "private schools" means schools nearly all of which were under clerical auspices) increased rapidly.[26] This annoyed the government of the Directory, which then passed laws limiting the rights of private schools. But primary education was available to so few chil-

---

[25] G. H. Van Duzer, *Contribution of the Ideologues to French Revolutionary Thought* (Baltimore, 1935), pp. 108–09, 115; Allain, *op. cit.,* pp. 23–25, 58–59; Aulard, *op. cit.,* pp. 1–3.

[26] R. Niderst, *L'enseignement primaire en France 1789–1914* (Strasbourg, 1935), pp. 11–20, Van Duzer, *op. cit.,* p. 132; Allain, *op. cit.,* p. 79; Aulard, *op. cit.,* pp. 16–17.

dren that Napoleon in 1802 increased the rights of private schools, and soon the *Frères des écoles chrétiennes* and other orders were opening primary schools. Napoleon's great solution, his comprehensive scheme for one single educational order, the *Université de France* (1808), tried to combine state inspection with a liberal policy toward private schools. Fontanes, the head of the *Université,* was so lax that not only did church schools increase rapidly, but lay pupils in large numbers were allowed to enter the seminaries for the preliminary training of priests. Here the lay pupils received a primary education under purely clerical auspices.

The net results of twenty-five years (1789–1815) of experimentation in primary education were first that clericalism had made it impossible for the state to control education, and second that both the quality and the number of primary schools in France were lower in 1815 than they had been in 1789.[27] Indeed, the same was true in 1830. The backwardness in primary education after 1789 meant that at least two generations grew up with fewer opportunities to learn to read, to write, and to figure than they would have had had they lived under the *Ancien Régime*. This situation in primary education inevitably retarded all the higher types of education, including technical training. This setback, so far as technical education was concerned, was partly offset by a number of new elementary and advanced technical schools established by the revolutionary governments.

The history of secondary education during the period of the

[27] Niderst, *op. cit.,* pp. 21–23; Van Duzer, *op. cit.,* pp. 133–134; Aulard, *op. cit.,* pp. 48–49, 52–56, 190–191, 239–248, 261–265. On the work of the elementary church schools, cf. also A. Chevalier, *Les Frères des écoles chrétiennes et l'enseignement primaire 1799–1830* (Paris, 1887); L. Combarieu, *Instruction primaire dans le département du Lot pendant la Révolution* (Cahors, 1882); H. Libois, *Instruction primaire dans le département du Jura pendant la Révolution* (Lons-le-Saunier, 1897); P. Gregoire, *Les écoles et la Révolution* (Nantes, 1911); J. Tramond, *L'Instruction primaire de 1789 à 1815 dans une commune du Bas-Limousin* (Tulle, 1905); and M. Soulice, *L'Instruction primaire dans les Basses-Pyrénées 1385–1880* (Paris, 1881).

Revolution follows much the same course as that of the primary instruction. The Revolutionary governments instituted programs which had to be modified because of the confusion of the time, because of the lack of funds and of adequate teaching personnel, and because of clerical opposition. Laws of 1795 and 1796 established secondary *écoles centrales* in the towns, at least one for each *département*. Nearly one hundred were set up. In these new secondary schools, the sciences formed the heart of the curriculum, and the humanities were taught — so far as possible — from the ethical point of view and with the purpose also of teaching the students how to improve their French composition. The courses were divided into three series of two years each. The pupil usually entered at the age of twelve and finished at eighteen. The different courses in the *écoles centrales* were each taught by special teachers, and the pupil could elect most of his courses and also determine the number of years he would stay in the school. In each case these matters depended on the pupil's capacities and interests and on his previous training. Thus, the old method of the *collèges* of the *Ancien Régime,* where everyone took the same courses in the same order, was abandoned. Moreover, the courses were now taught by different teachers — a striking innovation — and the pupils went from one teacher to another as in the modern high school or college.[28]

[28] The fullest discussion of the *écoles centrales* is a very sympathetic one by F. Vial, *Trois siècles d'histoire de l'enseignement secondaire* (Paris, 1936), Livre II, cf. also L. Liard, *L'enseignement supérieur en France 1789–1889* (2 vols., Paris, 1888, 1894); G. Weill, *Histoire de l'enseignement secondaire en France, 1801–1920* (Paris, 1921) Chaps. 1 and 2; and E. Durkheim, ref. 15, vol. 2, pp. 158–68. The role of Destutt de Tracy and the Idéologues in framing the curriculum is discussed in Van Duzer, *op. cit.,* esp. Chaps. 3 and 4. Three contemporary discussions of the *écoles centrales* are of special importance: Destutt de Tracy, *Observations sur le système actuel d'instruction publique* (Paris, An IX), A. Fourcroy, *Rapport sur la résolution du 8 Messidor, an IV, relatif au placement des écoles centrales* (Paris, An IV); and L. Lacroix, *Essais sur l'enseignement en général et sur celui des mathématiques en particulier* (2nd ed., Paris, 1816); for other contemporary

The curriculum in the *écoles centrales,* with its emphasis on science and on studies supposed to have a social utility, embodied many of the favorite ideas of the eighteenth-century reformers. Mathematics, physics, and chemistry, languages and literature, ethics and politics formed the fundamental division of subjects. The content of the individual courses shows the practical intent of the framers of the scheme. Drawing was emphasized especially in connection with the science courses because, as Lacroix said, "all the arts of imitation and of construction have drawing as their bases."[29] Drawing, says

writings, cf. the bibliography in Van Duzer, ref. 25, pp. 167–169. The *Enquête de l'an IX* on secondary education in France is reprinted in full in an appendix to Allain, ref. 23, pp. 349–432. There are good monographs on special ones of the *écoles centrales:* G. Quignon, *L'école centrale de l'Oise* (Beauvais, 1913), A. Troux, *L'école centrale du Doubs* (Besançon, 1926), and J. Dutheil, *Histoire de l'école centrale de la Creuse* (Gap, 1933). Cf. also L. de Launay, *Le grand Ampère* (Paris, 1925), Chap. 5. Some of the histories of secondary schools covering their whole background contain discussions of the *écoles centrales:* J. Quicherat, *Histoire de Sainte-Barbe* (3 vols., Paris, 1860–1864); M. Berthomé, *L'enseignement secondaire dans la Haute-Vienne 1789–1804* (Paris, 1913); C. Chabot and M. S. Charléty, *Histoire de l'enseignement secondaire dans le Rhône de 1789 à 1900* (Paris, 1901); A. Gain, "L'enseignement supérieur à Nancy de 1789 à 1896," *Annales de l'est,* 1933–1934; Godart, "L'école centrale de Seine-et-Oise," *Revue de l'histoire de Versailles,* 1909–1911; J. Peter, *L'enseignement secondaire dans le département du Nord pendant la Révolution* (Lille, 1912); and E. Quernau-Lamerie, "L'instruction secondaire pendant la Révolution: le collège et les écoles d'Angers," *Revue de la Révolution,* 1887. Finally, cf. H. Bernier, *Notice historique sur le collège de Beaupreau* (Angers, 1854); A. Bitton, *L'Enseignement secondaire en Vendée pendant la Révolution* (La Roche-sur-Yon, 1891); M. Bruchet, *L'Enseignement dans les collèges du département du Mont Blanc en 1793* (Annecy, 1893); L. Canet, *Le Collège de Tarbes pendant la Révolution* (Tarbes, 1900); V. Chauvin, *Histoire des lycées et collèges de Paris* (Paris, 1866); E. Cheylud, *L'École centrale du département du Cantal* (Paris, 1904); J. Combet, *L'Enseignement à Nice sous le Consulat* (Largentière, 1916); M. Deries, *L'École centrale de la Manche* (Paris, 1922); G. Mathieu, *L'Instruction publique en Corrèze pendant la Révolution* (Paris, 1912); H. Mosnier, *L'École centrale de la Haute-Loire* (Paris, 1822); F. N. Nicollet, *L'École centrale de Gap* (Gap, 1892); B. Paumès, *Le collège royal et les origines du lycée de Cahors* (Cahors, 1907); and L. Tiffonnet, *L'École centrale de la Haute Vienne* (Limoges, 1893).

[29] Lacroix, *op. cit.,* p. 63.

another, in substance, serves not only the painter and the sculptor, but also the architect, the engineer, the army officer, the naval officer, the physician, the surveyor, and even the simple artisan; it also teaches the youth to observe with exactness, for drawing "is the geometry of the eyes as music is that of the ear."[30] This last is clearly derived from the sensualist philosophy; if ideas are derived from the senses, studies should begin by the observation and reproduction of objects. The courses in drawing were the most attended of all in the *écoles centrales*.[31] The courses in natural history were devoted to the structure and functioning of plants and animals with a great deal of work in drawing.[32] The mathematics courses included arithmetic, algebra, geometry, and trigonometry, and the problems studied were usually those that would be presented in business transactions, engineering, the building trades, and in various industrial processes. Again a philosophic theory was combined with a practical outlook; mathematics was supposed to teach the youth to think clearly. The same ideas were embodied in the teaching of physics and chemistry.[33] For the work in natural history, physics, and chemistry each school, besides being supplied with a reference library, was to have a botanical garden, a natural-history collection, laboratories for physics and chemistry and a museum of machines and models for the industrial arts and trades. Unfortunately, the shortage of funds and the lack of teachers seriously restricted this interesting program for the teaching of the sciences.[34]

The teaching of languages and literature in the *écoles centrales* shows again the interests and the biases of the

[30] Guillaume, ed., ref. 16, Vol. 5, pp. 305–6; Destutt de Tracy, *op. cit.*, p. 10.

[31] Vial, ref. 28, pp. 77, 110; Aulard, ref. 23, p. 23.

[32] Vial, *op. cit.*, p. 77.

[33] Lacroix, ref. 28, pp. 65–68, Vial, *op. cit.*, pp. 106–08, Fourcroy, ref. 28, pp. 10ff.

[34] Aulard, ref. 23, p. 24; Allain, ref. 23, p. 128.

founders. Latin, the basis of the curriculum in the *collèges* of the *Ancien Régime,* was still taught, but the amount of time spent on it was sharply reduced, and the emphasis was laid on its usefulness in mastering French. The study of French composition and literature was emphasized, and other modern languages were taught, Italian and Spanish in the south of France, English and German in the north and east.[35] Finally, the courses in history and "legislation" were intended to make good Liberals. The instruction in history was no longer, as in the old *collèges,* confined to ancient and church history; the emphasis was now on modern and contemporary history and on the changes in government and in social conditions and ideas since the sixteenth century. The courses in "legislation" explained the purposes and the organization of the French state, and they also taught personal and group ethics independently of any religious system.[36] Three other courses had been proposed as additions to the curriculum of the *écoles centrales*: courses in hygiene, in scientific and logical methods of thought, and in applied industrial arts, but the idea was dropped.[37] Public lectures on subjects of practical utility were, according to the law, to be given monthly in each *école centrale.*[38]

The *écoles centrales* lasted only a few years, from 1795 to 1802, and it is difficult to judge the results. The subjects most studied were those which prepared students for administrative, industrial, military, and naval positions, or to enter special schools like the *École polytechnique*: drawing, mathematics, chemistry, and physics; the courses in the social sciences and in the humanities were less popular and often languished. Few of the *écoles centrales* had an adequate staff of teachers; instruc-

---

[35] Lacroix, ref. 28, pp. 69–70; Vial, ref. 28, pp. 79–80, 90–91, 108–09.

[36] Vial, *op. cit.,* pp. 91–99, 109. I have discussed the curriculum of the *éoles centrales* at some length because they show very clearly the general educational ideals and purposes of the time.

[37] Vial, *op. cit.,* p. 100.

[38] Van Duzer, ref. 25, p. 106.

tors who could handle these courses well were simply not available. Few of the schools were properly equipped with classrooms, laboratories, and books. Moreover, the primary schools were so disorganized that the pupils who entered the *écoles centrales* were usually badly prepared. Finally, religious bias and the fact that the *écoles centrales* took only day pupils and no boarders caused many parents to send their children to private secondary schools. As the teachers in the *écoles centrales* lived partly from the tuition paid by the pupils, the abstention or the withdrawal of large numbers of youths reduced some teachers to near starvation. Much depended on the local prefect; if he was sympathetic, the *école centrale* flourished; if he were indifferent or hostile, it usually languished.[39] In spite of their disappearance, the *écoles centrales* represent the most interesting experiment in secondary education in France between the foundation of the Jesuit schools in the seventeenth century and the opening of the modern *lycées* in the second half of the nineteenth century. The modern French *lycée,* moreover, derived many of its methods from those of the *écoles centrales.*[40]

Before the closing of the *écoles centrales* (1802), both the Directory and the Consulate tried to curb public criticism by making changes. But these secondary schools were the work of the *Convention,* and the growing Catholic reaction, to which was added the indifference and finally the opposition of

[39] Van Duzer, *op. cit.,* pp. 130, 133, 136, 139, 142; Aulard, ref. 23, pp. 30–33; Weill, ref. 28, pp. 14–16. There are some interesting statistics and some documents relating to the *écoles centrales* in Allain, ref. 23, pp. 349–432. Vial's account of the *écoles centrales* is very favorable; for an unfavorable estimate, cf. Allain, *op. cit.,* pp. 49–51, 60–62, 115–16, 120 *note,* 134–38, 141, 150–52.

[40] For a final estimate of the *écoles centrales,* cf., besides the other works already referred to, A. Cournot, *Les institutions d'instruction publique en France* (Paris, 1864); P. Arbelet, *La jeunesse de Stendhal* (2 vols., Paris, 1919), Vol. 1, pp. 283ff.; the documents in F. Rocquain, *L'État de la France au 18 Brumaire* (Paris, 1874); and a remarkable manuscript report of A. Fourcroy, *Arch. nat.* A.F. IV, 1018.

Bonaparte, brought on their dissolution. The *écoles centrales* were replaced by *lycées* set up by the state (Law of 1 May 1802), and by *écoles secondaires,* preparatory schools for the *lycées,* to be run either by town governments or by private individuals or groups. The *écoles secondaires* were later brought under government supervision, and, in the case of those run by the municipalities, their names changed to *collèges.* Latin was restored to an important place in the curriculum, the Christian religion was reintroduced, the elective system and the regime of having each subject taught by a different teacher of the *écoles centrales* was now replaced, in both the new *lycées* and *écoles secondaires* by the old fixed curriculum and class system of the *collèges* of the *Ancien Régime.*[41]

Among the sciences formerly taught in the *écoles centrales,* mathematics was the only one not reduced in the new *lycées;* this was because mathematics was needed for officers in the army and navy as well as for students who intended to enter the *École polytechnique* and the military and naval schools. The mathematics courses in the *lycées* included some work in physics, chemistry, astronomy, and mineralogy, and the practical exercises embraced the drawing of maps, plans of buildings and fortifications, some machine designing, and a study of minerals in relation to their utility. Mathematics — theoretical and applied, though usually without laboratory work — was the one science whose importance Bonaparte could understand. Boarding students were taken in large numbers, and all secondary schools were put under a military discipline which became more rigid after 1808; the *lycée,* especially, became a sort of combination barracks and monastery.[42] By 1806, there

[41] Durkheim points out that between 1802 and 1887 there were, at least, seventy-five significant changes in the curriculum of French secondary schools. Durkheim, ref. 15, Vol. 2, pp. 172–75.

[42] Vial, ref. 28, pp. 170–81. Cf. the opening pages of A. de Musset's *Confession d'un enfant du siècle.* Fourcroy was concerned over the loss involved in abolishing laboratory work: "Instead of real courses in physics and

were three hundred state *écoles secondaires,* three hundred
and seventy-seven privately owned schools of the same grade,
and four thousand five hundred other private secondary
schools of one sort or another. Every school not run by the
government had to have a special license from the state, which
both the Consulate and the *Empire* were liberal in granting.[43]
In 1808 there were thirty-seven *lycées* of the forty-five projected. Each had at least eight teachers and a library of fifteen
hundred volumes. The laboratories, botanical gardens, and
collections of models, of machines, and of natural history of
the *écoles centrales* were not continued.[44]

The history of the *lycées* and of the *écoles secondaires* shows
that they had to meet a steadily increasing competition from all
sorts and conditions of private secondary schools, most of
which were under clerical direction. Parents objected to the
inadequacy of the religious instruction in the state schools
and still more to the apparent intention of the government to
direct so much of the training to forming soldiers. This belief
was due not only to the strict discipline but to the fact that
out of about sixty-four hundred scholarships granted to boarding pupils in the *lycées* between 1802 and 1808, about twenty-
four hundred were given to sons of soldiers and of state
functionaries.[45]

The astonishingly rapid increase in private primary and

---

in natural history, a demonstrator shows a few electrical and magnetic
phenomena, and experiments with a vacuum, shows the circulation of
blood in a frog, and how objects are magnified by the microscope." Aulard,
ref. 23, pp. 78 *note,* 112.

[43] The law establishing the *lycées* and *écoles secondaires* put the privately
owned schools under government supervision, Aulard, *op. cit.,* pp. 62–63,
67, 69–74, and Weill, ref. 28, pp. 20–21; for the organization and administration of the secondary schools of France from 1802 to 1815, Aulard's
study is the best.

[44] Aulard, *op. cit.,* pp. 84–85, 87, 97–99, 103.

[45] Weill, *op. cit.,* pp. 18–19, 40–41; Aulard, *op. cit.,* pp. 105–09. The
original model for the *Lycées* had been a preparatory military school. Aulard,
op. cit., pp. 33–35.

secondary schools led finally to the establishment of the *Université de France* by laws of 1806 and 1808. This new national system of education, organized — at least, on paper — to cover everything from the primary school through the universities, aimed at creating a state teaching corps somewhat like the Society of Jesus. All private schools were to be heavily taxed and were to be placed under a very strict system of state inspection. In practice, Fontanes and the central administration of Napoleon's *Université* never enforced the regulations; in 1815 less than half of the secondary schools in France were state schools. The chief complaints from the private schools stemmed not from their annoyances with state inspection but from the taxes they were obliged to pay.[46]

There is no record of a private school being closed by state action after 1806. The growth of the *petits seminaires* was even more striking evidence of the power of clericalism in primary and secondary education. Existing in every diocese, these seminaries were supposed to devote themselves to the preliminary education of boys who would later enter the regular seminaries which trained for the priesthood. In practice, they took large numbers of children who had no intention of becoming priests.[47] Among many other advantages from the point of view of parents, the instruction was gratis. The rapid growth of lay students in the *petits seminaires* may be taken as a symbol of the failure of the French state either to improve or to control primary and secondary education in the whole period from 1795 to 1815.

When the *Empire* collapsed in 1815, there were fewer pupils in French primary and secondary schools than there had been in the last half century of the *Ancien Régime,* and of those

---

[46] Weill, *op. cit.,* pp. 22–26, 32–38; Aulard, *op. cit.,* pp. 140–45, 164–67, 170–72, 180–88, 268–76, 289–94, 305–13, 363–70. The prejudice against the teaching of science which was part of the anti-Jacobin reaction during the period after 1808 brought a vigorous protest from Cuvier in the *Moniteur,* reprinted in the *Revue internationale de l'enseignement,* Vol. 10.

[47] Aulard, *op. cit.,* pp. 298–99; Weill, *op. cit.,* pp. 45–46.

enrolled in such schools less than half were in state schools.[48] The significance of the revolutionary period in the history of primary and secondary education in France certainly does not lie in any immediate results obtained. Only by looking ahead into the nineteenth century does one see that much of French educational development centered in the filling out of programs laid down between 1789 and 1815. So far as elementary scientific and technical education is concerned, the primary and secondary schools of revolutionary France were — with the possible exception of the short-lived *écoles centrales* — largely a failure. The failure was, however, offset by the establishment of a whole series of special elementary and advanced technical schools of the type of the *écoles des arts et métiers,* the *Conservatoire des arts et métiers,* the *École polytechnique,* and a number of state military and naval schools.

2. *The écoles des arts et métiers*

The *écoles des arts et métiers* were an outgrowth of the *écoles de dessin* of the eighteenth century and — more specifically — of a trade school set up, just before the Revolution, by the great philanthropist, the Duc de La Rochefoucauld-Liancourt. This school, near the village of Liancourt, had been approved by a royal ordinance of 1786; instruction in reading, writing, arithmetic, and a number of trades, such as tailoring, shoemaking, and carpentry, was to be provided for a hundred boys who, at the age of sixteen, were to enter the army for a period of eight years.[49] Classes did not actually open until 1788, when twenty orphans of soldiers in the Duc's regiment began to receive instruction from subordinate army officers and from the regiment's shoemaker, tailor, and gunsmith. The

---

[48] Tilley, ed., *Modern France* (Cambridge, 1922), pp. 380–81.

[49] For the *écoles de dessin,* cf. J. Isambert, ed., *Recueil général des anciennes lois françaises* (29 vols., Paris, 1833ff.), vol. 28, pp. 223–24.

discipline was military and severe. The early years of the Revolution left this school — as many others in France — undisturbed, and in 1791 there were eighty pupils.[50] By 1793, however, difficulties had begun to multiply: The noble patron, the Duc, had emigrated; it was hard to get food and supplies, the suffering was sometimes acute, and the government frequently changed the regulations. Still, a report made to the *Convention* in 1795 shows that in addition to the three R's and drawing, the following trades were taught: tailoring, shoemaking, carpentry, cabinetmaking and locksmithing, and that there were two hundred and fifty pupils in the school.[51]

In 1800, the school at Liancourt was transferred to Compiègne, and was made part of a series of three special schools, at Paris, Saint-Cyr, and Compiègne, for the training of the children of officers; the three schools together were called the *Prytanée français*. All except the one at Compiègne were elementary military schools; at Compiègne a real trade school was set up, and the plans of Liancourt were continued. The

[50] H. Barnard, *Systems, Institutions and Statistics of Scientific Instruction* (New York, 1872), p. 453. There were several other very small private trade schools like the one at Liancourt. C. de Montzey, *Institutions d'éducation militaire jusqu'en 1789* (2 vols., Paris, 1866–1867), Vol. 2, pp. 7–9, 51–52.

[51] Guillaume, ref. 16, Vol. 6, pp. 217–21, 295, 712. F. Dreyfus, *La Rochefoucauld-Liancourt* (Paris, 1903), pp. 234–37. The difficulties encountered at the Liancourt school are recounted in E. Jomard, *Discours sur Wilhelm* (Paris, 1842). Cf. also P. Crouzet, *Observations justicatives sur l'école nationale de Liancourt* (Paris, 1798), J. B. Mestre, "La fondation de la première école des arts et métiers et son séjour à Compiègne" in *Bulletin de la société historique de Compiègne*, Vol. 18, pp. 149–70, and the articles "Wilhelm" and "Crouzet" in F. Buisson, ref. 4. There is a good general history of the *écoles des arts et métiers* with many of the important documents quoted, in A. Guettier, *Histoire des écoles des arts et métiers,* 2nd ed. (Paris, 1880); cf. especially Chap. 2 and the corresponding documents. A copy of this work is in the library of the University of Illinois. A list of the names of all the pupils in the various *écoles des arts et métiers* up to 1900 appears in *Société des anciens élèves des écoles nationales des arts et métiers, Liste générale alphabétique . . . des anciens élèves* (Paris, 1900).

boys were divided into classes according to their age and their previous training. Bonaparte visited the school soon after its removal to Compiègne. When he asked some of the older boys what career they wanted to follow, they answered, "that of a soldier." This displeased the First Consul, who at the time was absorbed in plans for internal reconstruction and peaceful reforms. He lamented the number of skilled workers in France who could not draw and who did not understand any of the scientific principles back of their crafts. "This," he concluded, "is a great defect, and I will provide here the means for remedying it." Chaptal also took an interest in the school at Compiègne; in 1803 it was definitely named the *École des arts et métiers,* and the course of study was reorganized by a distinguished committee which included Monge, Berthollet, and Laplace. The next year a second trade school was set up at Beaupréau; it was moved in 1815 to Angers. A third school was established at Aix in 1843.

In 1805 the Duc de La Rochefoucauld-Liancourt, returned from his exile, visited his old school now at Compiègne; he had not seen it since its removal from Liancourt. He found the younger boys, from about the ages of eight to twelve, being taught reading, writing, French grammar, arithmetic, drawing, and the first elements of geometry. The older boys were at work on descriptive geometry and trigonometry, and more advanced drawing. Shopwork was required of all the boys; here the instruction was being given by blacksmiths, machinists, metal turners, foundrymen, carpenters, cabinetmakers, and wheelwrights. Although he expressed satisfaction with some of the work done, he repeated a complaint heard in all types of technical schools since the seventeenth century: Too many pupils who could not read or write were being admitted! In 1806 the school at Compiègne, now well organized, was uprooted in the typical Bonaparte fashion, moved to Châlons-sur-Marne, and set up in an old seminary. In the process some of the equipment was broken and some was lost. However, all the evidence shows that within a short time the school was again running well; it continued to prosper. In the years 1812 to 1815 it was short of supplies, and many of the students were forced into the army. Between 1806 and 1812 this *École des arts et métiers* at Châlons seems to have been the best elementary trade school in Europe. Much of this success lay in the excellence of the teachers chosen, their skill in combining the theoretical training with the shopwork, and the refusal after 1806 to admit pupils who were too young or too poorly prepared to profit from the instruction.

The pupils stayed in the school from three to ten years; this was left to the management of the school. A report of 1807, now in the *Archives nationales,* shows that the instruction was divided into four parts; first mathematics, including advanced arithmetic, algebra, geometry, conic sections, descriptive geometry, trigonometry, and calculus all with practical applications and problems; second, the drawing of machines and buildings in whole and in detail; third, French grammar; and fourth, physics and chemistry. Among the textbooks used were Bossut on mechanics, the chemistry texts of Fourcroy and of Chaptal, and Hassenfratz's treatise on wood construction. The practical shopwork, like the class work, was carefully graded, and was everywhere integrated with the theoretical work. The principal shops in 1807 were for forges and metalworking in iron and copper, for carpentry and cabinetwork, for wheelwrights' work, and for weaving. The hours varied for pupils at different levels. A typical day for the older boys ran as follows, 6 to 8 A.M. shopwork, 8 to 9 A.M. breakfast, 9 to 12:30 shopwork, 12:30 to 1:30 lunch, 1:30 to 7 P.M. theoretical work, 7 to 8 P.M. dinner, 8 to 9 P.M. study—a heavy day's work. In general the boys worked from two to five and a half hours a day in classrooms and about six to eight hours a day in the shops. The more advanced pupils were sent for periods to work in some of the best manufactories in France;

those who went to Paris enjoyed special trips to the newly organized *Conservatoire des arts et métiers*.[52]

In the minds of the early backers and administrators of the *écoles des arts et métiers* there was great concern over finding something to replace the old system of apprenticeship. This time-honored method of teaching all sorts of crafts and trades to the young had been, as a part of the guild system, abolished — at least on paper — near the beginning of the Revolution. The *cahiers* of the third estate (1789) had contained numerous demands for lightening the terms of apprenticeship to the advantage of boys preparing themselves to earn their living

[52] The school at Beaupréau — established near the Vendée in the hope of improving the district economically — had fewer pupils and poorer equipment than the school at Compiègne. The budget of 1808 shows that the government spent 250,000 francs on the Compiègne school (now moved to Châlons-sur-Marne), as much as was spent that year on the *École polytechnique* in Paris, but only 50,000 francs on the school at Beaupréau. Aulard, ref. 23, p. 138. Aulard gives a summary of the budget for all the special schools in 1808. On the school at Beaupréau, cf. Guettier, ref. 51, pp. 85–88, 116–24. Further details on the Liancourt-Compiègne-Châlons school are in Dreyfus, ref. 51, pp. 372–405; in F. Euvrard, *Historique de l'école nationale des arts et métiers de Châlons* (Châlons-sur-Marne, 1895), esp. pp. 3–28; a few important documents are reprinted conveniently in E. P. Cubberley, *Readings in the History of Education* (Boston, 1920), pp. 491–92. An extended manuscript report on the *écoles des arts et métiers* will be found in *Arch. nat.* F[12] 1085. The Compiègne school was moved to Châlons because the latter is within easy access of Paris, Rheims, and Troyes, and the cost of living was low. Projects for new *écoles des arts et métiers* to be set up in the Napoleonic Empire outside of France at Trèves, Laibach, and Prato can be found in *Arch. nat.* F[12] 1227. Only the one at Trèves was opened. A law of 1 May 1802 proposed the founding of four schools of natural history, physics, and chemistry with four professors in each, two schools of mechanical arts, each with three professors, and an advanced school of applied art. Each of these schools was to be placed near a *lycée* whose equipment it was to share; none of these proposals was ever carried out. Aulard, ref. 23, pp. 117–19, 128. The *écoles des arts et métiers* in France continued to go ahead and to do good work, judging from a report on them made during the Second Empire, *Ministère de l'agriculture, du commerce, et des travaux publics, Enquête sur l'enseignement professionnel* (2 vols., Paris, 1864–1865), Vol. 1, pp. 220, 388–89, 402–08; Vol. 2, pp. 583–89. Cf. also, *L'éducation technique en France, étude publiée à l'occasion de l'exposition de 1900* (5 vols., Paris, 1900), Vol. 1, pp. 271–75.

through some sort of manual skill. Instead of trying reforms, the government abolished the guilds, and since these had regulated and controlled apprenticeship, any effective and uniform management of the relation of the apprentice to his master went too. Such arrangements now became a merely private affair. In 1803 the government tried to regulate the conditions of apprenticeship through a *Chambre des arts et manufactures.* This seems to have been mostly a well-meant gesture. Apprenticeship did not end with the Revolution; in many industries it went right on, but it was in a more chaotic condition than it had been before 1789. There were too few youths learning some trades, too many trying to learn others; some boys were badly exploited by their families and by the masters to whom they were apprenticed by their parents. In the name of both efficiency and justice, this practically unregulated situation for apprentices was worse than it had been during the *Ancien Régime.*[53]

The introduction of machine processes into various types of manufacture would have created new problems in the matter of apprenticeship even in a well-regulated system where apprenticeship was controlled either by the old guilds or by the state or both. As no effective control now existed, chaos reigned. These problems of the induction of boys into industries of various types were only slightly improved by the new *écoles des arts et métiers;* there were too few of them. Other schools were proposed; for example, in 1800 there was serious consideration as to the advisability of opening six special sewing, dressmaking, and embroidery schools for girls to supply the dressmaking trades of Paris. The project, like dozens of others, remained on paper. An *École nationale de dessin pour les jeunes filles* was founded privately in 1803 in Paris and was

---

[53] J. H. Cagninacci, *L'instruction professionnelle de l'ouvrier* (Paris, 1910), pp. 8–9; J. Hayem, *Histoire de l'apprentissage* (Paris 1868), p. 63; J. Marcelin, *Écoles professionnelles* (Paris, 1900), pp. 4–5; J. B. Paquier, *L'enseignement professionnel en France* (Paris, 1908), pp. 22ff.

taken over by the state in 1810. After 1800, *écoles de dessin* for boys, like those of the eighteenth century, were founded all over northern and eastern France, in the districts where most of the manufacturing was done. Some of these were supported by the state, some by the municipal governments, and some by private subscription. In 1810 there were successful *écoles de dessin* at Strasbourg, Metz, Mulhouse, Colmar, Bar-le-Duc, Besançon, Rheims, Nancy, Dijon, Langres, and Saint-Étienne. All were of an elementary nature; none was as well equipped or as well attended as it should have been, considering the needs of both handicraft and machine industry for well-trained workers. In a number of the larger cities various lectureships on applied chemistry and physics were established; their success depended on the backing of local authorities and on the ability of the teachers available. A few private trade schools, usually for evening classes, were opened in the larger cities. In view of the needs, such efforts seem well meant but haphazard, irregular, and without either adequate national planning or state backing.[54]

The far-sighted Duc de La Rochefoucauld-Liancourt realized, as clearly as any educational reformer of the period in France, the need for and the great possibilities of good elementary and secondary technical education. In a manuscript memoir of 15 January 1807, now in the *Archives nationales,* he says of the school at Châlons, the best elementary and secondary trade school in France, "the purpose of this institution . . . is to place in the workshops of France trained and skilled artisans who are able to reason about their work instead of stupid workers who are mechanically — a type to which belong the majority of workers today. So we will advance and perfect the industrial arts. The industrial instruction . . . will give youths all the knowledge necessary for becoming distinguished craftsmen and capable and enlightened foremen . . .

[54] *Arch. nat.* F[17] 1144, Barnard, ref. 50, pp. 409–11; Aulard, ref. 23, pp. 136–37, and Paquier, *op. cit.,* p. 27.

The instruction should be neither too formal nor directed merely to making scholars, nor should it merely teach a routine use of tools." [55] The *École des arts et métiers* at Châlons-sur-Marne realized the ideals of its founder, though the number of young workers there trained — only between one and two hundred a year — was wholly inadequate for meeting the needs of French industry.

A number of interesting proposals for schools of commercial and business education were made in the period 1800 to 1815. Schools of this type had existed in Italy since the twelfth century and in France since the Renaissance. Those in France were usually very small enterprises. In 1800 Roux, a successful businessman of Paris and one-time regent of the *Banque de*

[55] *Arch. nat.* F[12], 1085. There were others who were aware of these needs, such as Chaptal. Pigeire, ref. 23, pp. 261, 268–69, 270–73. In an early number of the *Bulletin de la Société d'encouragement pour l'industrie nationale* (1804), Vol. 3, p. 4, Chaptal writes, "The only difference which exists between the artist whom we call 'practical,' and the scholar whom we call a 'theorist' is that the former begins at the practical task and arrives through his experience at creating a theory, while the second arrives at the practical by the application of laws derived earlier from practice. There is no difference except in the points of departure. . . . To be a good artisan, one must have a good practical training, . . . but, also, he must have with this a theoretical knowledge which will give him the means to observe and to estimate his practice."

There seems to be no clear evidence that either the French writers on technical education or the organizers of these French technical schools (1789–1815) paid any serious attention to what was being done elsewhere, especially in the German states and in Switzerland, though some of these Frenchmen, like the Duc de La Rochefoucauld-Liancourt, had traveled in these countries. Guettier, ref. 51, Chap. 24. Most of the German and Swiss trade schools were small and of a very elementary nature and were more moral and cultural in their purposes than were the French *écoles des arts et métiers*. The French might, however, have learned something from the Francke Institut in Halle, and from a dozen eighteenth-century *Realschulen* in Germany. Cf. L. F. Anderson, *History of Manual and Industrial School Education* (New York, 1926), Chaps. 3 and 4, and C. A. Bennett, *History of Manual and Industrial Education up to 1870* (Peoria, Ill., 1926), Chaps. 3 and 8, also the references in Chaps. 1 and 2 of this study. The only important foreign influences on any field of French technical education before 1815 were in the field of mining education.

France, published a study of some of the various things the government could do to improve business. One section is devoted to business education. This opens with the statement that, while young Frenchmen are thinking now only of making money through adventure and speculation, they will soon, when peace returns, find such opportunities closed. Fortune which has for some time been the result of chance and intrigue will become the reward of hard work and ability. Then one can perceive the necessity of having solid knowledge and it will become evident how few competent businessmen there are. Moreover, some sound theoretical training will also help to replace the businessmen killed or ruined by the Revolution.

Roux acknowledges that school instruction cannot take the place of practical experience, but it can enable young men to learn more rapidly and to use their practical experience more judiciously. Accounting, the practices of foreign exchange, business methods to be used both at home and abroad, and commercial law have been successfully taught for centuries, especially in Italy, in Flanders, and in the German states. To prove his points, Roux describes at length a commercial school at Ghent whose organization he had investigated. Here the students were divided into companies, and each company is supposed to exist in a different nation. Practical problems were assigned in the buying and selling of materials and in the management of shipments and payments. Meeting together, the students formed a stock exchange.

Roux proposes such a school for France, the course to cover two years. The first part of the work would be concerned with simple types of transactions; the students would be assigned to hypothetical local companies organized in the manner of French companies engaged in domestic trade. During this first period the students would be taught the fundamentals of accounting, the products of commerce, the forms of commercial correspondence, the rudiments of commercial law, and the mechanism of the various types of domestic commercial transaction. Theory and practice would go along together, and at the end of each six months a general reckoning would be made. The more advanced work would concern itself with the problems of banking and of international trade. Throughout, the students should be taught to go ahead on their own, and everything should be done to stimulate a keen rivalry among them. It will be hard, he believes, to find the proper teachers and to organize the courses, and the textbooks for such courses are yet to be written. But these difficulties, Roux believes, will not prove insurmountable.[56]

Boucher, another French businessman, published a similar, though less detailed, project in 1807. He pointed out that Paris now had a number of schools of applied science but no adequate school of commerce, though such schools had now come into existence even in countries like Portugal and Russia. Further comments on Boucher's proposals were made by a state official, Davillier, and in 1807 the Minister of the Interior sent out the Boucher-Davillier proposals to the prefects.[57] The answers, now in the *Archives nationales,* must not have been encouraging. One prefect from the great commercial city of Genoa, at that time under French rule, wrote that political economy was too controversial a subject to be taught; evidently the hand of the tyrant was growing heavier. Other reports from the Chambers of Commerce of Avignon, Toulouse, Marseille, Lyons, Bruges, and Antwerp raise other objections: that such schools would cost too much, that practice in a good commercial house was better training for business than anything given in a school, that the courses given in some of the

[56] There is a good general study of the history of business education by E. Gottmann, *Die Wirtschaftsoberschule und ihre Entwicklung* (Eisfeld, 1932). V. Roux's project is discussed in his *De l'influence du gouvernement sur la prosperité du commerce* (Paris, 1800), pp. 306–37.

[57] P. B. Boucher, *Projet de l'établissement d'une école de commerce à Paris* (Paris, 1807). The only available copy of this rare pamphlet is in the library of the *Chambre de Commerce de Paris.* It contains the commentary on Boucher's proposals by Davillier. Though neither Boucher nor Davillier refer to Roux's book, they had evidently read it.

Flemish commercial schools were too complicated and needed simplification, that it was sufficient to teach bookkeeping, accounting, foreign exchange, and banking methods. One replied that the idea is good, that if youths had some theoretical knowledge they would advance more rapidly in banks and commercial houses. At present, when they go to work in such establishments they are given minor routine jobs and so have no real opportunity to learn how the whole enterprise works; thus, much time and effort is wasted, and both French youths and French business suffer. Nearly all the reports were skeptical or unfavorable; the bureaucracy was not interested except to find reasons for quashing the whole idea.[58] In this, as in other fields of education, a few leaders of each generation rediscover — and make some small additions to — theories already known, and still one ends the period with no practical results.

3. The Early Years of the Conservatoire des arts et métiers (1794–1815) and of Similar Institutions

The organization of the *Conservatoire des arts et métiers* in Paris into what soon became the greatest industrial museum in Europe shows again the lively interest of men of science and of some members of the *Convention* in organizing institutions that would improve the quality of French manufactures and agriculture. The *Conservatoire* was to be another organ of social utility of which Frenchmen had long dreamed; it was indeed the "Solomon's House" of Francis Bacon and Descartes's museum of machines come true.

The collecting of models and of machines by learned societies and by wealthy dilettantes had formed an interesting chapter in the intellectual history of the seventeenth and eighteenth centuries. Much of this material in the collections of the *Académie des sciences* had been described in a series

[58] *Arch. nat.* F^{12} 618, and F^{12} 2470.

of printed descriptions of machines and models passed on or given prizes by the *Académie,* and in a long series of monographs on industrial processes that had appeared as supplements to the *Encyclopédie.* The general public, however, had not been freely admitted either to the state or to most of the private industrial museums, and the suggestions made by Bachelier, the great advocate of *écoles de dessin,* that public lectures be given on these scientific collections was never taken up. One wealthy inventor, Vaucanson, had in 1775 installed his collections in the Hôtel de Mortagne in the Faubourg Saint-Antoine, and he had admitted all classes to inspect his material. When this collection, which was especially rich in spinning and weaving machines, was willed to the king in 1782, it was divided between the *Académie des sciences,* which got the pure curiosities, and the *Administration des finances* which got all the material valuable for industry. The government bought Vaucanson's Hôtel de Mortagne and made Vandermonde, a member of the *Académie des sciences,* director of the industrial parts of the collection. Between 1785 and 1792, Vandermonde added over five hundred models and machines, including a number from England and Holland. The purpose of the collection was not only to improve French manufactures and, to a lesser extent, French agriculture, but also to enable the government to know more about new inventions so that the inventors could be encouraged and recompensed and their inventions not turned over to foreigners, as had often happened earlier.

A second collection of machines and models was opened in 1793 in the Hôtel d'Aiguillon in the Rue de l'Université; decrees of 15 and 18 August had charged the *Comité d'instruction publique* of the *Convention* to go through the state warehouses and through scattered private collections to gather this material. A year later, the *Convention,* following the suggestions of the Abbé Grégoire, voted to use these machines and models of the Hôtel d'Aiguillon as the basis of a huge scientific and industrial museum. The founding act of 13 October 1794 says, "there shall be formed at Paris, under the name of the *Conservatoire des arts et métiers,* . . . a collection of machines, models, tools, drawings, descriptions, and books in all the . . . arts and sciences. The originals of instruments and machines invented and perfected shall be deposited at the *Conservatoire.*" Other articles provide for three demonstrators and a draftsman to explain the exhibitions to the public. The collections increased rapidly through the obligation of inventors to deposit models or copies of their inventions, and also by gift, purchase, and confiscation. Especially significant additions were Berthoud's collection of clocks, the physical apparatus of the Abbé Nollet, whose laboratory in one of the *collèges* of Paris had before 1789 been one of the best teaching laboratories for physics in eighteenth-century France, and part of the apparatus of Lavoisier. But up to 1798 there was no place adequate for the exhibition of these collections. Some of the material was still in the old rooms of the *Académie des sciences* in the Louvre, some of the state collections were in Vaucanson's Hôtel de Mortagne, and most of the rest was stuffed into the Hôtel d'Aiguillon. Finally, by a law of 10 June 1798, the old Priory of *Saint-Martin-des-Champs,* with its collection of splendid buildings which dated from the twelfth century through the eighteenth, was taken over. The securing of *Saint-Martin-des-Champs* was due again chiefly to the Abbé Grégoire who insisted that it was meaningless to collect materials unless they could be properly seen and studied. The government began in April 1799 to move in and to install a vast amount of material, including a magnificent library, from various sources including at least ten wealthy religious houses. After some delays, all the scattered exhibitions from the Vaucanson, the *Académie des sciences,* and the *Hôtel d'Aiguillon* collections were handsomely displayed in one place.

The administration of this vast museum remained, from

1794 to 1801, in the hands of a committee made up of three demonstrators and the draftsman. In 1801 this committee control was given up, and from 1801 to 1816 Molard, one of the original four, was head. He was an able and energetic man to whom the institution owes much of its early success. Molard had in 1796, in the crowded quarters of the Hôtel d'Aiguillon, given the first regular course of lectures offered by the new *Conservatoire,* a course in drawing as applied to the industrial arts. In 1806, the energetic Chaptal, Minister of the Interior, organized a regular series of courses in drawing, applied geometry, and statistics, all of a rather elementary nature. From 1804 to 1814 a weaving school, established by Chaptal, was run in connection with the *Conservatoire.* Among the many men trained in these early courses of the *Conservatoire des arts et métiers* a few became inventors and others the founders or directors of a number of important manufactories; Schneider, the director of the great Creusot iron works, and Jacquard, inventor of the famous mechanical loom for weaving figured silks out of which arose the prosperity of Lyons, were among the early students of these popular courses. Others later became professors in the *École des mines,* the *École des ponts et chaussées,* and the *École polytechnique.* By 1810 three hundred students were regularly enrolled in these courses; in 1811 prizes were for the first time offered for the best work done.[59]

[59] The history of the *Conservatoire* has been pretty thoroughly worked over. Cf. esp. *Notice historique sur l'ancien prieuré de Saint-Martin-des-Champs et sur le Conservatoire nationale des arts et métiers* (Paris, 1882), pp. 24–41; E. M. Lévy, "Le Conservatoire national des arts et métiers la création," *Annales du conservatoire* (4ème série, numéro spéciale 1933); *L'Enseignement technique en France* (5 vols., Paris, 1900), Vol. 1, pp. 1–90, a full account. Cf. also, A. de Montzie, *Histoire du Conservatoire des arts et métiers* (Paris, 1949); and R. Tesse, "Les origines du Conservatoire des arts et métiers," *Revue des travaux de l'académie des sciences morales et politiques,* 1952. The laws concerning the *Conservatoire* have been published in *Recueil des lois, décrets, ordonnances, etc., relatifs . . . au Conservatoire, etc.* (Paris, 1889); the footnotes contain historical material from the archives of the institution, and in the appendices there are lists, complete to 1889, of

The *Conservatoire des arts et métiers* was the first significant industrial museum in the modern world. It combined a vast series of exhibitions of applied science with a great scientific and technical library, a group of distinguished teachers of science, and a number of laboratories for tests and research. Visited by throngs of Frenchmen, it was also one of the great sights of Paris for all visiting foreigners. It was widely imitated all over the world. Its collections, from the viewpoint of the historian of technology, are still among the best in existence.[60]

Inspired by many of the same motives that led to the creation of the *écoles des arts et métiers* and of the *Conservatoire* was a whole series of special educational enterprises which were set up in the decade 1793 to 1803. The French faith that anything could be improved by founding a school to teach it led to the opening of new schools for soldiers, sailors, midwives, pharmacists, veterinarians, schoolteachers, the blind, deaf-mutes, students of the fine arts, of music, and of living oriental languages, miners, and agriculturists. It seemed that, with this veritable welter of new special schools, all the ideas and ideals of all types of professional schools dreamed of in the whole period since 1500 were suddenly to be realized.[61]

all the administrators and teachers of the *Conservatoire*. Some of the discussions of the committee of the *Convention* that discussed the founding of the *Conservatoire* are in Guillaume, ref. 16, Vol. 5, esp. pp. 61–65. The purposes of the founders are vividly set forth in a speech of Grégoire to the Council of 500 (15 May 1798), reprinted in the *Recueil des lois . . . ,* pp. 28–40. Chaptal thought more courses should be given. Pigeire, ref. 23, p. 427. For some excellent pictures of the *Conservatoire,* cf. *Illustration,* 19 Aug. 1933.

[60] The *Royal Institution* of Great Britain, founded in 1796 by Count Rumford, was inspired by the French *Conservatoire*. A. Wolf, *A History of Science, Technology and Philosophy in the 18th Century* (London, 1938), pp. 42–44.

[61] Most of these proposals yielded no substantial results. For example, in spite of many discussions on agricultural schools, of which there was great need, there were no important gains made in the period 1789 to 1815. Thus, in the important field of agricultural education, the Restoration and the July Monarchy continued the work of the *Ancien Régime* rather than any work of the Revolutionary era.

Unfortunately, many of these schools hardly got beyond the blueprint stage.

The desire to increase the quality and the quantity of French manufactures by applying science to industry and by training workers reached, at times, a fever pitch. In 1793, Monge suggested that rapid-fire courses be offered to men engaged in the production of war supplies. Such courses were given for several years, both in Paris and in the provinces. Workers were released to attend lectures and demonstrations, usually given in series of seven or eight, with one lecture a day. Men as eminent as Monge, Fourcroy, and Hassenfratz were among the teachers. Eight lectures on the manufacture of saltpeter covered the following subjects: the nature and properties of saltpeter, the art of separating saltpeter, its refinement, and its varied uses in the manufacture of munitions. For cannon manufactures, the lectures and demonstrations included methods of iron mining and smelting, general practices of foundries, and the methods of casting, finishing, and testing cannon. At the close of each series of lectures, printed summaries that devoted one or two pages to each of the seven or eight lectures were distributed to the pupil-workers. The government rejected proposals to extend these courses to one or two months.[62] The same hurried methods, as we shall see, were also used in a vast military school, the *École de Mars,* and in a series of naval schools. The short-lived experiment with such courses in industrial processes was not forgotten, and after 1815 this all came to life again in the popular courses for workers organized by men like the Baron Dupin, and by the early Mechanics Institutes.

[62] C. Richard, ref. 23, pp. 469–86; L. de Launay, ref. 23, p. 113. Other material will be found in the works by Ballot, Patterson, Pigeire, and Mathiez referred to in footnote 23 and in G. Pinet, *Histoire de l'école polytechnique* (Paris, 1887), pp. 353–56. On the great advances in powder manufacture made by the French before 1789, cf. R. Payant, *L'évolution d'un monopole, industrie des poudres avant la loi du 13 Fructidor, An V* (Paris, 1934); cf. also, J. C. Dawson, *Lakanal* (University, Alabama, 1948).

More closely allied to the ideas back of the founding of the *Conservatoire des arts et métiers* were the efforts of the government to provide elaborate industrial exhibitions. Such exhibitions had been held before 1789; now they were greatly increased in size and scope. Notable exhibitions were held in 1798, in 1801, 1802, and 1806; those of 1801 and 1802 were chiefly the work of the indefatigable and resourceful Chaptal.[63] The incessant wars interfered with these exhibitions, as they did with other parts of the government's program of technological improvement.

In 1801 a group of scholars, businessmen, and state officials, including Monge, Berthollet, Fourcroy, Ternaux, Chaptal, and Montgolfier, a demonstrator in the *Conservatoire des arts et métiers,* founded the *Société d'encouragement pour l'industrie nationale*. This society, in part modeled on one in England, proposed, through prizes and publications, to encourage improvements in manufactures, commerce, and agriculture. Chaptal was its president for thirty-one years, and Gérando its secretary for forty-two.[64] The regular publications of the *Société* specialized in studies of all sorts of technological improvements; it was fully illustrated and handsomely printed. It had a large circulation throughout Europe and the Americas, and it has continued publication down to the present.

The same idea of popularizing practical knowledge led to the transformation of the old *Jardin du roi* into the *Muséum d'histoire naturelle*. In 1635, in the reign of Louis XIII, and just at the time when Richelieu was organizing the *Académie Française,* the royal botanical garden, the royal menagerie and the museum of natural history were brought together into one *Jardin du roi*. The collections were famous all over Europe, and they grew rapidly. In 1636 eighteen hundred different plants were grown, and by 1665 the number had risen to four thousand. During the eighteenth century, admirable courses

---

[63] Dreyfus, ref. 51, p. 417.
[64] Dreyfus, *op. cit.,* p. 419; Pigeire, ref. 23, pp. 399–402.

were given in botany, pharmacy, chemistry, and anatomy, and members of the staff published a long series of scientific studies. Buffon became head of the *Jardin* in 1739; he greatly enlarged the collections, attracted many students to the courses, and through his teaching and writing made it the greatest center of natural history in Europe. The collections were greatly increased in the early years of the Revolution; most of the additions came from other royal sources, but the teaching was disrupted, and the collections suffered from rapid changes of administration and from neglect. The work of reconstruction was largely due to Lakanal, who got the *Convention* to change the name to the *Muséum d'histoire naturelle*. More funds were now provided for its upkeep, and courses of lectures were given in geology (two courses), mineralogy, general chemistry, chemical arts, botany (two courses), horticulture, agriculture, zoology, anatomy (two courses), and drawing.

By 1802 everything was running in good order; among those giving courses were Fourcroy, Lamarck, Cuvier, and Geoffroy Saint-Hilaire. During the *Empire,* courses were added in anthropology and paleontology, and the library was increased to a hundred and fifty-five thousand volumes, as good a scientific library as then existed anywhere in the world. Besides the hundreds who followed the courses, which could not have been very thorough, and the thousands of sight-seers, the work of the lectures reached a wide circle of readers through the monographs published by members of the staff and through its periodical *Annales du muséum d'histoire naturelle,* which began to appear in 1802, and which has continued under different names to the present.[65]

[65] J. P. Deleuze, *Histoire et description du muséum royale d'histoire naturelle* (2 vols., Paris, 1823), Vol. 1, pp. 6–100, and Guillaume, ref. 16, Vol. 1, pp. 476–86, Vol. 5, pp. 276–79. The list of teachers is in E. Allain, ref. 23, p. 203 *note* 2; cf. also E. T. Hamy, *Les derniers jours du jardin du roi et la fondation du muséum d'histoire naturelle* (Paris, 1893), and, by the same author, *Le muséum d'histoire naturelle, il y a un siècle* (Paris,

4. The École Polytechnique and Related Schools

The greatest achievement of the French Revolutionary era in the field of technical instruction, and in some ways the most significant advance in the whole history of higher technical education in Europe, was the launching of the *École polytechnique.* The best technical schools of the *Ancien Régime,* the *École du génie militaire* at Mézières and the *École des ponts et chaussées* in Paris, were by 1793 in a state of general disorder. Funds were lacking, the older students were called into the army and their places taken by good Republicans who all too often were ignorant of even the rudiments of science. The idea of creating a good central school for the training of all types of engineers, a school that would not only take over the work done at Mézières and in Paris but would also meet a large number of other needs seems to have occurred to a number of men at about the same time.

Such an idea had, in a very general way, appeared in a number of the educational projects of the early years of the Revolution, notably in those of Concordet and of Romme. Much more specific suggestions appear in the correspondence of a group of scientists which included Monge, the genius of the school of Mézières, Lamblardie, Perroult's successor as head of the *École des ponts et chaussées,* Lakanal, Carnot, and Lecointe-Puyraveau, head of the committee of bridges and roads in the *Convention.* Chief credit must go to Lamblardie and Monge; it was they who most clearly conceived the idea that a common training should be given to both civil and military engineers. Back of this collaboration stood the ideas

1896); Dresch, "La première oeuvre de Lakanal, organisation du muséum d'histoire naturelle," *Revue Soc. Ariègeoise,* 1897–8; *Muséum d'histoire naturelle, le centenaire de la fondation* (Paris, 1893). There are also some interesting items in the "Discours préliminaire of E. Geoffroy Saint-Hilaire," *Études progressives d'un naturaliste* (Paris, 1835), and in P. Cap, *Le muséum d'histoire naturelle, histoire de sa foundation et des développements successifs de l'établissement* (Paris, 1854).

and the experience of the two best technical schools just mentioned, that existed under the *Ancien Régime*. They were also, to a lesser degree, inspired by a new engineering school established by the government of Maria Theresa in Vienna, where advanced theoretical and practical training, especially in chemistry, was combined as it was in the schools of Mézières and Paris.[66] Besides trying to meet the practical need of training engineers, those who were considering the founding of the new school were also definitely interested in adding still another means of keeping alive and of spreading scientific work in France.[67]

A decree of the *Convention* (11 March 1794) created a *Com-*

[66] Pinet, ref. 61, pp. 358–61; *École polytechnique, Livre du centenaire* (3 vols., Paris, 1893), referred to hereinafter as *É. Poly. L. de Cen.*, Vol. 1, pp. 1–5. Pinet's whole account of the founding of the *École polytechnique* (pp. 351–77), though it contains a few minor errors pointed out in Guillaume, ref. 16, Vol. 5, pp. 627–53, also xxxvii and xxxviii, is the fullest and best account. The *É. Poly. L. de Cen.* has articles on all aspects of the school, by a large number of authors. P. Alvin, *L'école polytechnique et son quartier* (Paris, 1932), is chiefly valuable for its pictures, and its study of the school buildings. Cf. also, J. P. Callot, *Histoire de l'école polytechnique* (Paris, 1958). The old history by A. Fourcy, *Histoire de l'école polytechnique* (Paris, 1827), is still valuable. A long manuscript report of 1806 on the *École polytechnique* in the *Archives nationales* (A.F. IV, 1328), which contains a mass of detailed information and statistics, seems never to have been used by the historians of the school. The *École polytechnique* began in May 1795 to publish a monthly bulletin, which later became the *Journal de l'école polytechnique*. Cf. Fourcy, *op. cit.*, p. 82, and *É. Poly. L. de Cen.*, Vol. 1, pp. 19–20; this publication is useful for the history of the school. There is a list of the students in the *École polytechnique* together with information about their later careers, M. C. P. Marièlle, *Répertoire de l'école impériale polytechnique ou renseignements sur les élèves qui ont fait partie de l'institution 1794–1853* (Paris, 1855). There is no separate collection of the laws pertaining to the school. The account here given of the *École polytechnique* is deliberately condensed because there exist more good works on this school than on any other technical school in the world. Especially recommended are the older book by Fourcy, Pinet's history, and the *É. Poly. L. de Cen.*

[67] In addition to the references in note 66, cf. H. Barnard, *Scientific Instruction,* etc., 2nd ed. (New York, 1872), p. 405. The law of 16 Dec. 1799 in regard to the *École polytechnique* is especially definite on the point of fostering science in France.

mission des travaux publics, charged with reorganizing all the services of public works, both civil and military; one article of this decree ordered the establishment of an *École centrale des travaux publics.* A commission was created to organize the new school; it included, among others, Lamblardie, Monge, Fourcroy, Berthollet, Chaptal, and Hassenfratz, names that so often reappear in connection with other chapters of science and technology and technical education in this period. This group worked from April to July 1794; its final report, which Fourcroy drafted, was enacted into law 24 Sept. 1794.

The new school, at first called the *École des travaux publics* and after 1795 the *École polytechnique,* was designed to take the place of the older higher technical schools for military and civil engineering of all types. It opened in the Palais Bourbon, just across the Seine from the Place de la Concorde, in November 1794. The three hundred and eighty-six students, ranging in age from sixteen to twenty, had been selected by competitive examinations in algebra, geometry, trigonometry, and physics, held in twenty-two cities of France. Each student was provided with a stipend of twelve hundred francs a year; with this he was to clothe himself and to pay his board with some family approved for its recognized Republican ideas. No students boarded in the school. Lamblardie was made the first director. The organization of the courses and the method of instruction with lectures and *répétiteurs,* who acted as assistants and tutors, chiefly followed the ideas of Monge, and they were modeled on usages that prevailed in the engineering school at Mézières and in the school of bridges and highways in Paris. The severe admission examinations and the laboratory and practical exercises came from the Mézières school, the *répétiteurs* from the Paris school. Instruction was given in a series of classrooms, laboratories, and shops from eight until two each day. This was followed by the noon meal and recreation and private study; instruction was then resumed from five to eight in the evening. The students were divided into groups of twenty for their laboratory exercises and practical work. The curriculum was planned to cover three years; the first-year courses were in geometry, trigonometry, physics, and the fundamentals of chemistry with their practical applications — which involved a good deal of drawing and some laboratory and shopwork — in structural and mechanical engineering. The second- and third-year courses continued the same subjects with the application of the theoretical work turned to the building of roads, canals, and fortifications and to the making of munitions.[68]

After each lecture, the *répétiteur* went over the lecture, questioning the student and cleaning up all difficulties, and giving some suggestions for the private study, the drawing, laboratory, and shopwork each student had to do. The first students were so poorly prepared that only about a third of them could follow the courses intelligently. To remedy this, more *répétiteurs* were brought in, and the students were reclassified according to their ability. Within a year, the new school was running well. More able students were attracted, and complaints began to be heard that all the young men of ability in France were flocking to the sciences and especially to those studies that would assure them government employ, and that the humanities and philosophy were neglected.[69]

[68] De Launay, ref. 23, pp. 113–33. The entrance examinations were changed from time to time; there is a full description of them in H. Barnard, *Military Schools and Courses of Instruction in the Science and Art of War* (2 vols., Philadelphia, 1862), Vol. 1, pp. 66–70. These entrance examinations were always severe; between 1796 and 1837, 14,164 candidates took these examinations and only 5,502 passed them. A. D. Bache, *Report on Education in Europe to the Trustees of the Girard College for Orphans* (Philadelphia, 1839), p. 545. There is a full analysis of the courses given in the *École polytechnique,* in Fourcy, ref. 66, pp. 41–73; Pinet, ref. 61, pp. 377–92, and *É. Poly. L. de Cen.,* Vol. 1, pp. 14–16, 18–22, 24–31. The administrative organization is most fully explained in Pinet, *op. cit.,* pp. 385–90. For comparison with the courses given fifty years later, cf. Barnard, *op. cit.,* Vol. 1, pp. 91–130; for the classrooms and routine, cf. the same volume, pp. 70–84.

[69] The interest of young Frenchmen in scientific studies is discussed in Van Duzer, ref. 25, pp. 130–31.

The teachers included some of the best scientists in France, men who under the *Ancien Régime* were not in the universities. Indeed, the new faculty of the *École polytechnique* was now the most distinguished scientific faculty in the world. La Grange and Laplace taught mathematics; Prony, mechanics; Monge and Hachette, descriptive geometry and stereotomy; Delorme and Baltard, engineering design and architecture; Fourcroy, Vauquelin, Berthollet, Chaptal, and Gayton de Mourveau, chemistry.[70]

The original plan to abandon the special schools of engineering and have most of the state engineering students complete their training in the one *École polytechnique* was soon given up, and a compromise was arrived at in the law of 22 October 1795. The *École polytechnique* was now to give fundamental training to all engineering students, and those who were capable might then go on to a series of advanced and specialized *écoles d'application:* the *École d'artillerie,* the *École du génie militaire* (moved from Mézières to Metz), the *École des ponts et chaussées,* the *École des mines,* the *École des ingénieurs géographes,* and the *École des ingénieurs de vaisseaux.*[71]

The administration of the *École polytechnique,* in spite of the evident success of the enterprise, still had serious problems

[70] L. Liard, ref. 28, Vol. 1, p. 275. Liard also describes how the administration got together models and laboratory equipment from all sorts of sources, a brilliant job of rapid improvising. Cf. also Fourcy, ref. 66, pp. 17–18, 38–40, Pinet, ref. 61, pp. 372–77, and *É. Poly. L. de Cen.,* Vol. 1, p. 17.

[71] Other state services for which the *École polytechnique* trained were added; by 1837 there were eleven such services, most of which one might enter without further schooling. They were: land artillery, naval artillery, military engineering, headquarters corps, state manufactory of munitions, naval engineering, general naval service, hydraulic engineering, bridges and highways administration, mine inspection, and administration of state tobacco monopoly. For the history of each of these services in relation to the *École polytechnique,* cf. *Annuaire de l'école polytechnique* (Paris, 1837), pp. 66–75, and the summary of the history of the military engineering corps in France by E. Legrand-Girarde, "Étude historique sur le corps du génie," *Revue du génie militaire* (1897–1898), with bibliographical references.

to meet. It remained difficult, in spite of the number of applications, to find students with sufficient preparation to profit from the courses. The inflation made it very hard for the students to support themselves on the money allowed them by the government. And it was difficult to hold the students, especially the more capable ones, to the end of the course because of the demands made by the army. The school also had to face a great deal of criticism from the various services into which it sent its students, although the outside appreciation of the value of the training mounted steadily. The most common criticism was that there was no need for so much theoretical study, especially in mathematics; more practical exercises should be offered instead, and the time in the school shortened so that the students could get more apprentice training in the services they wanted to enter. A minor current of criticism came steadily from those who condemned the neglect of languages, literature, history, and philosophy, which were valuable in themselves and were needed to develop the young engineer as a man.[72]

As time went on, changes were made in every part of the school. The administration had at first been entirely in the hands of the faculty, organized into a *Conseil d'instruction,* each member presiding over the school for a month. In 1799 a new advisory body, the *Conseil de perfectionnement,* was set up; its members were chosen from the faculty and from eminent scientists and state officials outside. It acted as a sort of board of trustees and met once a month to discuss the activities of the institution: methods of admission, the organization of the curriculum, the system of instruction and examination, and the housing and discipline of the students. It made recommendations to the faculty council. The *Conseil de*

---

[72] Pinet, ref. 61, pp. 391–400. A representative collection of criticism of the *École polytechnique* is reprinted in Guillaume, ref. 16, Vol. 6, pp. 1, 3, 299–311, 774, 839; another typical piece, not cited by Guillaume, is that of J. F. Barailon, *Opinion sur l'école polytechnique* (Paris, 1798).

perfectionnement, from the beginning, included a number of able and distinguished men. It gave intelligent and disinterested advice and was able to shield the school from occasional ill-judged interference. In the period after 1800 the curriculum went through a series of changes, the most significant of which was the gradual reduction of the practical exercises, which were taken over by the *écoles d'application.*[73]

In spite of the growing esteem of the new institution, its critics remained numerous; there was complaint that, in theory at least if not always in practice, no one could enter the *écoles d'application* without first studying in the *École polytechnique,* a requirement more clearly fixed after 1799. The old criticisms were repeated, especially the one which insisted that the courses were too complicated and too theoretical and impractical, a line of attack that every good technical school in France had earlier faced. Fortunately the school found a strong friend in Bonaparte; soon after he became master of France he began to heap favors on the enterprise. In 1799 the number of students was fixed at three hundred, and for the benefit of those who had already done three years of military service the age of admission was increased from twenty to twenty-six years. In order to speed the entrance of the better students into the *écoles d'application,* the course was reduced from three years to two. These, and a number of other new regulations, including that defining the functions of the *Conseil de perfectionnement,* were summed up in the law of 16 Dec. 1799 which is fundamental in the later history of the institution.[74]

The Consulate moved steadily toward putting the school on a more military basis, although Monge and a number of other scientists protested. After 1804 the students were forced to live in barracks, and a military governor was appointed

---

[73] H. Barnard, ref. 67, pp. 406–07; *É. Poly. L. de Cen.,* Vol. I, p. 24, and de Launay, ref. 23, p. 130.

[74] Pinet, ref. 61, pp. 401–13.

by Napoleon. He was given such extensive powers that neither the *Conseil d'instruction* nor the *Conseil de perfectionnement* had much influence; this situation continued to the end of the *Empire*. On registering at the school, the students were now required to indicate just what service they eventually intended to enter. They were kept under severe discipline and were hard driven in their work. A tuition fee of eight hundred francs was now charged; this largely limited the students to young men from well-to-do families, though some free scholarships were established. In 1805, the school was moved from the Palais Bourbon to its present site, the old Collège de Navarre in the Sainte-Geneviève quarter. Napoleon kept changing the regulations; as a result of this and even more because of the need of men in the army, the students stayed a shorter time, many did not finish their course, and in general the training became less thorough. At the same time some students continued to be admitted to the supposedly advanced *écoles d'application* without any preliminary training in the *École polytechnique*.

The last years of the *Empire*, from 1813 through 1815, found both the number and the quality of the students declining; in 1813 alone, one hundred and twenty students were summarily pulled out of the school and put into the artillery. The general conditions in France were, moreover, so disturbed that those who stayed in the school found it difficult to work. Napoleon, who had once been honored as a friend of the *École polytechnique*, came to be hated by both the faculty and the students, as well as by a great many of the graduates. His military follies were blamed for the endless changes and the near ruination of the school. In spite of this dislike of Napoleon, the *polytechniciens* fought bravely in the defense of Paris in 1814.[75]

[75] Pinet, *op. cit.*, pp. 413, 421; *É. Poly. L. de Cen.*, Vol. 1, pp. 31–43. That Napoleon intended to make more sweeping changes in the *École*

In the first period of its existence, from 1794 to 1815, the *École polytechnique* annually furnished France about a hundred and twenty well-trained engineers. Until 1813 a large proportion of these took further training in the *écoles d'application*. By 1806, of the 1664 students admitted, about a thousand held various state positions: 312 had entered the artillery, 194 were in military engineering, 38 in naval engineering, 29 were with the department of mines, 194 were with the service of bridges and roads, 24 were geographers, 10 were in the infantry, 45 were with the state navy, 29 were in teaching, 14 were in the civil administration; most of the rest had entered commerce and manufacturing.[76]

In spite of the decline of the *École polytechnique* during the last years of the *Empire,* the institution was so solidly founded that it quickly recovered after Waterloo. Back of it lay the long traditions of French scientific studies and of French technical education, above all the extraordinary improvements made during the eighteenth century in the school of civil engineering in Paris, and still more those made in the teaching in the army engineering school at Mézières. The *École polytechnique* continued these traditions: a highly selective system of admission by competitive examinations, strict limitation of numbers, insistence upon a single course of closely integrated studies, mostly in mathematics, without any attempt to adapt the work to individual differences among the

---

polytechnique, such as reducing all the courses to an abbreviated quick survey of a few months, and that he even intended to change the name of the school to the *École napoléonienne des services publics* is shown in a manuscript memoir of 1807, *Arch. nat.* F[17] 1381 (dossier 4). There is a monograph on the students in the campaign of 1814, M. Sautai, *L'École polytechnique pendant la campagne de France, 1814* (Paris, 1910).

[76] *É. Poly. L. de Cen.,* Vol. I, p. 31. There is a detailed classification of where the students went when they left the school for the years 1795 to 1836 and of the number of students in the school in *Annuaire de l'école polytechnique* (Paris, 1837), pp. 74–77, 80, 268.

students, a regime of careful, thorough, and hard work, the use of the lecture system in teaching, supplemented by the work of *répétiteurs,* and the courses combined with drawing, laboratory work, and practical exercises, emphasis on oral rather than written examinations, and the main lectures given by the most eminent scientists available. At the very center of its striking success was the prestige and ability of its great teachers and the virtual monopoly of entrance which it commanded to many of the best careers in the state service. Thus, from its very foundation it was the most sought after and the most difficult of access of all the schools in France and probably in the world.

Though it was really more of a mathematical and scientific university than a technical school, it has, nevertheless, had a far greater influence on technical education than any other school. It attracted international attention from its very first years; it was visited by Volta, Rumford, Humboldt, and the leading scientists and educators of the German and Italian States, of England, Russia, Poland, Sweden, and the United States. Only the incessant wars prevented its immediate influence from being more extended. The French system of organizing the highest technical education separate and apart from the universities has been followed everywhere. It is interesting to see how the details of its entrance examinations, its curriculum — always with a pronounced emphasis on mathematics — its laboratories and its work rooms, its textbooks, methods of teaching, and its examinations began to be imitated in the technical schools of every European state.[77] One of its capable graduates, Crozet, who fled to the United States, brought its methods to West Point. There Thayer enlarged upon his methods after he had gone to the Virginia Military Institute at Lexington, Virginia. At the same time, Greene

[77] F. Klein, *Vorlesungen über die Entwicklung der Mathematik im 19. Jahrhundert* (2 vols., Berlin, 1926–1927), Vol. 1, Chap. 2.

introduced the same ideas at Rensselaer Polytechnic Institute at Troy, New York.[78]

One interesting result of all the improvements in technical education that had been made in France since the time of Colbert was the fact that by the early nineteenth century France was the only country in the world where engineering was clearly and definitely established as a learned profession. In England, it was only emerging as a profession; in most other places it was merely a skilled craft.[79] Moreover, so distinguished and influential were the graduates of the *École polytechnique* that many of the general ideas and attitudes

[78] W. Couper, *Crozet* (Charlottesville, Va., 1936), esp. Chap. 2, and W. E. Wickenden, *A Comparative Study of Engineering Education in the United States and Europe* (Lancaster, Pa., 1929), pp. 13–14; cf. also E. V. Willis, *The Growth of American Higher Education, Liberal, Professional, and Technical* (Philadelphia, 1936). The American educator Henry Barnard praises the combination of theoretical and practical work at the *École polytechnique* as well as the combination of the German university system of lecturing with the British and American system of recitation. He also admires the excellent balance between supervised and required study during most of the course and the period of complete freedom for review before the examinations. "The mainspring of the school's energy," he adds, "is the competition among the pupils" who are sure to get reward for good work in the state services. As the result of the work of the *École polytechnique* and the *écoles d'application,* Barnard concludes, the French have the best-trained corps of civil and military engineers in the world. All of Barnard's conclusions show unusual insight. He is one of the best sources for the study of every aspect of European education in the first half of the nineteenth century. H. Barnard, ref. 67, pp. 84–87.

[79] Cf. A. Gibb, *The Story of Telford* (London, 1935); T. P. Hughes, ed., *Selections from Samuel Smiles, Lives of the Engineers* (Cambridge, Mass., 1966); J. W. Roe, *English and American Tool Builders* (New Haven, 1916); W. Porter, *History of the Corps of Royal Engineers* (3 vols., London, 1889–1915); A. M. Carr-Saunders and P. A. Wilson, *The Professions* (Oxford, 1933); and by the same authors, *Professions, Their Organization and Place in Society* (Oxford, 1928); E. Cressy, *A Hundred Years of Mechanical Engineering* (London, 1937); M. S. Briggs, *A Short History of the Building Crafts* (Oxford, 1925); R. S. Kirby and P. G. Laurson, *The Early Years of Modern Civil Engineering* (New Haven, 1932); and a Radcliffe doctoral dissertation, which is in the Radcliffe College Library, Esther C. Wright, *The Genesis of the Civil Engineer in Great Britain* (1931).

for which the school stood passed over into the main currents of French thought and life. Something of a polytechnician's point of view, compounded of scientific and democratic idealism and a desire to work for human progress, is distinctly marked in nineteenth-century France; to all this the *École polytechnique* made a deep contribution.

When the *École polytechnique* was opened in 1794, it was expected to take the place of most, or even all, of the other higher state technical schools such as the schools of bridges and roads, of mines, and of military and naval engineering. In the meantime, until the *École polytechnique* could get under way, these schools were kept going. It was soon seen that the *École polytechnique* could not fully replace the older and more specialized institutions which were then reconstructed as advanced *écoles d'application*.[80] In the field of civil engineering — the schools of military and naval engineering will be considered later — this meant the reorganization of the old *École des ponts et chaussées,* the *École des mines* and the *École des ingénieurs géographes*. These schools, after 1795, were supposed to admit only students who had studied in the *École polytechnique;* to this they usually adhered, though, on occasion, others were admitted.

Lamblardie, after a short period as the head of the *École polytechnique,* returned to spend all of his time as director of the *École des ponts et chaussées*.[81] There were usually three professors, and from twenty to thirty students in the school each year, though between 1804 and 1812 the number of students was higher. The sessions ran from November to May and the practical work from June to the end of October. The theoretical work consisted of the theory of stereotomy, architecture, mathematics, mechanics, and mineralogy, subjects as would be useful in canal, road, bridge, sewage, drainage and

[80] Guillaume, ref. 16, Vol. 5, p. 650.

[81] Guillaume, *op. cit.,* Vol. 5, pp. 632–35, 652. *É. Poly. L. de Cen.,* Vol. 3, pp. 1–58.

harbor construction. Some students studied administrative law, English, and German with private teachers.

The students received state pay during the three-year course, and on its completion were usually appointed state engineers of the third class. After three years of satisfactory service with the state *corps des ponts et chaussées,* they were eligible for advancement to the position of engineers of the second class. These were evidently considered good positions, for the *École des ponts et chaussées* was the favorite choice with the graduates of the *École polytechnique* among all the *écoles d'application.* Some foreigners were admitted to the *École des ponts et chaussées* provided they could pass a special entrance examination that was considered very difficult. Graduates of the school were occasionally permitted to accept private employment.[82]

The *École des mines,* founded in 1783, was undergoing some reorganization at the time it was made into an *école d'application.* After having been closed for a while, it was reopened in 1794 for twelve students taking a four-month course given during the winter by some of the state mining inspectors. The next year, when the school was raised to an *école d'application,* a regular faculty was set up, the collections and equipment were enlarged, and the school began to get the best-qualified students it had ever had. The courses included mineralogy, metallurgy, mine-construction and general mining methods, advanced physics, drawing, trigonometry, and German. German was given in order to make a number of important German books and periodicals on mining available

---

[82] M. d'Ocagne, *Les grandes écoles de France* (new ed., Paris, 1887), 370–72. *Bulletin des lois,* 1ᵉ série. no, 1196, 4ᵉ série, no, 1068; H. Barnard, *Systems, Institutions and Statistics of Scientific Instruction* (New York, 1872), p. 462, and by the same author, *National Education in Europe* (2nd ed., Hartford, 1854), pp. 89, 462. All the engineers belonging to the corps of bridges and highways between 1716 and 1884 are listed in F. P. H. Tarbé de St. Hardouin, *Notices biographiques sur les ingénieurs des ponts et chaussées depuis la création du corps en 1716* (Paris, 1884).

to the students. The school in Paris had two professors and about twenty students in the years 1796 to 1802. The course covered two years, after which the students could either find employment with mine owners or operators or join the state corps of mining inspectors. The hope was that by this means French mining methods would rise to the level of those used in England and in some of the German states. The Minister of the Interior decided, however, that the courses were not sufficiently practical, and the school was closed in 1802. At the same time, two schools were opened near mines, one at Geislautern in the Saar Basin for coal and iron mining, and one at Pesey in Savoy for lead, copper, and silver mining. Each was to have ten students supported by the state, and any others who might want to come. A good secondary education was now all that, for most of the students, was required for admission. The school at Geislautern was never really organized; a few students were trained in the mines by an apprenticeship system. In the Pesey school the equipment was poor, the teachers mediocre, and the students few. There were never more than twenty-four students at a time; of all those who attended the Pesey school between 1802 and 1816, only eight were graduates of the *École polytechnique*. The *École des mines* in Paris was reopened for a few students in 1814, but the collections and laboratories were moved twice in 1814 and 1815, and the school was not properly running again until January 1816.[83]

---

[83] L. Aguillon, "Notice historique de l'école des mines," *Annales des mines* 1889, a long, carefully prepared history of French mining education. Fourcy, ref. 66, pp. 225–27; A. Guillaume, ref. 16, Vol. 5, pp. 650, 884–885, and Pigeire, ref. 23, p. 351. Aguillon gives a list of the teachers in French mining schools and statistics about the students between 1783 and 1900 in an article in *Programmes des cours de l'école nationale supérieure des mines* (Paris, 1900). For the history of the state *corps des mines,* cf. *É. Poly. L. de Cen.,* Vol. 3, pp. 101–279; for legislation, cf. L. Fleury, *Recueil des lois, décrets, ordonnances . . . concernant le service des ingénieurs des mines* (2 vols., Paris, 1856–1857). After 1816 the two mining schools of Geislautern and Pesey were united in one school at Saint-Étienne, and in 1845 another

A small school for teaching map making, the *École des ingénieurs géographes,* had already been developed before the Revolution.[84] This was closed in 1791, and the old *corps des ingénieurs géographes militaires,* which went back to the days of Vauban in the seventeenth century, was abolished. Most of its members took positions in some part or other of the army. There was a great need for skilled cartographers, and in 1795 the old *École des ingénieurs géographes* was revived and reorganized as an *école d'application.* It had three teachers, one of applied mathematics, one of mechanical and cartographical drawing, and a third of landscape drawing and engraving. The school provided a two-year course with about four months of field work each year, and it was usually attended by about twenty graduates of the *École polytechnique* and ten others. The men who finished the course took positions in the army or the navy or with the department of public works. Some became teachers of geography and map making in the higher military and naval schools. The school was temporarily closed in 1802 but was reopened soon after. It seems to have been difficult to get students to enter the school; the army and navy usually used members of their own staffs, who had learned their map making on the job, to do their map work for them, and it was not easy to get the right sort of positions for the graduates of the *écoles des ingénieurs géographes.*[85]

-----

school was opened at Alais. These were schools of a more elementary type than the Paris *École des mines;* cf. *L'École nationale des mines de Saint-Étienne* (Saint-Étienne, 1921).

[84] For the work of the *ingénieurs géographes,* cf. de Montzey, ref. 50, Vol. 1, p. 214; *É. Poly. L. de Cen.,* Vol. 2, pp. 277–79; Fourcy, ref. 66, p. 11; and the two important works of H. M. A. Berthaut, *La carte de France 1750–1898* (2 vols., Paris, 1898–1899), and *Les ingénieurs géographes militaires 1624–1831* (2 vols., Paris, 1902).

[85] *É. Poly. L. de Cen.,* Vol. 2, pp. 279–86. Fourcy, *op. cit.,* p. 227; Berthaut, *Les ingénieurs géographes, . . . ,* Vol. 1, pp. 83, 230, 283, Vol. 2, pp. 78, 231. A. de Ganniers, "Les écoles militaires en France sous la Révolution et l'Empire," *Revue des questions historiques,* 1902, pp. 72,

In all the *écoles d'application,* including those for military and naval training, it became the usage after 1800 to have the examinations set by the commandant of the school, an officer of the corps for which the school gave training, and a member of the examining board of the *École polytechnique.* In the final classification of a student in any of the *écoles d'application,* his earlier work in the *École polytechnique* was usually counted one third. The *écoles d'application* suffered even more than the *École polytechnique* from changes in regulations, lack of financial support, and inability to get capable students. The whole system never functioned well until after 1815.

The era of the French Revolution thus presented many curious contradictions. The fact that the *Convention* abolished the *Académie des sciences* and voted for the execution of Lavoisier, which caused one revolutionary enthusiast to say that "the Revolution has no use for scholars," once led to the general idea that the French Revolution was unfavorable to science. But, seen as a whole, the exact contrary is the fact. For besides organizing the *École polytechnique* and *Conservatoire des arts et métiers,* two of the greatest landmarks in the history of technical education and of the growth of technology, the Revolutionary era, in spite of its ups and downs, also made notable contributions to military and naval science and education.

5. *Military Education*

France had, for several centuries, been the leader in starting various types of military education, but at the outbreak of the

---

137. There is an admirable guide to all aspects of the history of the French army, de Favitsky de Probobysz, *Répertoire bibliographique de la littérature militaire et coloniale française depuis cent ans* (Paris, 1935). M. Jaryc has published a list of "Périodiques d'histoire militaire" in *Revue internationale d'histoire militaire* (1939); this included periodicals devoted to both military and naval history.

Revolution her military schools showed the evil results of endlessly changing regulations and of financial stringency, both of which — in spite of all the high hopes of the Revolutionary era — became worse after 1791. The famous *École militaire* had been finally closed in 1787. This left, in 1789, twelve elementary military schools run by different religious orders; from these one might enter various branches of the army as a cadet officer or one might go on to the army engineering school at Mézières or to any one of a number of artillery schools. In 1791 the artillery schools were united into one establishment at Châlons-sur-Marne. In 1793 the *Convention* condemned the military schools as strongholds of the old aristocracy, and decreed the closing of all of them except the artillery school at Châlons and one of the preparatory schools at Auxerre.[86] The *Convention* now having gone far toward cleaning the slate, started out to rebuild military education along what it considered to be truly Republican and scientific lines.

Before following the main traditions of military education during the rest of the period down to 1815, let us look for a moment at one special military school, the short-lived *École de mars* (1794) that was peculiarly a product of the *Convention* and was, educationally, without either definite ancestors or descendants. The *Convention* established the *École de mars* in June 1794, to train officers for the huge army that was defending the republic. The three thousand students,

---

[86] *Arch. nat.* A.D. VI, 49; A. Augoyat, *Aperçu historique sur les fortifications, les ingénieurs et sur le corps du génie en France* (3 vols., Paris, 1860–1864), Vol. 3, pp. 38–39; de Ganniers, *op. cit.,* pp. 172–78; Guillaume, ref. 16, Vol. 4, pp. 522–29; de Montzey, ref. 50, Vol. 2, pp. 11–41; J. B. Valentin de Lapelouze, "Lettre à Lamartine 1847," in *La Révolution française, LX* describes life in the *École de mars.* There is an attack on the old military schools by Lakanal in the *Moniteur* 21 June 1793. The so-called "closing of the elementary military schools" is not exactly correct; these schools belonged to various religious orders, and all the government did at the time was to withdraw the tuition and boarding expenses of such students as were receiving aid from the state. Some pupils stayed on.

whose ages ranged from sixteen to eighteen years and who were recruited from all parts of France, had to show little more than an ability to read and write and do simple arithmetic. They lived in tents on the Plaine des Sablons near Neuilly. Some were selected for an intensive teacher-training course and were then used to help in the training of the others. Very elementary military instruction was given in a vast wooden hall built for the purpose. Here lectures were given on physics, chemistry, army maneuvers and tactics, fortification, army administration, and hygiene. The lectures were printed and were distributed at the end of each discourse. Actually about all the students got out of the whole experience was some military drill and a little gun practice. The students helped to give Paris a military air, and they furnished troops to appear at state functions. The school was closed after three and a half months in October, 1794. It came to almost nothing. It proved to be very expensive to run, the students were too young and too ill-prepared to profit by the training offered, the teaching staff was inadequate; it was jerry-built, and it was closed before it could accomplish anything. It was all very grandiose and very sterile; one historian speaks of it as "military buffoonery." [87]

Through all kinds of difficulties, the older traditions of military education were continued. In 1791, the artillery schools, which were drifting into disorganization, were united into a

[87] There is a good monograph on the *École de mars* by A. Chuquet (Paris, 1899). A report by Barère, who was chiefly responsible for the schools, shows the temper of the time. After a high-flown discourse on the necessity of education for patriotism and for forming the minds of Republicans, Barère denounces the older military schools: "To enter a royal military school, one had to be descended from some feudal brigand, from some privileged trifler, or from some ridiculous marquis. . . . To go to the *École de mars* one must belong to a Republican family, come from poor parents, from useful farmers, from simple artisans and from volunteers wounded in defending our freedom." L. Barère, *Rapport fait à la Convention nationale sur l'éducation révolutionnaire républicaine, et militaire* (Paris, 1794), pp. 3–9.

central *École d'artillerie* at Châlons. Even this heroic attempt to bolster the situation was not immediately successful. Those who were working to get the school under way found it difficult to get adequately prepared students and to find the necessary teachers, equipment, and supplies — always the same story. The thirty-six youths first admitted averaged sixteen years in age; they came partly from the *écoles militaires* of the *Ancien Régime*. Before being admitted at Châlons, they had passed examinations in arithmetic, algebra, and geometry. The following year the school admitted sixty-seven students, and in spite of difficulties the teachers, by hard work and by dividing the students on the basis of ability and previous training, began to achieve results. Duroc, Foy, and Marmont, who later became Napoleonic generals, seem to have learned something during these first years of the Châlons *École d'artillerie*. In twelve years the school furnished the army three hundred and sixty artillery officers. The one-year course included work in drawing and architecture but was largely mathematical, with practice problems in fortification, and siege and field operations. Nothing seems to have been taught about the relations of artillery to the infantry and cavalry. The equipment was poor; the library had less than three hundred volumes. There was no physics laboratory and very little military gear and equipment. The further one got from 1789 or 1791 the harder it was to get students who had had any good elementary schooling. The students in the school suffered from the inflation, and from the poor food, clothing, and quarters the government furnished them. Though the course was only one year long, students were frequently pulled out during the term and put directly into the army.[88]

While the *École d'artillerie* was struggling along at Châlons,

[88] De Ganniers, ref. 85, pp. 158–64; T. Le Puillon de Boblaye, *Esquisse historique sur les écoles d'artillerie* (Paris, 1858), esp. Chap. 3, which contains a full account of every aspect of the school during the Châlons period; in the appendix, pp. 137–59, there is a complete list of the teachers and students in the Châlons school before it was moved to Metz.

the famous *École du génie* at Mézières, which before 1789 was the best higher technical school in the world, was uprooted and transported to Metz near the eastern frontier. The real reason was that it would take the institution away from the aristocratic traditions that still hung about it at Mézières; the reasons given were that it would be better to have the school in a larger center and nearer the frontier where defense was needed. In the process of transfer, part of the Mézières equipment was moved to the *École des ponts et chaussées* in Paris, and part was ruined en route. There were at first twenty students in the new quarters at Metz, with a few teachers and a little equipment; the school was barely kept in existence. The years 1791 to 1795 saw two of the very best types of technical schools in Europe, the French artillery schools and the army engineering school, almost collapse because of the disorders in France. In 1795, both were rescued by being integrated with the new *École polytechnique* as *écoles d'application,* and then in 1802 by a thorough reorganization that united all advanced artillery and army engineering training in a single school at Metz.[89]

The enlarged *École du génie et d'artillerie* at Metz now received most of its students from among the graduates of the *École polytechnique;* each year about seventy students entered to study artillery and about thirty to study military engineering. The subjects taught and the methods of teaching were about the same as in the *École polytechnique,* though the courses and the practical exercises were more specialized. For some of their courses, the artillery and engineering students followed the same lectures, for others they worked separately. The course lasted for two years, with study at Metz in the fall, winter, and spring, and field work in various parts of France in the summer. At the end of the course, the students entered into full military service as second lieutenants. Here

[89] Fourcy, ref. 66, pp. 5–7; Augoyat, ref. 86, Vol. 3, pp. 51–53.

again, the wars of the *Empire* called many of the students into active duty before they had finished their course.[90]

The lack of trained officers in the huge armies built up by the revolutionary governments remained a serious problem which could never be solved by the comparatively small number of young men who came out of the *École polytechnique* and the school of Metz. A number of proposals to establish elementary military schools were made between 1790 and 1799, the most important being one made in 1797 by Jourdan to the *Council of Five Hundred*. But nothing substantial was done until Bonaparte came into power in 1799. He hated uneducated officers, and often said so. He found plenty to hate in an army in which, on the basis of a recent order, no one could be named general "who did not know how to read and write." Laws of 1801 to 1803 reorganized a type of secondary military school, *Le Prytanée français*. This system had included four schools, the only one of which that ever gave good military training was the one at Saint-Cyr which in 1808 was moved to La Flèche. Here about four hundred boys between the ages of seven and sixteen were given a secondary education which included some substantial courses in mathematics and a good deal of military drill.[91]

[90] *É. Poly. L. de Cen.*, Vol. 2, pp. 404–09. There is an elaborate account of the school at Metz with details of its administration, disciplinary regulations, and its courses in H. Barnard, ref. 68, pp. 137–224. Cf. also Le Puillon de Boblaye, ref. 88. Besides this advanced school for the training of army engineers and artillery officers at Metz, many regiments in the army ran regimental schools in which the rudiments of army engineering and artillery practice were taught to some of the officers and even to some of the enlisted men by the older officers.

[91] Aulard, ref. 23, pp. 33–35; de Ganniers, ref. 85, pp. 179–84. In the *Archives nationales* (A.D. VI, 49) there is an undated document, apparently of about 1796, which contains a proposal for the opening of twenty-three military schools, each to give a two-year course in the principles of government, and in drawing, mathematics, physics, geography, history, English, German, and finally dancing and fencing. Nothing came of the proposal. On the *Prytanée* at Saint-Cyr, cf. E. Titeux, *Saint-Cyr et l'école spéciale*

The first real fulfillment of Napoleon's ideas was the *École spéciale militaire* which he established at Fontainebleau in 1803 and in 1808 moved to Saint-Cyr. This military school at Saint-Cyr, which is still in existence and is a sort of French West Point or Sandhurst, accepted such young men from sixteen to eighteen years of age as could pass the entrance exami-

------

militaire en France (Paris, 1898), Chap. 4; J. Clère, *Histoire de l'école de La Flèche* (Paris, 1853), Chap. 9; also G. Desmages, *Saint-Cyr, son histoire, ses gloires, ses leçons* (Paris, 1948).

Le Prytanée français had a curious history which shows the ups and downs of educational usage during the Revolutionary Era. The idea was launched in 1795 when the old *Collège Louis-le-Grand,* whose name had been changed to *Collège égalité,* was taken over and made into a boarding home for the sons of soldiers. The name *Prytanée* was taken from that of a home in ancient Athens, where citizens who had made unusual contributions to the state might eat. At first, in 1795, the pupils were merely boarded in the *Prytanée* and went out to study in one of the state schools. In 1800 the *Prytanée* was reorganized, and four secondary schools were established at Paris, Compiègne, Saint-Cyr, and Saint-Germain, all four to be called together *Le Prytanée français.* Each school was to have a hundred scholarship pupils selected from families where the father was in military service or had died in such service. Other paying pupils were also to be admitted. The four schools were just getting started when in 1801 Chaptal raised the number of scholarship pupils to two hundred in the Paris, Saint-Cyr, and Saint-Germain sections and to three hundred in the Compiègne section. Paying pupils were fixed at one hundred for each school; regulations now allowed pupils to enter at ten years of age and to stay until they were eighteen. The pupils were divided into a military and a civil section. The training for the pupils in the second section was directed toward preparing them to go into medical, law, or technical schools; those in the military section were to be prepared for careers in the army and the navy. In the case of the Compiègne section, emphasis was to be laid on training skilled mechanics for industry and for the navy. The next year, 1802, the Paris and the Saint-Germain sections were closed. In 1803 the Compiègne section was joined with the Compiègne *École des arts et métiers.* This left only the school at Saint-Cyr to bear the name of *Le Prytanée français.* It was this school at Saint-Cyr that in 1808 was moved to La Flèche, to make way at Saint-Cyr for a military school that from 1803 to 1808 had been at Fontainebleau. At La Flèche, the *Prytanée* was set up in the buildings of the famous seventeenth-century Jesuit school in which Descartes had been educated. The *Prytanée* lasted at La Flèche from 1808 to 1814; in 1811 an artillery school was set up alongside it. Cf. Buisson, ref. 4, articles "Prytanée français" and "Prytanée militaire de La Flèche."

nations in arithmetic, geometry, and French grammar. The tuition was high, twelve hundred francs a year, but some were admitted on scholarships. The admissions policy had, at least at first, to be very lenient; for example, of forty-six admitted at one time only five had really fulfilled the requirements. As time went on, the quality of the two hundred students steadily improved. Evidently the school was favored by the government, for during this same period the quality of the students deteriorated in nearly all of the other technical schools in France. The work remained of a somewhat elementary character until after 1815. The two-year course included history, French literature and composition, geography, a good deal of mathematics, drawing including map making and fortifications, infantry and cavalry maneuvers and tactics, the principles of attack and of defense, and a great deal of military drill and practical exercises. The hours of work were long, the discipline was severe, and the students during their course were rarely allowed to go outside the school, which was set up in the old buildings of Madame de Maintenon's school for girls, closed since 1793. The Saint-Cyr school, in the years 1804 to 1807, furnished 1,348 second lieutenants to the army; of these, two thirds were killed in the campaigns of 1805, 1806, and 1807. More students were admitted. In 1809, 458, in 1810, 229, in 1811, 145, in 1812, 603, in 1813, 715, and in 1814, 252 alumni were in Napoleon's armies. The Saint-Cyr school, from Napoleon's point of view, was a success.[92]

[92] Aulard, ref. 23, pp. 128–29, de Ganniers, ref. 85, pp. 184–203, 214–20; *Arch. nat.* A.D. VI, 49, a full report on the school, including methods of admission, content of courses, and administration. Chaptal was chiefly responsible for the Saint-Cyr *École spéciale militaire;* Napoleon told him one day he wanted a plan for it the next day. Chaptal worked all night, took his plan to Napoleon in the morning. In three hours, Napoleon went over it, made some changes, and issued a decree. Pigeire, ref. 23, p. 349. There are detailed accounts of the school in Titeux, ref. 91, Chaps. 2 and 5, and in Barnard, ref. 68, pp. 225–40. To provide men trained in balloon service, an *École aérostatique* with two teachers and sixty students was set up in 1794 at Meudon. *Almanach national de France, l'an sixième* (Paris, 1797–1798), pp. 151–52.

In 1809 Napoleon established, somewhat along the lines of Saint-Cyr, a cavalry school at Saint-Germain. For this purpose he closed a small and poor cavalry school at Versailles — one of three that had been established in 1796, the other two at Lunéville and at Angers having already been closed — and moved some of the men and equipment to Saint-Germain. The course at the new *École spéciale de cavalerie* was much like that at Saint-Cyr, though the tuition was higher, the quarters more comfortable, and the discipline less severe. Napoleon hoped in all this to attract a more aristocratic student body than the one found at Saint-Cyr or at the *École polytechnique*. Quarters were provided for six hundred men, but the school never had more than two hundred students. The institution had a poor reputation; the instruction was mediocre, the administration sloppy, and the students lazy and unruly. The number of students declined, and by the end of the Russian campaign there were actually only ten students left at Saint-Germain.[93]

The school at Saint-Germain, like the others, was drained to fill Napoleon's armies. In 1809 the calls were very heavy. The small *École spéciale de cavalerie,* for example, furnished 6 officers in 1810, 13 in 1811, 59 in 1812, 134 in 1813, and 9 in 1814. In 1809 the following numbers of students were taken from technical schools and put into the army: 168 from the *École spéciale militaire* at Saint-Cyr, 400 from the *Prytanée français* at La Flèche, 50 from the *École polytechnique,* 150 from the *écoles des arts et métiers,* and equally large numbers from the other technical schools. Most of these youths were between sixteen and eighteen years of age. A lull occurred in the years 1810 and 1812, when more students were allowed to finish their courses, but beginning with the Russian campaign all the military schools, and many schools not so closely con-

---

[93] De Ganniers, ref. 85, pp. 206–14; Titeux, *op. cit.,* Chap. 6, and L. Picard, *Origines de l'école de cavalerie et de ses traditions équestres* (2 vols., Saumur, 1889), Vol. 1, Chaps. 19–21.

nected with the army, were nearly emptied. Many of those who were left in the years 1812 to 1815 were from the conquered peoples who had been forced to send their sons to France to be educated.[94]

6. Naval Education

In naval education, as in all other fields of instruction in France, the older educational enterprises were not suddenly closed at the opening of the Revolution in 1789 but lasted on into the early 1790's. Then the growing hatred of all things royal, clerical, and aristocratic, combined with a naïve and doctrinaire enthusiasm for change and reform, led to a closing of old schools and the creation of new ones — often only on paper. In 1791 the old naval corps and the old naval schools that had developed in the last two centuries of the monarchy were dissolved. A single naval corps combining the state navy and the merchant marine was set up.[95] The same law of 1791 ordered the opening of two types of centers of instruction in hydrography and mathematics in the principal parts of France; twenty-four were to be quite elementary schools under the name of *écoles d'hydrographie* (their name was soon changed

[94] De Ganniers, *op. cit.*, pp. 216–21.

[95] The old naval apprentice corps *gardes de la marine* and the *gardes du pavillon* had been abolished in 1786. For the regulations for the navy 1791–1795, cf. J. de Crisenoy, "Les écoles navales et les officiers des vaisseaux depuis Richelieu jusqu'à nos jours," *Revue maritime et coloniale,* 1864 Vol. 2, pp. 102–11; the standard (anonymous) *Histoire de l'école navale* (Paris, 1889), pp. 144ff.; A. Anthiaume, *Évolution et enseignement de la science nautique en France* (2 vols., Paris, 1920), Vol. 2, p. 240, de Montzey, ref. 50, pp. 150–155. Of great usefulness on all aspects of the history of the French naval organization are A. Jal, *Glossaire nautique, répertoire polyglotte de termes de marine anciens et modernes* (Paris, 1848), and M. Blanchard, *Répertoire général des lois, décrets, ordonnances, règlements, et instructions sur la marine* (3 vols., Paris, 1849–1859). The standard histories of the French navy, even those by Ch. de la Roncière and Tramond, are chiefly concerned with the details of naval engagements and are very brief on the organization of the navy.

to *écoles de navigation*) and twelve were to be somewhat more advanced and for older students, and were to be called *écoles des mathématiques et d'hydrographie*. The government seems to have hoped that the twelve *écoles des mathématiques et d'hydrographie* (Toulon, Cette, Marseille, Bayonne, Bordeaux, Rochefort, Nantes, Lorient, Brest, Saint-Malo, Le Havre, and Dunkerque) would train sailors for the state navy, and that the more elementary *écoles de navigation* in twenty-four lesser ports would train sailors for the merchant fleet.

To enter either of these types of schools, one had only to prove that he was at least thirteen years of age, could read and write, and knew the four rules of arithmetic. There were no tuition charges, but each pupil had to board and clothe himself. The port authorities were to provide teachers, the central government furnished only inspectors and advice. After the schools had been under way for a few years, the central government was to give examinations in mathematics, physics, and the elements of navigation. No student could take these examinations if he was under fifteen years of age or over twenty. Those who passed the examinations were to obtain apprentice positions on ships. Here they would receive small wages from the state until they were assigned definite positions. Schools of this type were organized, with a good deal of variation in the courses and in the quality of teachers and students, in some twenty-four ports of France. Most of the teachers were men who had taught in similar schools of navigation before the Revolution. They gave elementary training in mathematics, drawing, map making, and navigation to over a thousand youths, most of whom got positions in commercial shipping. Anthiaume, who has studied them in detail, is convinced that although a great many students were turned out these schools were inferior to similar schools that existed in nearly all the French ports before 1789.[96]

[96] Anthiaume, *op. cit.*, Vol. 2, pp. 230–313; *Histoire de l'école navale* (Paris, 1889), pp. 145–53; Porentree, "L'école d'hydrographie de Saint-

In 1796, the government decreed a more advanced type of school, the *École navale,* with branches at Brest, Toulon, and Rochefort. Students who wished to enter one of these establishments had to pass examinations in arithmetic, geometry, physics, and such rudiments of navigation and naval usage as they might acquire from studying several of the stock compends on the subject. Besides the classroom instruction and demonstrations inside the school, they were to receive practical training in the shipbuilding yards attached to each port and in addition to have practical training on a small warship. At the end of two years of such training, a whole year was to be spent on board a training ship. Those who finished the whole three years' course satisfactorily were then to join a corps of *aspirants de la marine* in which they were to remain until they were assigned definite positions. The whole scheme was a good one, but it remained on paper for the time being.[97]

After 1789 the first successful step toward establishing higher naval education came in the years 1795 to 1799 when the *École du génie maritime* (sometimes called the *École des*

Malo pendant la Révolution," *Annales de la société historique de l'arrondissement de Saint-Malo,* 1923–1924. Guillaume, ref. 16, Vol. IV, XXXV; Chuquet, ref. 87, p. 11. A manuscript report (*Arch. nat. Marine* G 87) shows that the largest of the schools were at Le Havre, Brest, and Toulon, each with over six hundred pupils; the smallest was at La Rochelle with a hundred and twenty. A report of 1799 insists on the need of improving naval education. "French naval schools which were neglected during the storms of the Revolution are still languishing. Most of them are without good teachers, many consider them mere 'hors d'œuvres.' The good naval schools of the eighteenth century should be copied. Better teachers of the mechanical arts in the great ports would do much good. In all these ports, all the work with ropes, levers, pulleys, etc., is done by old rule-of-thumb methods; much material and effort is wasted. Teachers of drawing are also needed for teaching ship designing and map making." L. Rollin, *Rapport sur l'organisation des écoles de la marine* (Paris, 1799), pp. 1–17. For the English parallels to French naval education of various grades, cf. E. C. Millington, *Seamen in the Making, a Short History of Nautical Training* (London, 1933), esp. Chaps. 2 and 3.

[97] De Crisenoy, ref. 95, p. 108 *note; Histoire de l'école navale* (Paris, 1889), p. 151; and de Montzey, ref. 50, pp. 155–57.

éléves ingénieurs de vaisseau), the *École des ingénieurs constructeurs,* and the *École d'artillerie de la marine* were reconstituted as *écoles d'application* for graduates of the *École polytechnique.* These small schools, each with only a few students, had been started in the eighteenth century but had fallen into a state of disorganization during the years following 1790. As they were reopened one by one, they each had places for only about a dozen students. No one of the three schools seems to have had a very active life until after 1815. The *École du génie maritime* was established in Paris; in 1801 it was moved to Brest, in 1810 to Antwerp, and in 1816 it was back in Brest. (In 1830 it went to Lorient, in 1854 it returned to Paris, and in 1872 was finally settled again in Brest.)

The largest of the three schools was the *École d'artillerie de marine.* In addition to their course in the *École polytechnique,* the students admitted here had to take a year's work in the army artillery school. They then finished their training with a year in the *École d'artillerie de la marine* and a year of apprentice duty in the port of Brest. Few students entered this long training, but the school, small as it was, did help to keep alive in France the traditions of good and thorough naval training.

In the small *École des ingénieurs constructeurs* the teaching was done by a professor of drawing and design, an experienced naval engineer, two master carpenters, and two master ship-riggers. The students drew all types of ship plans, studied and built models, and during several months of the year had practical work in construction in the best shipyards in France, where they worked on ships that were being built or repaired. During the three-year course each student had not only to pass his examinations but had also to serve on a long cruise at sea. This school gave excellent training in ship designing and construction, but it never had more than a handful of students.[98]

[98] *É. Poly. L. de Cen.,* Vol. 2, pp. 160–65, 380–81, de Montzey, *op. cit.,* pp. 161–62. J. R. Soley, *Report on Foreign Systems of Naval Education*

During the *Empire* the great shipyards of France introduced a large number of improvements in construction because of new ideas picked up in Holland, Italy, and Spain, and from a study of English ship design. Napoleon was interested in the navy, as in other services, trying to introduce more regularity and order into every part of French administration. To improve conditions in both merchant shipping and the state navy, he appointed special maritime prefects to look after shipping, shipbuilding, arsenals, and naval schools in all the coastal parts of France; later the same system was extended throughout the Empire. During the Directory Napoleon gave to the whole *Corps de marine,* on land and on the sea, an administration more centralized than it had ever had before. These excellent reforms survived the fall of the *Empire.*[99]

The one really new experiment in advanced naval education undertaken during the Revolutionary era was the establishment in 1810 of two full-fledged naval schools on shipboard. The "Tourville" at Brest and the "Duquesne" at Toulon were rebuilt for each to receive three hundred pupils who might enter between the ages of thirteen and fifteen. No student was supposed to stay in school beyond the age of eighteen; a few, however, remained till they were nineteen. Each school was put under the supervision of the local maritime prefect. Entrance examinations included arithmetic; soon algebra and geometry were added. Later plane trigonometry, physics, and drawing were also required. Each ship had teachers for mathematics, physics, geography, drawing, and the principles of navigation. The courses were planned in a three-year cycle

---

(Washington, 1880), pp. 101–02; D. Dislère, "Notice historique sur le corps du génie maritime," *Revue maritime* (1921), pp. 438–39. Cf. also remarks by Fourcroy in *Moniteur,* 2 Sept. 1794; L. Villaret, "Notions historiques sur le service des constructions navales dans les ports maritimes," *Mémorial du génie maritime,* 1902. There is interesting material on the *corps du génie maritime* in *É. Poly. L. de Cen.,* Vol. 2, pp. 161–249 and on the *corps d'artillerie de marine* in the same work, Vol. 2, pp. 375–402.

[99] De Crisenoy, ref. 95, pp. 111–16.

and combined theoretical and practical training in ship designing and building, in navigation, and in gunnery. Part of the teaching was done in school buildings in the cities of Brest and Toulon, but most of it was given aboard the two ships on which the students lived. Some of the students paid eight hundred francs a year tuition; others were on state scholarships.

The first year of the new schools on board the "Tourville" and the "Duquesne" was not very successful, but during the next five years things went better. The older boys were used to help discipline and train the younger ones. Both schools failed to have their full quota of three hundred youths, and of those admitted not all had passed the entrance examinations. Neither the equipment nor the teachers nor the clothing and rations furnished were very good. In spite of all difficulties, these two floating naval schools were to leave a permanent mark on French naval training. For though both were closed in 1816 and their place taken for the next fourteen years by a naval school at Angoulême — a curious sort of a naval Saint-Cyr — it was to Napoleon's training-ship plan that the government returned in 1830.[100]

7. Conclusion

The purpose of the educators, the scientists, and the legislators of the Revolutionary era was to turn the young away from the study of God, of men, and of the past and to direct their attention to nature and to science, to the state, to what was believed to be socially useful, and to the future.

The first impression of a close study of their educational experiments, however, is that of much bold planning outlined on paper and sometimes enacted into law, of some interesting starts and promising beginnings, and then of a gradual peter-

---

[100] De Crisenoy, *op. cit.,* pp. 116–17; *Histoire de l'école navale* (Paris, 1889), Chap. 14, and de Montzey, *op. cit.,* pp. 169–72.

ing-out due to lack of experience, to failure to get equipment and to find competent teachers and sufficient funds, to rising clerical and antidemocratic and then anti-Bonapartist opposition, and finally to the exhaustion of long wars. Viewed at close range it is all a pretty confused and depressing picture.

If, however, one moves into the nineteenth or twentieth century and looks at the Revolutionary era from a longer perspective, it is immediately evident that this period not only continued the older types of technical training but that it also bequeathed to modern France and to the whole modern world important new types of technical education. Although before the Revolution France had, through schools like the *École des ponts et chaussées* and the *École du génie militaire,* taken the lead in developing the highest type of technical instruction, certainly this leadership was made even more evident by the launching of institutions like the *écoles des arts et métiers,* the *Conservatoire des arts et métiers* and the *École polytechnique.* There were shortcomings aplenty in all types of French technical schools, but in spite of these there were nowhere in the world, even in the disastrous years 1814 and 1815, better schools offering training for industry, for the army and the navy, and for the designing and constructing of public works than those in France.

The Constitutional Monarchy
1814–1848

A quarter century of revolution and war left the French nation defeated, exhausted, and deeply divided politically and culturally. More is the wonder, then, that France after Waterloo was able to go on making contributions of first-rate importance to all the arts and sciences. The decades between the two Napoleons again show that France was one of the leaders in European culture.

In the field of education the period is marked by few new experiments, but programs that had earlier been projected and in some cases started, now, under peaceful conditions, came to remarkable fruition. Unlike all the earlier periods we have considered, the age of the Constitutional Monarchy was not a period of bold starts followed by sudden changes or by disappointing neglect. Progress was steady. France during the first half of the nineteenth century not only improved her primary and secondary education but continued to take the lead in nearly every field of technical education.

1. Scientific and Technical Instruction in Primary and Secondary Schools

The strong clerical reaction that had followed the "restoration of order" in 1795 had steadily increased, and, as we have seen, the government — in spite of the setting up of the *Université de France* — had accepted the extension of church schools alongside those run by various state agencies. After 1815 the clerical reaction was even more evident. Having failed to destroy the Napoleonic *Université,* the Ultra-Royalists by 1822 got it put under clerical control. "Youth needs a religious and monarchical direction," says an ordinance of 1821.

In 1815, in the fields of primary and secondary education, the communes provided a number of schools; other schools were run by private individuals and by the church, both with easily procured state licenses. According to law, all public, private, and church schools were subject to government inspection; in practice, however, government inspectors found it expedient to pay little attention to private and church schools. The government of the Restoration (1814–1830) in its early years appropriated a small sum each year toward primary education; this was spent almost entirely on the printing of schoolbooks and on brief reports on the primary-school systems of other countries. Gradually the amounts spent by the national government increased, the appropriations going chiefly for scholarships for poor students. The burden of supporting the state primary schools thus fell on the local departmental, cantonal, and municipal governments, which collected taxes for this purpose. Support also came from the tuition fees paid by the families of the pupils.

Among the reasons always used by the church to prove the advantages of sending pupils to church schools were that it cost the parents less (as most of the church schools charged no tuition) and that the teachers were more competent. Both these considerations influenced parents who would not otherwise have patronized church schools. Most of the church schools were conducted by teaching orders, especially by the *Frères des écoles chrétiennes.* The diocesan authorities conducted primary schools, the *petits séminaires,* for the training of young boys who later intended to enter the priesthood. In practice, however, though it was against the law, they accepted many pupils who had no intention of ever becoming priests.

The pay of the schoolmasters in the government schools was often too small to attract men of ability. So the teachers in state primary schools were usually poorly trained and too few in number; in addition, they were often badly overworked. Much time was wasted by having the boys and girls taught separately, either in separate rooms or on different days of the week.

Guizot's famous report of 1833 shows a deplorable state of ignorance both among the teachers in the state schools and among the population of France. The condition of primary education, as shown in this report, is definitely much worse than it was before the Revolution. In spite of all the fine educational plans and laws of the whole Revolutionary era, and in spite of a well-meant ordinance of 1816 which said that every commune in France must support a school, there were only 28,000 primary schools of all types in 1821, and only 30,000 in 1829. At the beginning of the July Monarchy (1830–1848) only about ten million out of twenty-five million adults were literate, and only 10,000 out of about 39,000 communes had primary schools. Out of every hundred conscripts in the army only forty-two could read. All this backwardness, around 1830, stands in contrast with the vast educational plans of the periods of the Revolution and Napoleon, though it should be pointed out that the situation was even worse in nearly all the large states of Europe, including England. Only in Holland and some of the German states were conditions better.[1]

The inadequacy of primary education, the clerical influence in the schools, and the type of subjects taught, all drew criticism in the period between the fall of the First Empire and the passing of the reforming law of 1833. During the Hundred Days of 1815 a *Société pour l'encouragement de l'instruction élémentaire* was founded by a group of philanthropists, including La Rochefoucauld-Liancourt, Gérando, and Laborde. They collected funds and opened a number of primary schools which followed two English plans, one by an Anglican, Bell, and another by a Quaker, Lancaster, where the older pupils were used to help in the instruction of the younger ones. By 1830, in spite of a great deal of clerical opposition, 904 of these so-called *écoles mutuelles* were in operation, mostly in Paris and the larger cities. The pupils were taught reading, writing, and arithmetic, but little more. The whole enterprise was aimed at interesting people in extending primary education rather than in reforming it. Under the auspices of the society there were opened the first kindergartens in France, the *salles d'asile*.[2]

[1] F. B. Artz, *France under the Bourbon Restoration* (Cambridge, Mass., 1931), pp. 138–39, and bibliography pp. 405–6; R. Niderst, *L'enseignement primaire en France 1789–1914* (Strasbourg, 1935), pp. 29–31. Niderst's account is the best available summary of the history of French primary education since the beginning of the Revolution. Some interesting details for local areas will be found in E. L'Hommedé, *Un département français sous la monarchie de juillet* (Paris, 1933), pp. 61–65; in L. Bideau, ed., *État de l'instruction primaire dans le département de la Marne sous la Restauration* (Paris, 1914); in A. Decap *et al.*, eds., *L'instruction primaire en France au XVIII*e *et XIX*e *siècles* (Paris, 1914); M. Soulice, *L'instruction primaire dans les Basses Pyrénées 1385–1880* (Paris, 1881); and M. Schnerb, *L'enseignement primaire dans le Puy-de-Dôme avant et après la loi Guizant* (Clermont-Ferrand, 1937). The state schoolmaster and the local priest often quarreled. Cf. A. Mater, "L'histoire d'une paroisse au XIX*e siècle," *Revue d'histoire moderne,* 1905.

[2] No state kindergartens were opened till 1837. Niderst, *op. cit.,* pp. 27–28; F. Dreyfus, *La Rochefoucauld-Liancourt* (Paris, 1903), Chap. 10; C. H. Pouthas, *Guizot sous la Restauration* (Paris, 1923), pp. 356–57; articles

The demands for educating the masses and for giving a practical turn to instruction in the primary schools became very numerous after the return of peace in 1815. The *Saint-Simoniens,* the followers of Fournier, and of Auguste Comte took up the demands of Rousseau and of eighteenth-century writers and insisted that not only must all children be given an opportunity to learn, but that they should be taught to work with their hands and should from the beginning learn about things that have a social utility. Free thought, democracy, and the improvement of society through applied science were veritable religious dogmas in these radical circles. Cabet, during the July Monarchy, carried this radical dislike of older types of education to the limit; he proposed that all the old schoolbooks be burned and that a new start, along more practical lines, be made.[3]

In less radical and more definitely bourgeois circles, the same ideas were widely expressed. Both Dupin and Chaptal, the leading economic writers of the Restoration, were very critical of the existing educational regime. A periodical of 1825 says, "The enlightened spirits of the last century were fully aware of the importance of teaching the sciences; through their application they realized that the mechanical arts, the chemical manufactures, and agriculture could make no progress without the help of the physical and mathematical sciences. The practice of the arts without the flame of science is limited by a blind routine that will never improve anything. Instead of

---

"Gérando" and "Laborde" in F. Buisson, ed., *Dictionnaire de pédagogie* (4 vols., Paris, 1888). The *Société de la morale chrétienne* devoted much attention to discussing education. It was at a session of this society in 1824 that Guizot read a report on the competition he had started in the *Tablettes universelles* for suggestions for primary education, Pouthas, *op. cit.,* pp. 336–37. For the use of *l'enseignement mutuel,* cf. R. Lemoine, *L'enseignement mutuel dans la Somme* (Abbeville, 1933).

[3] M. Ferraz, *Étude sur la philosophie en France au XIXe siècle* (Paris, 1877), p. 48; G. Weill, "Les théories Saint-Simoniens sur l'éducation," and "Les républicains et l'enseignement sous Louis Philippe," *Revue internationale de l'enseignement,* 1896 and 1899.

learning Latin, youths should devote themselves to the study of mathematics, physics, chemistry, natural history and the mechanical arts." [4]

In 1823 the *Tablettes universelles* opened a contest for the best essay on the subject: "Is there not in our system of public instruction a gap between the primary schools and the *collèges,* devoted to classical studies, which should be filled by schools of another type?" The prize was won by Renouard, *Considérations sur les lacunes de l'éducation secondaire* (published in 1824). This treatise greatly impressed Cousin, who in 1831 made a tour of the German states where he found that the *Bürgerschulen* were doing the work advocated by Renouard. Out of all this came, after 1833, the *écoles primaires supérieures.* During the Restoration (1814–1830) there seems to have been universal agreement that, until the number of primary and secondary schools were greatly increased and some changes

---

[4] *Journal des connaissances usuelles* (May 1825), pp. 89–92, and A. Corbon, *De l'enseignement professionnel* (Paris, 1859), p. 122. The importance of extending primary schools and of introducing into all primary schools some scientific, mechanical, and agricultural teaching is repeated over and over again. Buret, in his study of the lower classes, says that all children "should be taught to know the basic truths of the physical order; each commune, including even the poorest, should possess about its school fields, flocks, and machines. These should be the true school of the people. The primary teacher should teach his pupils natural history and the instruments of work which they are later to use. For this teaching, the more skilled workers of the community should be brought in." E. Buret, *De la misère des classes laborieuses en France et en Angleterre* (2 vols., Paris, 1840), Vol. 2, pp. 461–64. Cf. also C. Dupin, *Discours sur le progrès des connaissances de géométrie et de mécanique dans la classe industrielle* (Paris, 1829) and J. Willm, *Essai sur l'éducation du peuple* (Paris, 1843), esp. pp. 244–48, 439–42. In 1821 there was founded a short-lived *Société des méthodes d'enseignement;* its purposes were similar to those of the *Société d'enseignement élémentaire.* A. C. Renouard, *Considérations sur les lacunes de l'éducation secondaire en France* (Paris, 1824), p. 11. Renouard's pamphlet is typical of the sort of attacks made on primary and secondary education; he wonders how you can hope to train a farmer by preparing a youth to read Virgil's *Georgics,* a sheep raiser by preparing him to read Theocritus, or a sailor by introducing him to the voyages of Ulysses! Cf. also, C. P. Collard, *Coup d'œil sur l'état de l'instruction en France* (Paris, 1835).

were made in the quality of teaching and the subjects taught, it would never be possible to improve the trade schools or the higher schools of advanced engineering training.

Soon after the establishment of the July Monarchy, Guizot and a group of Liberal statesmen and scholars began to investigate the whole system of French primary education. Out of this, plans were formed to extend state primary education to every commune in France, and to make a number of other educational reforms. The result was the famous *Law of 1833*. The principal provisions of the Law were these: one elementary school must be established in every commune; in all communes over 6000, besides primary schools, *écoles primaires supérieures*, a *collège royal* (a secondary school), infant schools, and evening classes for adults were to be organized. The management of the primary schools was to be entrusted to local committees, each to include the mayor, the president of the town council, the priest or the pastor, and one other person appointed by the educational committee of the *arrondissement* in which the commune was situated. The educational committee of the *arrondissement* (including the mayor of the chief town, a judge, several members of the local clergy, a teacher from some advanced school in the district, three members of the council of the local district, and the members of the general council of the *département* who reside in the *arrondissement*) was to inspect the local schools, to meet once a month, and to report from time to time directly to the Minister of Public Instruction in Paris. The running of a local normal school and the certification of teachers were given to a departmental council.

Besides all this machinery, the Minister of Public Instruction appointed inspectors for each department. Their duty was to visit every school at least once a year; copies of their reports were sent to the educational committees of the commune, the *arrondissement,* and the *département,* and the Minister of Public Instruction. (In 1843 there were 87 state inspectors and 114 assistant inspectors; they visited in that year 30,081 communes.) Each commune must provide at least a school-house and a residence for the teacher. The state provided one third of this initial expense; if this was insufficient, departmental or national funds were to be drawn upon. Most of the rest was to be provided by taxes in the commune. For the pupils who attended the schools the parents must pay tuition, though poor children were to be educated free. The instruction was to cover reading, writing, and arithmetic, French, moral instruction, the legal system of weights and measures, geography and history (especially of France), draw-ing, and singing. In each departmental capital, as in all com-munes of 6,000 and over, one or more *écoles primaires supé-rieures* were to be established as a link between the primary schools and industrial and commercial careers. Emphasis in these schools was to be on geometry, bookkeeping, chemistry, drawing, and modern languages. Special courses of instruction for artisans were to be given in these schools in the evening. In 1847 there were 6,877 evening classes in government schools, with 115,164 auditors. The instruction in these evening classes ranged from the three R's to courses in higher mathematics, and applied chemistry and physics.

These reforms of 1833 were vigorously opposed by the church, which was unfavorable to state schools and demanded for all parents the free right to choose between state and church schools. And the clergy, under the banner of "free-dom of teaching," kept up a steady attack on state edu-cation. As the church could not provide enough primary schools for the whole of France, and as the competition for students was keener on the level of secondary education, the church attacks on the state secondary schools and on the universities was more severe. During the July Monarchy all of this clerical agitation attracted an immense amount of public interest in educational questions, though this tremen-dous fight between church and state belongs more properly to the political history of modern France than to the general history of education. Guizot and his chief collaborators Villemain and Cousin were not anticlerical; their great interest was not in fighting church education but in the rapid expansion of educational opportunities for the masses.[5]

As a result of the Law of 1833, primary schools multiplied; in 1832 there were in France 42,092 primary schools of all types; by 1847 their number had risen to 63,028. In the same period, the number of pupils in primary schools rose from 1,937,582 to 3,530,135; the number of normal schools increased from fourteen to seventy-six. Illiteracy dwindled; in 1829 more than half of the army recruits could neither read nor write; by 1847 the number had been reduced to one third. Some critics thought improvements moved too slowly. In 1838 Buret complained that five thousand communes still had not set up schools, that twenty thousand communes conducted schools in rented buildings, that there were only three million out of five million children in elementary schools, that the provisions for educating girls were grossly inadequate, and that fourteen million adults in France could not read and write. Criticisms of this sort should not obscure the fact that it was the July Monarchy that finally created state primary education in France. The dream of the eighteenth-century *Philosophes* and of the Revolutionary reformers was, at long last, coming true.[6]

The record for the *écoles primaires supérieures* was not as

[5] For a summary and exposition of the Law of 1833, cf. *American Journal of Education*, 1870, pp. 244–80; for the quarrels between church and state, cf. A. Debidour, *Histoire des rapports de l'église et de l'état en France de 1789 à 1870*, 2nd ed. (Paris, 1911); G. Bonet-Maury, *La liberté de conscience en France 1598–1870* (Paris, 1910); the bibliography in Artz, ref. 1, pp. 404–09; and L. Grimaud, *Histoire de la liberté de l'enseignement en France*, Vol. 5: *La Restauration* (Paris, 1950); Vol. 6: *La monarchie de juillet* (Paris, 1954).

[6] E. P. Bush, *Guizot in the early years of the Orleanist Monarchy* (Urbana, Ill., 1927), pp. 153–57; Niderst, ref. 1, p. 35; S. Charléty, *La monarchie de juillet* (Paris, 1921), pp. 91–93, and R. Lemoine, *La loi Guizot 1833, son application dans le département de la Somme* (Abbeville, 1933); Buret, ref. 4, Vol. 2, pp. 454–56.

good as that for the elementary schools. Some parents who might have sent their children to the *écoles primaires supérieures* after they had finished the elementary school refused to do so because these schools did not teach Latin, and their legal name offended the vanity of many parents because it would be said that their son attended only a "primary" school. So, though the youth might be destined for business, he was often sent to a public or a church *collège* where the course was largely humanistic and mathematical. Latin had social prestige — science had not. By 1841 there were only one hundred and sixty-one of these *écoles primaires supérieures* and one hundred and ninety-one in church or private hands. In all these *écoles primaires supérieures* there were in 1837, 9,414 pupils, though by 1840 their number had risen to 15,215. Willm, inspector of schools in the district around Strasbourg, condemned them as a sort of "bastard instruction without any clear-cut character." Some he found were no better than ordinary primary schools, others were organized like the classical *collèges*. He suggested that they be turned into genuine trade schools with the courses directed toward the chief economic interests of the local district. The best of these schools were certainly those oriented toward the local situation, as those in Paris, Lyons, Mulhouse, Nîmes, Boulogne, Nantes, Rennes, Laval, Dieppe, Le Puy, Rheims, and Saint-Étienne. Many such *écoles primaires supérieures* became elementary trade schools and turned out men who later were factory foremen, bankers, shippers, merchants, and state employes.[7]

[7] J. B. Paquier, *L'Enseignement professionnel en France* (Paris, 1908), pp. 34ff.; L. Rétail, *Rôle économique de l'apprentissage et de l'enseignement technique* (Paris, 1925), p. 26; and A. D. Bache, *Report on Education in Europe to the Trustees of the Girard College for Orphans* (Philadelphia, 1836), p. 199. In the state normal schools for preparing teachers, courses were given in geometry, physics, natural history, and drawing as applied to industry and agriculture. *Académie des sciences morales et politiques, séances et travaux* (1846), Vol. 9, pp. 248–49. The best contemporary studies of the *écoles primaires supérieures* are those of Saint-Marc Girardin, *De l'instruction intermédiare et de son état dans le midi de l'Allemagne* (Paris, 1835)

In the field of higher secondary education, the old national *lycées* in 1814 were renamed *collèges royaux,* and the commercial secondary schools were called *collèges communaux.*[8] Military training was thrown out and attendance at mass made obligatory; many ecclesiastics and laymen favorable to the church were put into the *collèges* as administrators and teachers; and all *collèges* were inspected by the local bishop. The central *école normale* in Paris was hard hit; the teachers were put under police surveillance to be sure they did not teach too many Liberal ideas, and finally, in 1822 this excellent institution, widely regarded as the best normal school in the world, was closed for a time. In all the *collèges,* in spite of the reactionary attitude of the Bourbon government, there is much evidence of Liberal resistance on the part of teachers, especially for the decade 1820 to 1830. The government of the Bourbon Restoration largely ignored the laws regulating the schools run by the church. The church secondary schools multiplied,

---

and *De l'instruction intermédiare et de ses rapports avec l'instruction secondaire* (Paris, 1847). The *École primaire supérieure* at Nantes was opened in 1834 with sixty pupils; the number soon rose to one hundred. Among the subjects studied were physics, mechanics, industrial chemistry, mathematics including descriptive geometry, biology, bookkeeping, drawing, modeling, and English. The pupils came mostly from the homes of foremen, petty officials, small manufactures, and retail tradesmen. This report dates from 1863, but it gives a fair picture of what some of the intermediate schools came to. Ministère de l'agriculture, du commerce et des travaux publics, *Enquête sur l'enseignement professionnel* (2 vols., Paris, 1864), Vol. 1, pp. 319–27. Hereafter this very useful report will be referred to as *Enquête.* A translation of it appeared as a government document in England in 1868 under the title *Commission on Technical Education Appointed by Imperial Decree 22 June, 1863.*

[8] On higher secondary education for the 1815 to 1848 cf. G. Weill, *Histoire de l'enseignement secondaire en France 1802–1920* (Paris, 1921), Chap. 3; F. Vial, *Trois siècles d'histoire de l'enseignement secondaire* (Paris, 1936); F. Buisson, ref. 2, articles "Lycées et collèges," section on "La Restauration et la Monarchie de Juillet"; H. Bernier, *Notice historique sur le collège de Beaupreau* (Angers, 1854); V. Chauvin, *Histoire des lycées et collèges de Paris* (Paris, 1866); Kilian, *Tableau historique de l'enseignement secondaire en France* (Paris, 1841); and the references to secondary education in Chapter Three of this work.

and they — through sentiment or snobbery or because the tuition was either free or very low in cost — attracted many students.[9]

In the *collèges royaux* and in the *collèges communaux* of the Restoration the principal subjects taught were Latin and mathematics; the stiff four-year course in mathematics being an important legacy from the state secondary schools of the Empire. As clerical reaction grew, in 1821 the mathematics courses were reduced, the courses in Latin and French literature increased, the teaching of all sciences separated sharply from the literary courses, the courses in philosophy reduced in length, and all the instruction and examinations in philosophy conducted in Latin. Evidently science was to be played down and philosophy to be confined in scholastic forms and taught in a dead language that would not inflame young students. The whole *Université de France* was put under a bishop. A statute of the time declared, "In calling to the head of public instruction a man clothed in a sacred character, His Majesty makes known to France how he desires the youth of the kingdom to be raised in an atmosphere of religious and royal ideas. Moreover, anyone who has the misfortune to live without religion and who is not devoted to the royal family should feel that he is unworthy of teaching the young." Evidently Latin studies are favorable to the throne and the altar; scientific studies foster democracy and free thought. From the point of view of king and church, this was the first principle of education after 1815. The Liberals, in turn, bottomed their educational faith on modern languages and the sciences. Debates on these subjects in the chambers and in the press were endless.

In 1826 some changes were made, students taking science

[9] A royal ordinance of 27 Feb. 1821 declared, "The bases of education in the *collèges* are religion, monarchy, legitimacy, and the Charter of 1814." Buisson, ref. 2, Vol. 2, p. 1743; cf. also Debidour, ref. 5, pp. 335–36, 343, 359–60, 370–72, 377; Bonet-Maury, ref. 5, pp. 128–29, and an article by Dubois in *Le Globe,* 21 June 1828.

courses were no longer separated from those studying the humanities, and a required course in physics was integrated with the courses in philosophy. Further reforms introduced in 1828 kept Latin in each year's work but reduced the time spent on it; the time gained was opened to electives in mathematics, French history, and to courses in modern languages (English and German in the North, and Spanish and Italian in the South). In 1829, the teaching of philosophy was again given in French, and provision was made for special elective courses in applied science for students who intended "to enter the manufacturing professions." From these special courses set up in 1829 dates the beginning of what the French later called *bifurcation* in education, i.e., the running side by side, in secondary schools, of more or less independent classical and scientific courses of study. The changes in 1829 also raised the requirements for those who taught in the secondary schools.[10]

The science courses given in the *collèges royaux* and in the *collèges communaux* during the Restoration began in the first year with a review of arithmetic, followed by a first course in plane geometry; in the second year solid geometry and trigonometry were studied; in the third year all of geometry and trigonometry were reviewed, and for the first time algebra was studied; finally in the fourth year, all sorts of practical problems involving the application of mathematics were the center of interest. A good deal of physics, mechanics, chemistry, mineralogy, and elementary engineering was given in connection with all the mathematics courses. When separate courses were offered in physics, biology ("natural history"),

---

[10] Paquier, ref. 7, p. 28; E. Bertrand, *L'enseignement technique en France . . .* (Montpellier, 1913), p. 215; E. Durkheim, *L'Évolution pédagogique en France* (2 vols., Paris, 1938), Vol. 2, p. 175. The best of the *collèges royaux* were several in Paris, and those of Nantes, Valenciennes, Béziers, and Nancy.

and chemistry, they were usually given by the professor of philosophy.[11]

After the July Revolution, the new regime was more favorable to scientific studies and to the study of modern languages. In 1833 the time spent on mathematics was increased, and in 1838 the study of modern languages was made obligatory.[12] By 1842 the special elective courses established in 1829 had been organized in 9 *collèges royaux* out of 46, and in 51 *collèges communaux* out of 312. However, of 46,281 pupils in both the national and municipal secondary schools, only 1,191 were taking any of the special elective courses.[13]

In 1843, Villemain made a careful study of the whole situation in secondary education, the first thorough one made since 1802. According to this report there were 60,000 positions in the liberal professions and in the public administration, 3,000 of which fell vacant each year. The last was about the number graduated each year from the various types of secondary schools in France. Some of these graduates went on into the law, medical, normal, naval, military, and engineering schools; many went directly into business. Surprisingly few entered the Faculties of Letters and the Faculties of Science of the universities. The university professors devoted themselves chiefly to public lectures, to research, and to service as state examiners. In 1847 there were 54 *collèges royaux* with about 23,000 pupils (about 8,000 more than in 1830) and 312 *collèges communaux* with about 32,000 pupils (4,000 more than in 1830). There were 102 private secondary schools, 23 of which, with 9,000 pupils, gave full secondary-school courses of the sort given by the *collèges royaux;* 914 minor private schools with about 35,000 pupils gave a definitely inferior kind of

---

[11] *Journal d'instruction publique,* 1827, 326–36; Vial, ref. 8, pp. 187–93; and Durkheim, *op. cit.,* Vol. 2, pp. 174–75.

[12] Vial, *op. cit.,* pp. 193–201.

[13] O. Gréard, *Éducation et instruction* (4 vols., Paris, 1889), Vol. 2, p. 40.

secondary-school work; about 6,000 of their pupils went on into one of the state, municipal or church secondary schools. Altogether there were in the 1840's in France about 69,000 pupils in 1,374 state, communal, and private secondary schools. In the ecclesiastical secondary schools, mostly in the *petits seminaires,* there were about 20,000 more. This makes a grand total of about 90,000 secondary-school students in France in the 1840's.[14] With the great improvements in primary and in secondary education, there was by 1840 a large reservoir of trained youths from which both the trade schools and the higher schools of engineering might draw.

Salvandy, the Minister of Education in 1847, was anxious to extend a type of secondary education useful to the commercial and industrial classes, and so established in some of the *collèges royaux* a special set of courses in drawing, accounting, commercial law, and agriculture. This scheme, which carries further the *bifurcation* begun in 1829, is interesting because it looks back to the elective system of the *écoles centrales* of the Revolutionary era, and it foreshadows the separation of classical and scientific courses in the secondary

[14] *American Journal of Education,* 1870, p. 295. Charléty, ref. 6, pp. 217–18; Weill, ref. 8, Chaps. 4 and 5; and C. Dejob, "De l'établissement connu sous le nom de Lycée et d'Athénée et de quelques établissements analogues; *Revue internationale de l'enseignement,* Paris, 1889, p. 487; on poor salaries of teachers, cf. Dejob, *op. cit.,* pp. 219–26, 409–11, 416. Typical of the increase in students are the *collèges royaux* of Lyons and of Orléans; that at Lyons had 480 pupils in 1831 and 894 in 1847; that at Orléans had 120 more pupils in 1847 than it had in 1831. The periodicals of the July Monarchy are full of criticisms of the state system of education that trains doctors, lawyers, soldiers, teachers, and administrators but does not give sufficient training for engineering, manufacturing, commerce, and banking. This type of argument was heard sometimes in the Chamber of Deputies. Vial, ref. 8, pp. 196–201. The best place to follow the attacks on classical education in the press is perhaps in the articles in the *Journal des économistes.* While this quarrel between classicists and scientists was going on, the old quarrel over education between church and state was raging hotter than ever. Charléty, *op. cit.,* pp. 324–44, and Debidour, ref. 5, Chap. 4. Most of the important parts of Villemain's report of 1843 are quoted in Buisson, ref. 2, Vol. 2, pp. 1744–45; the whole report is in the *Moniteur* for 8 March 1843.

schools in the latter half of the nineteenth century. These special courses set up in 1847 were made fun of by the classicists who called them the *"pas latins"* or the *"classes des épiciers."* However, by the next year, 1848, these courses had been started in 9 *collèges royaux* and in 51 *collèges communaux.*[15]

In 1847 Dumas, a member of the *Faculté des sciences* of the University of Paris, published a remarkable report on the teaching of science in French schools and its relation to technical education. He first discusses the national and communal *collèges* as schools preparing youths who intend to enter the higher schools of civil and military engineering. He finds that students planning to take the entrance examinations for schools like the *École polytechnique,* the *École navale,* and the army school at Saint-Cyr regularly take two years of work in a *collège* and then go to a private tutoring school. Dumas points out that the preparation of such students is neglected by the *collèges.* The science courses in the *collèges* were, except in mathematics, insufficient in number; those taught in the first two years were inadequately connected with those given in the fourth year; also the timing of the science courses was bad; i.e., the candidates for the advanced technical schools have to take their entrance examinations at a date earlier than some of the most important applied scientific work in the last year of the *collège* was given. Dumas found the instruction in most of these private tutoring schools, which coached candidates for examinations, of a high order. The various scientific courses were not taught by one or two men as was often the case in a *collège,* where a single teacher often handled physics, chemistry, biology, geology, and philosophy, and *répétiteurs* were used to supervise carefully each student's work. This type of instruction was expensive and cost the families of the students a good deal, but Dumas believed that the state and communal

---

[15] Vial, ref. 8, pp. 205–08; Weill, ref. 8, pp. 109–15; Paquier, ref. 7, p. 37.

collèges could improve their methods of organizing the teaching of individual science courses and the timing of these courses by observing the private tutoring schools.

Dumas then goes on to analyze the curricula of the *collèges* of the July Monarchy. He insists that in a society where science and technology are so important every student, even if he is not to use science directly in his career as businessman, lawyer, teacher, writer, or government administrator, should know the rudiments of mathematics, physics, chemistry, and biology. These should be parts of the training of every educated man. This scientific instruction, he repeats, should run all through the years of training in the *collèges* and should not be concentrated at the beginning and the end. "As half the students leave the *collèges* before the last year to enter industrial, commercial and other careers . . . they finish their education with far too little science. Moreover, the science taught in the *collèges* should be taught by specialists with laboratory demonstrations and with adequate explanation of its applications." Dumas lays out a program of science courses that would run through the entire *collège* course: arithmetic applied to problems of industry, commerce, and agriculture, free-hand and mechanical drawing, theoretical and applied geometry, algebra, physics, mechanics, chemistry, and biology. Laboratory demonstrations should accompany all the work in physics, chemistry, and biology; some experiments should be performed by the students themselves, and field work should be used for the study of biology. Also factories and public works should be visited. This can be done, Dumas believes, by using for science courses some of the time otherwise devoted to other studies, or by a *bifurcation* system for the last three years of the *collège,* during which one course should be predominantly humanistic with some scientific courses given in each year and the other predominantly scientific with some literary and historical courses offered alongside. Villemain's division, which had just been announced when Dumas was writing, was, he believed, a step in the right direction, but it needed more study and clarification. "When improved scientific teaching will have gone on for a number of years, you will see agriculture, industry, and the arts entering a new life."

Dumas's study then considers the *écoles primaires supérieures* introduced fourteen years earlier by Guizot's Law of 1833. These schools, he says, were intended for those who would never go to a *collège;* their instruction included, among other subjects, applied arithmetic, geometry, drawing, elementary physics, mechanics, geography, and history. They were some help in preparing boys for industry, commerce, and agriculture. Since 1833 far too few of these schools had been opened, and even those started by the state and by the municipalities were too largely attended by boys of the upper middle class; very few future mechanics, skilled factory workers, and farmers attended. Dumas believes that more of these schools should be opened, that the central and local governments should furnish many more scholarships so that poor but able boys could profit by their instruction, and that the course should be expanded from two years to three or four. In this expansion, the courses in different schools should be varied to fit the local situation in farming, manufacturing, and commerce. The teachers in these schools should be paid to open evening and even Sunday classes; adult education should be greatly extended. Dumas's study of 1847 is the most interesting document of the period 1815 to 1848 on the subject of science teaching in the intermediary and secondary schools. The Revolution of 1848 and the confusion and reaction that followed it prevented, for some years, an extension of the reforms suggested.[16]

In brief, the progress of higher technical education, in France as elsewhere, depended to a large extent on the sort of

---

[16] A. Dumas, *Rapport sur l'enseignement scientifique dans les collèges, les écoles intermédiares et les écoles primaires* (Paris, 1847), esp. pp. 15–57 and conclusions, pp. 62–63.

students who could be recruited from the lower schools. If the primary and secondary schools were insufficient in number, poor in quality, and deficient in their teaching of mathematics and the sciences, no amount of improvement in such institutions as the *École polytechnique* could much offset the inadequacies of good primary and secondary instruction. The period of the Constitutional Monarchy (1814–1848) made definite improvements in both elementary and secondary education, especially after the July Revolution of 1830. The improvements in primary education, which consisted mostly in opening more elementary schools and in starting the *écoles primaires supérieures,* were more marked than the advances made in higher secondary education. The *écoles primaires supérieures* made a great contribution to the advances in agriculture, industry, and commerce. All evidence points to the fact that the improvements in higher secondary instruction were largely confined to the state and communal *collèges.* By the 1840's their teachers were better trained than in the private and church schools, and their courses were more diversified. The instruction in the church schools was by comparison mediocre, even in the field of Latin on which the ecclesiastical schools laid great emphasis.[17]

If one narrows his attention to the scientific courses in the state and communal *collèges,* he will find that the mathematics courses showed the emphasis laid on mathematics by the *écoles centrales* of the Empire. The textbooks in mathematics, physics, and mechanics were good, and excellent materials for laboratory demonstrations were often available.[18] In the preparation of students for advanced technical schools, the chief improvements lay in the *bifurcation* system which began in 1829, but which even by 1848 had not been properly organized.

[17] For *École normale* and the training of teachers cf. Weill, ref. 8, Chap. 4; also Dejob, ref. 14, p. 487.

[18] Cf. G. Weill, "L'Enseignement secondaire sous Louis Philippe jugé par un Allemand," *Revue universitaire,* 1928.

If the methods of instruction and the curricula in the *collèges* were definitely improving, the total number of pupils in all types of secondary schools was still, according to Villemain's report of 1843, less than the number receiving secondary-school training in the last decades of the *Ancien Régime*. The ratio in 1789, according to Villemain, was one pupil to every 382 inhabitants; in 1842 it was one pupil to every 493. No wonder that Villemain complained that for a country with a population like that of France there were still too few *collèges* to supply the needs of the nation.

2. *The Trade Schools and Trade Courses*

The improvements in state primary and secondary education in the years 1815 to 1848 did not seem to many businessmen and educational reformers to meet the practical educational needs of a growing industrial society. New techniques in manufacturing, mining, and transportation created shortages of engineers, of factory foremen, and of skilled workers. Impatient with what was being done and hopeful of spreading instruction to thousands of future workers, reformers concentrated their efforts on programs of improving and extending trade schools and trade courses. Writers like Dupin delighted in describing the Mechanics Institutes of Britain and the remarkable work they were doing in adult education for workingmen. Such institutions, he and others pointed out, have fine reading rooms and lectures, and are supplied with experimental apparatus and models of machines. Courses of lectures and demonstrations are given usually in the evenings. Workers so educated are more skilled, and through them industry is improved. Such workers also become better and more law-abiding citizens and are less liable to be led astray by political demagogues. The lesson is drawn that trained workers will improve French industry and enable it to compete successfully with British industry.

French writers, filled with enthusiasm for the application of science to industry, grew lyrical when they contemplated more and better trade schools.[19] After 1815, the faith in political

[19] *Journal des connaissances usuelles,* Oct. 1825, pp. 43–45, 91–94; Oct. 1828, pp. 38–39; Nov. 1828, p. 90; *Le Globe,* 4 Oct. 1824, 31 May 1825, 13 Dec. 1825. Cf. also C. Dupin's extended introduction to his course on applied mechanics in *Les Normands annales,* 1824, pp. 193–216, 225–52; and in the same periodical, 1820, pp. 322–23. A friendly rivalry grew up between England and France. The French praised what the English were doing in their trade schools, especially in the Mechanics Institutes, and declared that in all these matters the French are very backward. In turn, English writers insisted that in such affairs the French were superior. Cf. Birbeck's introduction to the translation of C. Dupin, *Mathematics Practically Applied to the Useful and Fine Arts* (2 vols., London, 1827), Vol. 1, pp. i–iv. Chaptal and Dupin were the ardent French advocates of trade schools; cf. articles on them in F. Buisson, ref. 2, and J. Pigeire, *La vie et l'œuvre de Chaptal* (Paris, 1931). Periodicals of the time, both in England and France, endlessly repeat the advantages of trade schools; for France, cf. *Revue britannique,* April 1826, p. 258; April 1828, p. 182; *Journal des connaissances usuelles,* 1829, 128–32, 174–81; *Moniteur,* Dec. 1839, pp. 18–20; A. Corbon, *De l'enseignement professionel* (Paris, 1859), pp. 122, 128–32; *Moniteur,* 28 June 1824; *Le Globe,* 1 Jan. 1828; J. A. Borgnis, *Traité complet de mécanique appliquée aux arts* (8 vols., Paris, 1818–1820), Vol. 1, Preface; *Journal réformateur,* 3 May 1835; *Journal des débats,* 3 May 1836; *Le national,* 26 March 1837; G. Lamé and E. Clapeyron, *Plan d'écoles générales et spéciales pour l'agriculture, l'industrie manufacturière, le commerce, et l'administration,* Paris, 1833, pp. 4, 14, 35–43 51–80; M. Chevalier, "De la nécessité de fonder l'enseignement professionnel," *Journal des économistes,* 1846; A. Blanqui, "Du désaccord de l'enseignement public avec les besoins publics," *Acad. des sciences morales et politiques, Séances et travaux,* 1846; A. Guettier, *Étude sur l'instruction industrielle,* Paris, 1961; P. Pompée, *Études sur l'éducation professionnelle en France* (Paris, 1863), p. 18; E. Bertrand, *Étude sur l'enseignement professionnel* (Brussels, 1864), pp. 10–11; G. Weill, "Les théories Saint-Simoniennes sur l'éducation," *Revue internationale de l'enseignement,* 1896, and J. B. Paquier, ref. 7, p. 28. Enough sample references are here given to show how much agitation for extending and improving trade schools and trade courses appeared after 1815. Curiously enough, a study of the regular educational periodicals of the period 1815 to 1848 showed very little space devoted to matters of technical education. The agitation for more trade schools and courses came from factory owners, economists, scientists, and statesmen, not from men connected with the public or church schools of France. For general notions of faults of technical education in France, and of what should be done about it, cf. Part II of *Commission on Technical Education* (British Documents, London, 1863). The Mechanics Institute movement in England greatly interested French observers, but no

democracy was at a low ebb; it did not begin to rise till after 1825 and did not again sweep France till in the 1840's. But the faith in regenerating society through increasing industrial production, which inevitably involved extending technical education, seems from the periodical literature of the period to have received no setback from the events of 1789 to 1815. The desire for better roads and bridges, for enlarged agricultural production, for increasing industrial output, indeed for everything that had social utility mounted steadily in the whole period after 1750. The French Revolution and the Age of Napoleon caused no setback in all this. Here indeed was a cause that "knew nothing but victories."

The ever-increasing demand for trade schools and trade courses was due not only to the growing needs of industry for various types of skilled workers, factory foremen, and engineers, but it was also due to the breakdown of the old apprentice system. Before 1789 the guild system had given industrial training to thousands of boys, but with the abolition of the guilds in 1791 the old system of apprentice training was also deeply changed. Many shop owners and especially small manufacturers still continued to take youths as apprentices on the basis of private arrangements made with the apprentice's family. But as there were now few legal protections for such apprentices, as even the existing government regulations were

---

such institutes seem to have been founded in France. On the Mechanics Institutes in England and the United States, cf. C. D. Burns, *A Short History of Birbeck College* (London, 1924); C. A. Bennett, *History of Manual and Industrial Education to 1870* (Peoria, Ill., 1926), Chap. 9; M. Turner, *History of Science Teaching in England* (London, 1927), pp. 62–64; A. Abbott, *Education for Industry and Commerce in England* (Oxford, 1933), pp. 11–16; J. W. Hudson, *History of Adult Education* (London, 1851); M. E. Sadler, *Continuation Schools in England and Elsewhere* (Manchester, 1907), p. 576; A. E. Dobbs, *Education and Social Movements, 1700–1850* (London, 1919), pp. 173–77; A. Audiganne, "L'Enseignement industriel, etc.," in *Revue des deux mondes,* 1851, pp. 864–67. Cf. H. M. Pollard, *Pioneers of Popular Education, 1760–1850* (Cambridge, Mass., 1957) and M. Tylecote, *Mechanics Institutes of Lancashire and Yorkshire before 1851* (Manchester, 1957).

often not enforced, many families were reluctant to enter into agreements that would cover the whole period of a boy's industrial training. Also, it was complained, employers frequently failed to teach their apprentices a trade, using them instead as errand boys and as domestic servants. In Paris and in some of the provincial cities, philanthropic societies like the *Société pour le placement des jeunes apprentis,* founded in 1822 by Barante, Gérando, Guizot, and Montalembert, interested themselves in the working and living conditions of apprentices. They sought to see that the apprentices were well treated, were taught the trade they were supposed to learn, were offered class instruction at least in the evenings and on Sundays, and were given legal protection when needed. Some large manufactures set up classes for apprentices in which boys were taught some of the principles of a trade and in addition were given lessons in French composition, arithmetic, and drawing. In practice those who went into skilled trades and manufactures went as ordinary workers for whose extended training the employer accepted no responsibility.

Thus, in this field of apprenticeship the situation was much worse after 1815 than it had been before 1789. Trade schools and trade courses were often proposed either as substitutes for apprenticeship or as valuable adjuncts to it. Some argued that boys needed both and that at the age of twelve, the usual age for entering an apprenticeship, a boy was too young to leave his family. It would be better to send him to a trade school for several years, then apprentice him when he is more mature and, in his knowledge of mathematics and mechanics, better grounded in theory. The critics who had the clearest insight into the situation realized that with the extension of large-scale production and the whole factory system, the old apprenticeship system, even had it been working effectively, was quite inadequate. It might still be useful in trades that did not lend themselves to mass production. But now with the standardization of factories the need was less to train operatives than to educate foremen and managers. The skills needed by foremen and managers were of a kind different from those needed in the handicraft trades. The factory foreman needed mental alertness and an ability to adjust hand movements to varying phases in the working and adjusting of machines. Moreover, he had no time or opportunity to train his assistants from the bottom up as had the old guildmasters working with a few apprentices. Both the factory foreman and the factory manager needed just such theoretical preparation as could be furnished by good trade schools.[20]

The old *écoles des arts et métiers,* established before 1815, were extended and greatly improved under the Constitutional Monarchy. Two older schools were at Chalon-sur-Saône and at Angers; a third school was set up at Aix in 1843. From 1815 to 1826 complaint was made that the two older schools were ill-equipped, that pupils were admitted without proper preparation, and that the discipline was bad. Each of the two older schools usually had about three hundred students. In 1826, the age of candidates was raised from eight to twelve years to thirteen to fifteen years; in 1832 the age was again raised, this time to fifteen to seventeen years. In both years, 1826 and 1832, the annually given entrance examinations in

[20] J. D. M. Cochin, *De l'extinction de la mendicité* (Paris, 1829), pp. 37–38; M. L. Boullangé, *De l'éducation professionnelle des enfants pauvres* (Paris, 1842), p. 15; C. Fichet, *Mémoire sur l'apprentissage et sur l'éducation industrielle* (Paris, 1847), pp. 26–33; A. Corbon, ref. 19 (1859), pp. 9–38, 128–32; P. Pompée, ref. 19, p. 20. The studies of Cochin, Boullangé, Fichet, Corbon, and Pompée, and also that of A. Guettier, ref. 19, furnish much contemporary material for the whole period 1815 to 1870. Cf. also *Enquête,* ref. 7, Vol. 1, pp. 410–11, 413, 416–17; J. H. Cagninacci, *L'instruction professionnelle de l'ouvrier* (Paris, 1910), pp. 8–9; article "Vocational education" in *Encyclopedia of Social Sciences* (8 vols., New York, 1937), Vol. 15, p. 273; and A. Abbott, *Education for Industry and Commerce in England* (Oxford, 1933), pp. 5–9. Cf. also M. Deslandres and A. Michelin, *Il y a cent ans, état physique et moral des ouvriers au temps du Liberalisme, témoignage de Villermé* (Paris, 1938); A. M. Gossez, "L'ouvrier lillois du textile et sa situation sociale autour de 1848," *Revue de 1848,* 1938; and R. E. Cameron, *France and the Economic Development of Europe, 1800–1914* (Princeton, 1960).

reading, writing, and arithmetic were made more severe. In addition to entrance examinations, pupils had to have had at least a year's training in some trade. Also parents had to agree after 1826 not to remove pupils from the school except by special permission. Tuition was five hundred francs a year with two hundred francs in addition for clothing. Competition for entrance was keen, and only about one fifth of the applicants were admitted. Over half of the pupils got some government support in the way of scholarships. Partial as well as full scholarships were distributed over the *départements* of France according to population.

The theoretical training in the schools included arithmetic, algebra, geometry, trigonometry, calculus, Monge's descriptive geometry with application to stone and woodwork of all sorts, machine construction and industrial mechanics, industrial chemistry, and freehand and mechanical drawing. The work was hard; after 1826 five and a half hours a day were spent on theoretical subjects and drawing, and five to seven hours on shopwork in such activities as joinery, patternmaking, foundrywork, and machine construction. Instruction was also given in French grammar and literature, in ethics, and geography. After 1815 all military drill was dropped. During the Restoration, the government hounded the directors of the schools on the subject of keeping the students uncorrupted by Liberal political and religious ideas. And it took the intervention of both the Duc de La Rochefoucauld-Liancourt and Dupin to prevent the removal of the Chalon school to Toulouse.

The training given on the practical side emphasized the following: drawing to scale, geometrical and projection drawing, elaborate machine drawing, including the making of sections and drawing of separate details, all with full mathematical calculations. The workrooms were equipped with machines and models of all sorts. These were taken apart or cut along horizontal or vertical planes so that all their details could be well understood. As in the case of nearly all technical training, some critics complained that in all stages of trade-school training too much emphasis was laid on theory and not enough attention was given to practical exercise. On the other hand, other critics insisted that too much time and energy were often wasted on practical exercises; it would be better to ground the pupil thoroughly in theory, and the practice could then later be learned, and learned better, in connection with a regular job. On the whole, the French practice, in comparison with trade schools in other states, was to lay greater stress on theory and to reduce practical training to a minimum. Complaints were also often voiced that too few workers had received technical training, that few working-class families could afford to send their children to such trade schools, that it was very difficult to obtain and to keep adequately trained teachers, and that there was too much uniformity in the types of courses given; for example, courses given in or near a spinning and weaving center were frequently exactly like those given in a center whose chief manufacture was hardware. Both might need mathematics, physics, and chemistry courses, but in addition more should be done with the special problems involved in the local industry.

The course was four and later three years, and the more able students were usually allowed to stay an extra year. The earlier purpose of the *écoles des arts et métiers* was to train skilled workers, but the changes made in 1826 and 1832 were intended, in part, to shift the emphasis toward the training of draftsmen, foremen, and factory superintendents. By 1840, while many of the graduates went into skilled trades, such as carpentry and the making of machine tools, the majority were in supervisory positions in factories, in road and bridge construction, in the navy and merchant marine, and in railroad construction. Some graduates went on to the *École centrale des arts et manufactures,* established in 1829, and to the *École polytechnique.* In spite of all criticisms, the French *écoles des arts et métiers* were by 1840 considered the best intermediate trade schools in Europe and were much visited and studied by men from most of the European states, including Russia.[21]

As the enrollments in the state *écoles des arts et métiers* were limited, there appeared all over France a great variety of local trade schools and courses. Some were supported privately either from endowments or from the fees of their pupils; others found financial help from city and departmental governments, from local chambers of commerce, and even from local manufacturers, as, for example, the Schneider Company at Creuzot. All over France these schools were founded by the dozen. Many followed the pattern of the *écoles de dessin* of the eighteenth century. Most of them gave courses for boys after school hours and for adults in the evening. Mathematics, mechanics, and chemistry, with exercises in freehand and mechanical drawing and the making of machine plans, were their stock in trade. By the end of the July Monarchy there were nearly fifty of such schools. They ranged from schools

[21] A. de Férussac, ed., *Bulletin des sciences technologiques,* 1826, p. 59; 1827, pp. 217–24; C. Dupin, *Les forces productives et commerciales de la France* (2 vols., Paris, 1829), Vol. 1, p. 60. Dupin is very critical of the *écoles des arts et métiers,* chiefly on three scores: that the pupils' attention is too diffused over a number of mechanical processes, and that he is given thorough training in none; that the schools, not being in important manufacturing centers, give the students little opportunity to observe manufacturing plants in operation, and that the instruction is always too theoretical. Cf. also A. Audiganne, "L'Enseignement industriel en France," *Revue des deux mondes,* 1851, pp. 875–76; *Bulletin des lois,* 7ᵉ série, p. 1781; 8ᵉ série, p. 4672; 9ᵉ série, pp. 6511, 9460, 10,750; *Enquête,* ref. 7, Vol. 1, references in index, pp. 411–12, and Vol. 2, pp. 583–605; H. Barnard, *Institutions and Statistics of Scientific Instruction* (New York, 1872), pp. 427, 451–62; A. Guettier, *Histoire des écoles des arts et métiers* (2nd ed., Paris, 1880); F. Euvrard, *Histoire de l'école des arts et métiers* (Châlons-sur-Marne, 1895), pp. 44–82; F. Dreyfus, ref. 2, pp. 330–31, 405–08; W. E. Wickenden, *A Comparative Study of Engineering Education in the United States and Europe* (Lancaster, Pa., 1929), pp. 15–16; A. L. Dunham, "How the First French Railroads Were Planned," *Journal of Economic History,* 1941, and R. Crozet, "Contribution à l'histoire de la voie ferrée de Paris à Toulouse, etc.," *Revue d'histoire moderne,* 1939.

that offered only a few courses to full-fledged institutions that offered two- to six-year courses.[22]

A number of these private and municipal schools achieved outstanding success. During the July Monarchy, the city government of Mulhouse established an excellent trade school, the nucleus of which was an earlier *école de dessin*. It admitted qualified boys at eight years of age and carried those who cared to continue through a series of general and specialized courses till they were eighteen. In practice, few stayed till they reached that age. The first six years were devoted to the type of general instruction given in other schools, except that English and German were taught instead of Greek and Latin. At the end of this six-year period, those who elected to do so stopped their general education and entered courses in applied

[22] *Journal de l'instruction publique* Vol. 2, p. 82; Vol. 3, pp. 110, 113; Vol. 4, p. 56; *Journal d'éducation*, 1817, p. 172; 1824, p. 126; *Bulletin de la société d'encouragement pour l'industrie nationale*, Vol. 19, p. 20; Vol. 24, pp. 375–80; *Annales de l'industrie nationale* Vol. 1, pp. 61, 282–83; Vol. 2, pp. 325, 328; *Le Globe*, 4 Nov. 1824, 10 Oct. 1826; Dupin, *op. cit.* Vol. 1, p. 71; Vol. 2, pp. 134, 279–81; L. S. Le Normand and J. de Moléon, eds., *Annales de l'industrie nationale et étrangère*, 1824, pp. 181–91; 1825, pp. 101–02, 161–68, 175–211, 313–16; 1826, pp. 153–61, 275–314; Buisson, ref. 2, article "Dessin," esp. Vol. 1, pp. 692–93; Audiganne, *op. cit.;* Lamé and Clapeyron, ref. 19, pp. 81–93, 108–29; de Férussac, ed., ref. 21, 1824, p. 112; 1826, p. 61; 1829, p. 98, 1830, pp. 305–307; Paquier, ref. 7, pp. 28–31; S. Charléty, *La Restauration* (Paris, 1921), p. 304, and by the same author, ref. 14, pp. 220–21; Dejob, ref. 14, *Revue internationale de l'enseignement*, 1889, pp. 36–37; *Enquête*, ref. 7, Vol. 1, references in index, pp. 119–421; Barnard, ref. 21, pp. 491, 494, 508; Corbon, ref. 19, pp. 167–68; *Le Centenaire de la société industrielle de Mulhouse*, Vol. 1, pp. 109, 118–234; *Bulletin de la société industrielle de Mulhouse*, Vol. 4, pp. 208–11; Vol. 5, pp. 330–33; Vol. 6, pp. 480–82; Vol. 7, p. 336; Vol. 8, pp. 383–84; Vol. 9, p. 332; Vol. 10, p. 467; Vol. 11, pp. 467–69; Vol. 12, p. 347; Vol. 13, p. 227; Vol. 20, p. 65; E. Duvernoy, "L'enseignement industriel et commercial à Nancy," *Pays Lorrain*, 1905, pp. 431–35; Bache, ref. 7, p. 572; J. Schoenhof, *Industrial Education in France* (Washington, 1882), p. 72; V. Deniée, *De l'enseignement professionnel, 1762–1852* (Paris, 1852), pp. 10–31; in H. Barnard, *op. cit.*, pp. 433–38 there is a list, with comments, on all the trade schools in every *département* of France.

mathematics, physics, and chemistry. In connection with these courses, the pupils had a minimum of two hours of shopwork a day. The school was only for the sons of men in comfortable circumstances, for the tuition was high, increasing from ninety francs for the first year to four hundred for the last. Most of the pupils were sons of factory owners or superintendents, or of professional men, or of government employees. It was always easy to find good positions for those who finished the course and even for some who had completed only part of the full program. The Mulhouse school was praised and copied all over France. Being near the borders of Germany and Switzerland, this school showed the influence of the ideas of Pestalozzi, of the trade school of Fellenberg, and of trade schools in Württemberg and Baden. Its work was, however, better organized and more thorough than that of any Swiss or German trade schools.[23]

The *Frères des écoles chrétiennes* had given some trade courses, along with other subjects, ever since the order was founded in 1709. During the Revolution these schools had been closed, but they were reopened in 1808. More trade courses were now offered, and after 1830 special courses were given, mostly in the evening, for older boys and men. The subjects included some mathematics, theoretical mechanics, and freehand and mechanical drawing, but the main emphasis was laid on practice in trades as carpentry, upholstery, stone-cutting, and locksmith's work. By 1863, the *Frères* had, in Paris alone, twenty thousand pupils between the ages of six

[23] On the Mulhouse school see *Enquête*, ref. 7, Vol. 2, references in index, p. 432; for contemporary accounts of Pestalozzi and Fellenberg, cf. *Revue britannique*, April 1828; *Edinburgh Review*, Dec. 1818; *Le Globe*, 22 Dec. 1824, 4 Jan. 1825, 25 Jan. 1825, and 22 March 1827; J. Griscom, *A Year in Europe*, 2nd ed. (New York, 1924), pp. 287–93. That all France stirred with new ideas about the value of trade schools, even in remote areas, is evidenced by the experiments of J. F. Oberlin in Alsace, *Journal de l'éducation*, 1816, pp. 245–50; C. Leenhardt, *Vie de J. F. Oberlin* (Toulouse, 1914); Buisson, ref. 2, article "Oberlin."

and fourteen and over four thousand adult pupils. They hired skilled workers to do part of the teaching. In addition they maintained employment offices to place their graduates and visited them after they were employed. Some of the more competent pupils entered one of the state *écoles des arts et métiers,* the *Collège Chaptal,* or the *École Turgot.*[24]

In 1827, a secular priest opened the *Œuvre de Saint-Nicolas,* a trade school for boys in Paris. By 1833 the school had one hundred pupils, and a good school building with six shops where the pupils received practical instruction in such fields as printing, shoemaking, and tailoring. The workshops were partly supported by industrialists who derived some income from the products made by the boys. By 1863 the number of shops had risen to twelve. The number of pupils increased to seven hundred seventy-seven by 1844, and to eleven hundred and thirty by 1858. Tuition was low, and many boys were admitted on scholarships. The pupils entered the school at eight years of age and usually left at the age of fourteen or sixteen. Most of the boys came from the families of skilled workmen or of small shopkeepers. In connection with the school there was a *Société de Saint-Joseph,* founded by the church as early as 1822, five years before the opening of the *Œuvre de Saint-Nicolas.* By 1830 it had a membership of about seven thousand mechanics of various sorts, and about twelve hundred office and store clerks. The *Société* gave evening lecture courses on trade subjects.[25]

Typical of a more advanced type of trade school that was founded by municipal governments all over France was the *Collège Chaptal,* established by the city government of Paris in 1844. Its purpose was to train young men who expected to

---

[24] *Enquête,* ref. 7, Vol. 1, references in index for extended details of contents of courses and methods of instruction.

[25] Corbon, ref. 19, pp. 166–67; and *Enquête,* Vol. 1, references in index p. 437.

enter industry, agriculture, commerce, and the arts. It offered a general six-year course for qualified pupils between the ages of fourteen and twenty. Many of its pupils received their earlier training in some sort of industrial school and then, after spending some time at the *Collège Chaptal,* went to more advanced schools, as the *École centrale des arts et manufactures,* the *École polytechnique,* or the *École des beaux arts.* The pupils in the *Collège Chaptal* came mostly from middle-class families who wanted their sons trained for executive positions in industry and commerce. The school seems to have been well run and successful from its beginning, and its curriculum and teaching methods were copied in other schools in France and abroad. In Paris, the following schools were all modeled on the *Collège Chaptal: Écoles Turgot* (1839), *Colbert* (1868), *Lavoisier* (1872), and *Say* (1873). By 1863 the *Collège Chaptal,* nineteen years after its foundation, had nine hundred and fifty pupils, six hundred of whom were boarded in the school.[26]

Among many elementary and secondary trade schools founded after 1815, the one that attracted most attention both in France and abroad was the *École de la Martinière* at Lyons, founded by a wealthy manufacturer in 1826. Pupils were admitted between the ages of twelve and fourteen and could remain for a two-year course, in a few cases extended to three years. As a rule, the boys were the sons of factory managers, foremen, artisans, and tradesmen. The pupils, in turn, were destined for careers of the same sort. The general courses consisted of arithmetic, algebra, geometry, and trigonometry, all with applied mechanical problems, drawing, accounting, ethics, and French composition and literature. The special courses were in subjects like applied chemistry and weaving and other industrial processes. Instruction was given to about five hundred pupils, besides an evening school for about three hundred

---

[26] *Enquête,* ref. 7, Vol. 1, pp. 1–5, 8–10, 226–28; Bertrand, ref. 19, p. 217; and Buisson, ref. 2, article "Turgot, École."

adults. To enter, the candidate had to pass an examination in reading, writing, and arithmetic. No tuition was charged, and only day pupils were admitted.

The administration was in the hands of a board of trustees, including the mayor of Lyons, the executors of the donor's large estate, and seven others chosen by the municipal council with the approval of the prefect. They regulated expenditures, selected the faculty, and supervised the curriculum. The director of the school made a quarterly report to the directors and to the parents of the students. The teaching was done by a corps of teachers aided, as in the *École polytechnique,* by a group of *répétiteurs* who supervised the study hours and carefully reviewed each day's lessons. The school had a large income, and could afford to hire an excellent faculty. The sessions were eight hours a day, broken by meals, shopwork, and short recreation periods. Of the eight hours of classwork, about two and one-half hours were spent on theoretical subjects: mathematics, physics, and mechanics; two hours in drawing; one and a half hours on chemistry; and the rest of the time on French grammar, composition, and literature, ethics, and the study of manufacturing processes. The evenings were spent in study. In some courses, the pupils were divided into sections on the basis of ability. The term ran from November through March. By 1856 there were six hundred pupils in the day school and about two hundred in the special evening classes for adults. The buildings, workshops, equipment, and teachers were the best available in any secondary trade school in Europe. By 1856, twenty years after the foundation of the *Martinière,* the majority of the skilled workers, shop managers, and foremen in Lyons had passed through this school, besides hundreds of graduates and former students who were active in commerce, manufacturing, and banking, scattered all over the whole of France. The school was also an important center for preparing candidates for the two advanced engineering schools of France, the *École polytechnique* and the *École centrale des arts et manufactures.* By 1888 the school had graduated twenty thousand pupils.[27]

Much was done, in the years of the Constitutional Monarchy, 1815–1848, to spread new ideas about industrial education and about industrial production through periodicals and books, both of an elementary and advanced type. In 1795 the *Journal de l'école polytechnique* had begun to appear. The reconstituted *Académie des sciences* started in 1835 a series: *Notices sur les titres et travaux scientifiques.* The *École centrale des arts et manufactures* soon after its foundation in 1829 published both a *Bulletin* and the *Annales de l'industrie française et étrangère.* Other important periodicals were: *Bulletin de la société d'encouragement pour l'industrie nationale* (1803ff.); L. S. Le Normand and J. de Moléon, eds., *Annales de l'industrie nationale et étrangère* (1820–1827); *Bulletin des sciences technologiques* (1824ff.); *Journal des connaissances utiles* (1831ff.); *Journal des connaissances usuelles et pratiques* (1825ff.); *L'industriel, journal destiné à répandre les connaissances utiles* (1826ff.); *Encyclopédie populaire des sciences utiles* (1827ff.); *Journal des connaissances utiles* (1831ff.); *Annales des ponts et chaussées* (1831ff.); *Bibliothèque industrielle* (1827ff.); *Bulletin de l'enseignement technique* (1827ff.); *Bulletin de la société industrielle de Mulhouse* (1827ff.); *Bulletin des sciences technologiques, encyclopédie populaire des sciences utiles* (1827ff.); translation from an English publication brought out by the *Society for the Propagation of Useful Knowledge; Journal des sciences militaires* (1825ff.); and, finally, *Annales maritimes* (1815ff.).

Most of these journals lasted from five to ten years after the date of their foundation, some more, some less, but their

[27] *Le Globe,* 8 July 1826; *Journal de l'instruction publique,* 1827, pp. 16–18; *Bulletin des lois,* 9ᵉ série, 1 Oct. 1833; A. D. Bache, ref. 7, pp. 318–21. Some of the unique teaching methods used at the *Martinière,* especially those developed by Tabareau, are described in Buisson, ref. 2, article "Martinière"; cf. also *Enquête, ref.* 7, Vol. 1, references in index pp. 430–31.

places were usually taken by new journals. In addition to journals devoted specifically to problems of technological education and technological improvements, many of the general periodicals, as for example *le Globe* and the *Revue britannique,* contained articles on these matters. It would be more difficult to list the books on technology that appeared in large numbers after the return of peace in 1815. The leading publisher of such works was Bachelier of Paris; a list of his publications, printed at the close of the *Annuaire de l'école polytechnique pour l'an 1837,* shows a surprising range of titles.

The work of spreading technical information was also furthered by popular lecture courses, usually given in the evenings. Many of these, as we have seen, were run in connection with regular trade schools, but in addition numerous courses were given that had no connection with any industrial school. Dupin was very active in starting these courses, beginning in 1819, and others took them up. After 1830 some of these courses were given by graduates of the *École polytechnique* who were members of the *Association polytechnique* and, after 1848, of the *Association philotechnique.* Other courses were given in the factories under the direction of the factory owners. The lecturers were often foremen or engineers from the factory itself or from the neighborhood. Sometimes a secondary-school teacher would do the teaching. This lecturing was frequently done without pay; in other cases a factory owner or the town government paid the teachers. The municipal authorities would usually, at least, furnish rooms for such classes. These courses of lectures were ordinarily very poorly supplied with illustrative materials, and they had no laboratories or workshops, such as were attached to the *écoles des arts et métiers* and special schools of the type of the *Martinière* of Lyons. On the other hand, they were given to adults who already had factory experience and were less in need of the shop exercises on which emphasis was laid in the trade schools. These lectures were frequently criticized for being too theoretical. They existed all over France but were especially common in Paris and other large manufacturing and commercial centers.

Probably the best of this type of special lecture courses were those given by the *Conservatoire des arts et métiers.* Founded during the Revolution, it had grown rapidly. Its collections of models and machines set up in the former monastic house of *Saint-Martin-des-Champs,* was, even before the fall of the *Empire,* by far the best in Europe. The exhibitions were well displayed; guides were provided to explain them, and crowds of visitors frequented the galleries. In 1818 the *Conservatoire* published the first catalogue of its collections, with full and excellent descriptions of all that was exhibited. (The *Annales du Conservatoire* did not begin till 1852.) In addition to its exhibitions, it had by 1815 built up a splendid technical library of over fifteen thousand volumes and about five thousand drawings and had opened a series of lecture halls. Two small classes, one for training weavers and one for instruction in drawing, had been opened before 1815.

An advisory committee, the *Conseil de perfectionnement,* like the one for the *École polytechnique* was set up in 1817. This was composed of a very distinguished group of scholars and industrialists, including Berthollet, Chaptal, Gay-Lussac, Arago, Molard, Ternaux, and Delessert. It met once every three months to supervise the *Conseil d'administration,* the governing body, which met twice a month. After 1840 the *Conseil de perfectionnement* was composed entirely of teachers in the *Conservatoire.* The first *Conseil de perfectionnement* was presided over by the Duc de La Rochefoucauld-Liancourt. Under his leadership and with the advice of a young scientist, Charles Dupin, who had made an extensive study of English industry and education, a series of three evening courses in applied science were opened in 1819. These courses were given on two evenings a week between 7:45 and 10 o'clock from the first of November to the first of May. Dupin gave a course in applied mechanics, Clément-Desormes one in industrial chemistry, and J. B. Say one in business economics. The success was immediate; by 1824 the three courses were attended by two thousand students. The auditors at the evening lectures and demonstrations were chiefly skilled workers, factory foremen, and clerks in all kinds of business establishments. In 1829 a course in experimental physics was inaugurated. By 1839, a decade later, the number of courses offered had risen to ten. These included courses in geometry applied to the arts, descriptive geometry, industrial mechanics, applied physics, two courses in applied chemistry, two in agriculture, industrial economics, and business law.

It was in the *Conservatoire* in 1853 that General Morin installed the first teaching laboratory of engineering in the world. Only the ablest men were employed as lecturers, most of them members of the *Institut de France*. The *Conservatoire* came to be called the *"Sorbonne de l'industrie"* by one writer, the *"Collège de France de l'agriculture, du commerce, et de l'industrie"* by another.[29]

Somewhat similar to the *Conservatoire des arts et métiers* was the *Muséum d'histoire naturelle* which, during the Revolutionary era, had been reorganized out of the old *Jardin du roi*. Besides its large library of nearly two hundred thousand volumes (as fine a scientific library as there was in Europe) and its world-famous collections of living and preserved plants and animals, which attracted crowds of visitors, it offered popular lecture courses to several hundred students in geology, mineralogy, chemistry, botany, agriculture, horticulture, zool-

[28] *Enquête,* ref. 7, Vol. 1, pp. 29–34 and references in index 417–19.

[29] There is an extensive literature on the *Conservatoire des arts et métiers.* Cf. reference 59 in notes to Chap. 3, also esp. *Notice historique sur l'ancien prieuré de Saint-Martin-des-Champs et sur le Conservatoire des arts et métiers* (Paris, 1882), pp. 41–63; *Le Globe,* 13 Nov. 1824; H. Barnard, ref. 21, pp. 407, 444–49; A. Audiganne, ref. 21, p. 874; "A. Liesse, J. B. Say au Conservatoire etc.," *Journal des économistes,* 1901, pp. 161, 169–73; and E. Levasseur, "L'Enseignement de l'économie politique au Conservatoire, etc.," *Revue internationale de l'enseignement,* 1901, pp. 211–15.

ogy, the anatomy of men and animals, anthropology, and paleontology. Many of these courses were given by members of the *Institut de France,* by scholars of the caliber of Cuvier and Geoffroy Saint-Hilaire. Its series of published monographs and studies and its *Annales* carried its influence all over France and Europe.[30]

Parallel with the various types of trade schools and trade courses were the *écoles de commerce.* The upheaval of the Revolution had destroyed the few schools of this type that had appeared in the eighteenth century. A number of proposals for opening better organized schools of commerce had attracted the attention of some of the leading businessmen and public officials in France in the years 1800 to 1815, but no new school was founded till 1820. In that year, a group of Parisian capitalists, including Ternaux, Laffitte, and Casimir-Périer, with the help of government officials like Chaptal, opened the *École supérieure de commerce de Paris.* The first important director was the well-known economist Adolphe Blanqui. At the time it was opened it had sixty students, but this number soon rose to over two hundred. Among these were quite a few foreigners, English, Belgian, Swiss, Italian, Spanish, and South American. Its first decade saw the school struggling with financial difficulties, and it was forced to move several times. In 1839, the government reorganized the school, gave it aid, and established a number of scholarships. Snobbism and the habit of educating boys of the upper classes in law and the humanities deprived the school of many youths who might well have been trained there. Not till after 1840 did it begin to be considered good form for a well-to-do bourgeois family to send its sons to the *École de commerce.* Blanqui was not only a very successful organizer of the school, but through his writings on economics (such as his life of J. B. Say of 1840, his *Précis d'économie politique* of 1841, and his

[30] Cf. J. P. F. Deleuze, *Histoire et description du Muséum royal d'histoire naturelle* (2 vols., Paris, 1823), and P. Cap, *Le Muséum d'histoire naturelle* (Paris, 1854).

Huskisson et la réforme économique of 1842), his founding of the famous *Journal des économistes,* his position as a member of the *Chambre de Députés,* and his membership in the *Académie des sciences morales et politiques* helped advertise the school not only in France but all over Europe and Latin America.

The first courses taken by the students, who entered at the age of fifteen or sixteen, were in commercial correspondence, commercial arithmetic and accounting, and commercial geography. They then went on to study advanced accounting, commercial law, economic theory, statistics, chemistry, comparative coinages, weights and measures, commercial usages of foreign states, and foreign languages: English, German, and Spanish. The practical exercises included all sorts of transactions among groups of students organized as imaginary commercial corporations. In the summer, supervised visits were made to ports, banks, and factories. The full course lasted three years. A large museum connected with the school contained extensive collections of raw materials and manufactured articles commonly handled in commerce. A *conseil de perfectionnement,* in imitation of similar bodies in the *École polytechnique* and the *Conservatoire des arts et métiers,* was set up in 1824. It included a group of outstanding business leaders and scholars, among them Chaptal, Laffitte, Ternaux, Casimir-Périer, J. B. Say, and Dupin. The conditions of admission to the school were so high and the course of study so difficult that, though there were by 1825 a hundred and seventy students, there were only four graduated in 1825, eight in 1826, thirteen in 1827, and eighteen in 1828. The number of graduates rose rapidly thereafter, and, by the 1840's the school had its alumni in many of the banks of France, besides others who had entered manufacturing, commerce, and government service.[31]

[31] Blanqui represented the ideas of a substantial group of forward-looking businessmen and economists when he declared, "Commerce has become a science; even the less important branches of it have attained an un-

Estimating the exact influence of all these varied types of trade schools and courses on the growing industrialization of France after 1815 is impossible, but certainly they helped this growth, not only by improving the skills of many factory workers but also by supplying factory managers, engineers, and trained clerks for all sorts of government or private-industry projects. In spite of all the efforts of these most diversified types of training, there remained in the periodical literature of the July Monarchy continual complaints that too few men were being trained for industry and that the work of these schools and courses needed greatly to be extended.

3. Agricultural and Mining Schools

The idea of agricultural education had had its start in France during the eighteenth century. In 1753 the *Académie des sciences* had first admitted observations and studies on agriculture to its publications. In 1762 de Goyon, a well-known writer on agriculture, proposed the establishment of a number

precedented development. The businessman worthy of the name ought to know the usages and the products of various regions and countries. He should speak foreign languages. There is, moreover, an art of buying and selling which has certain analogues with the art of warfare. It is the ensemble of these fields of knowledge which constitutes the science of commerce." C. Coquelin and A. Guillaumin, *Dictionnaire d'économie politique,* 4th ed. (2 vols., Paris, 1873), Vol. 1, pp. 641–42. On the *École de commerce,* cf. *Bulletin de la société d'encouragement pour l'industrie nationale,* 1820, pp. 323–24; 1828, pp. 50–51; *Journal de l'instruction publique,* 1827, pp. 7–12; Férussac, ref. 21, (1826), 205–07; *Le Globe,* 18 July 1826, 27 July 1827; A. Renouard, *Histoire de l'école supérieure de commerce,* 3rd ed. (Paris, 1920); H. Barnard, ref. 21, pp. 533–38; E. Léautey, *L'Enseignement commerciale et les écoles de commerce* (Paris, 1895), pp. 3–12; *Enseignement technique en France* (5 vols., Paris, 1900), Vol. 1, pp. 143ff.; P. Lacroix, *Notice sur l'école supérieure de commerce de Paris* (Paris, 1898). The original name of the school was *L'École spéciale de commerce et d'industrie;* this was closed in 1822 and later the same year reopened as *L'École spéciale de commerce.* In 1852 the name was again changed to *L'École supérieure de commerce de Paris;* cf. also E. Jourdan and G. Dumont, *Les écoles de commerce en France et à l'Allemagne* (Paris, 1899), and E. Gottmann, *Die Wirtschaftsoberschule und ihre Entwicklung* (Eisfeld, 1932).

of agricultural schools. In 1775 the Abbé Rosier submitted to Turgot a plan for an agricultural school to be set up in the park of the Château de Chambord, a plan that was brought to the Constituent Assembly in 1789. In the four decades between 1760 and 1800, France had been flooded with writings on education, many of which contained suggestions for the setting up of agricultural schools. The first such school actually established was founded in 1767 for twenty-four foundlings. It was a small affair and not very well managed; it closed down in 1780. Several other small agricultural schools did not even last as long as that. In 1786 Louis XVI founded an experimental farm at Rambouillet which took a few pupils to train. Then came the Revolution, with a series of governments, each of which made extended plans on paper for reorganizing and extending educational opportunities. Plans for founding agricultural schools were included in many of these projects.[32]

But in spite of over a half century of agitation and discussion, the first good agricultural school in France was not opened until 1822. In that year, Mathieu de Dombasle established an agricultural school in connection with his experimental farm at Roville. A number of large landholders in Lorraine contributed funds, and the project had the enthusiastic backing of the enlightened prefect of La Meurthe, Villeneuve-Bargemont. This was followed in 1826 by a school at Grignon set up by Auguste Bella. Both schools show the influence of a school lately opened by Fellenberg in Switzerland.

At Roville, the school opened with five students, but the number soon rose to twenty. About half of the pupils re-

[32] The best brief accounts of agricultural education in the nineteenth century in all the European states is in Buisson, ref. 2, article "Agriculture (Enseignement de l')"; cf. also article on "Agricultural education" in *Encyclopedia of the Social Sciences,* and *Enquête,* ref. 7, Vol. 1, references in index, p. 409. Also H. Barnard, "National Education in Europe," *American Journal of Education,* 1870, pp. 544–76; the last has a multitude of details about agricultural education in France, its history and organization.

ceived government scholarships. The teaching was done by Mathieu de Dombasle, a wealthy and scientific-minded landed proprietor, and a few helpers. The courses offered included general biology, mineralogy, the elements of veterinary medicine, agricultural accounting, drawing, and land measurement. Beginning in 1831 this school, which had struggled along against great financial odds, got some government subsidies. About this time, a small factory for the manufacture of agricultural implements was added. The work of this model farm and school at Roville was widely advertised through its periodical, the *Annales de Roville*. The school lasted till 1842 when it was closed for lack of funds. It had been in existence long enough to stimulate an interest in improving agriculture and in extending agricultural education. By this time (1842) other agricultural schools were under way.[33]

The agricultural school at Grignon, founded in 1827, was a more substantial affair than the one at Roville. The initiative had been taken by a society for improving agriculture in the district about Paris, and this society got from the government a forty-year lease on an excellent and productive property of eleven hundred and seventy acres about twenty-five miles from Paris. This included an area of land twice the size and much more productive than the acreage connected with the school at Roville. The Grignon school, which only got under way in 1832, was run by the private society that had founded it until 1848, when the French government took it over. By that time the school had come to be considered the equal, if not the superior, of any agricultural school in Europe. It was visited by experts and agricultural reformers from all over England and the Continent, and its work was made widely known through its periodical, the *Annales de Grignon*. The course

---

[33] F. Lullin de Châteaurieux, *Voyages agronomiques en France* (2 vols., Paris, 1843), Vol. 1, pp. 262–63; *Gazette des écoles,* 8 July 1830; Villeneuve-Bargemont, *Économie politique chrétienne* (3 vols., Paris, 1834), Vol. 3, pp. 584–86.

was two years in length and included both theoretical instruction and practical exercises in all branches of agriculture. Most of the pupils lived in the school dormitories; some, however, were boarded on neighboring farms. The system was arranged so that poor boys attending the school might help support themselves by work on the school farm or on privately owned farms round about. All the pupils had to do some of the general work of the farm. In addition, each one had a small plot of land assigned directly to him which he had to cultivate and look after. Also, certain pupils were appointed for periods to help take care of the different departments of the farm, such as the hog, sheep, cattle, or horse departments. The day began at four in summer and at four thirty in winter, with cleaning stables and feeding the stock, and ended with "lights out" at nine. The class instruction and the farm work went along side by side in any given day.[34]

A third important school was set up by a private company which had established a model farm at Grand-Jouan in Brittany in 1830. The leading spirit in this enterprise had once been a pupil at Roville. In 1833, the departmental council of the Loire Inférieure gave the farm a subsidy, provided the management would undertake to train twenty boys. A school in imitation of the one at Roville was at once set up. The school seems to have been successful from the beginning, and in 1842 the state took it over, greatly enlarging it, and made it into an agricultural school for the whole district.[35]

The demand for more agricultural schools, which had begun before the French Revolution, was not abated by the setting up of a few schools. Critics pointed out that the state schools

[34] For the school at Grignon, there is a full description in *American Journal of Education*, 1870, pp. 564–71; cf. also *École nationale d'agriculture, centenaire de Gringon* (Paris, 1926), pp. 129–45.

[35] *Le centenaire de l'école nationale d'agriculture de Grand-Jouan* (Rennes, 1930) contains speeches made at the centennial celebration, some pictures, and a list of teachers at the school. Cf. also *American Journal of Education*, 1870, pp. 557–63, 572–73.

were teaching Greek and Latin, and other foreign languages including Chinese, and yet did little to extend agricultural education or even to get proper instruction in agricultural subjects in the ordinary primary and secondary schools. It was pointed out that the agricultural classes in France paid over half of the total taxes collected by the state, that farming methods in France were very backward, and that agricultural courses and agricultural schools were needed as an important means of raising the total national income of France. Many of the arguments resemble those used to push the extension of industrial and engineering education.[36]

After 1830 a few new agricultural schools were founded both by private individuals and by groups, some of whom got help from the state. To stimulate interest in improving agricultural methods, the *Conservatoire des arts et métiers* in Paris, in the 1830's, rearranged its exhibits of agricultural instruments. In 1836 the government established three new professorships at the *Conservatoire,* one on general principles of agriculture, one on agricultural mechanics, and one on agricultural chemistry. At the same time, demonstration lectures on grafting were opened in the *Jardin de Luxembourg,* and the *Muséum d'histoire naturelle* gave a number of excellent courses on agricultural subjects. The information contained in these courses was spread by means of government publications as well as by textbooks published by the lecturers.

By 1848 there were twenty-five agricultural schools in operation. Some were small, and some were attached to orphanages and to penal colonies. Only the schools at Grignon and at Grand-Jouan were of much importance. Nearly all of these schools were connected with model farms, and the financial risks were taken in many cases by the individual or groups who owned the model farms. State help usually took the form

---

[36] *Bulletin de la société d'encouragement pour l'industrie nationale,* 1819, 237–38; *Gazette des écoles,* 18 April 1830; *Journal des économistes,* Vol. 57, p. 281.

of granting scholarships and of paying the teachers' salaries. Only the most careful management could make these model farm schools pay.

The revolutionary government of 1848 tried to institute a wholesale reform of the whole situation. By a law of 3 October 1848, three types of agricultural schools were to be established, all to be supported by the national government. First, there was to be a farm school in each *département* and later in each *arrondissement;* second, a higher district school for two or more *départements* to train farm managers; and finally, a central national agricultural school for the education of teachers of agriculture. The lowest schools were to take pupils sixteen years of age who had completed their primary education. No school was to be maintained for less than twenty-four pupils, the estimated minimum number of those considered necessary to run the model farm connected with such a school. The aim was to have enough pupils on each farm to carry out all its operations without any help other than that of the teachers. Each school was to be staffed with at least a director, a head workman, a nursery gardener, and a veterinary. The course was to cover three years. Besides agricultural subjects of all sorts, the pupils were to be taught bookkeeping and surveying. The director of each farm school was to work the model farm at his own risk. The government would pay the tuition and board of the pupils, the salaries of the teachers, and supply other subsidies. These farm schools and model farms were not only to train youths in the best agricultural methods but also to furnish a good example of tillage and stock breeding to the farmers in the surrounding district and to spread among them new ideas that would transform some of their backward methods of farming.

Seventy-one of these departmental agricultural schools, with fifteen hundred pupils, had been set up by the end of 1851. The larger district schools, each for several *départements,* were not only to run more advanced courses in agriculture but were also to be equipped with libraries, laboratories, and museums, and were to conduct advanced experimental work. Their courses were to include practical agriculture, care of livestock, forestry, botany, chemistry, physics, geology, and surveying. This part of the program was never carried out. A central national agricultural school was opened at Versailles in 1849 but was closed in 1852 and not reopened until 1876.[37]

In spite of the critics of French agricultural education, France by 1850 was ahead of any country in Europe in agricultural instruction. But French agriculture still remained very backward in its methods, far behind the agricultural methods used in England and East Prussia. This backwardness seems to have been due primarily to the conservatism of the large landowners in France and their indifference to, and ignorance of, the sort of improved agricultural methods used on the large estates of England and East Prussia.

The perennial French idea that in order to improve any public service or private occupation a school should be started appears in the setting up of a forestry school. The French state had maintained a regular forestry inspection service since 1554. In the eighteenth century a number of state officials believed that the service needed improvement, and they considered the idea of making available better training for young men who wished to enter the department of forestry. In a law of 1791, it was provided that each forest inspector spend part of his time training young apprentices, who after three years of instruction, at the age of about twenty-five, might apply for a state position. There is no indication that the law

[37] *American Journal of Education*, 1870, pp. 545–63. Typical of private agricultural schools was the agricultural school for orphans at Mettray (described in *American Journal of Education*). Founded in 1839 by private subscription, it got help from the state in the form of scholarships. Within a decade of its foundation it had nearly seven hundred youths enrolled. The boys lived in twelve large dormitories, in each of which there was a house director and his family. Each dormitory was three stories high, with workshops on the ground floor. Besides instruction in agriculture, some boys were also taught such trades as shoemaking, tailoring, and carpentry.

was carried out. In a pamphlet published in Paris in 1807, *Observations sur la nécessité d'établir en France des écoles forestières,* a member of the *Corps législatif* described the good forestry schools in some of the German states where were taught natural history, physics, chemistry, mathematics, drawing, and map making, and he made a strong plea for the establishment of such schools in France. A more comprehensive discussion of the whole subject by Baudrillart, a state forestry inspector, appeared in 1821 in the *Encyclopédie méthodique.* He outlined a two-year course, partly theoretical and partly practical, based on the experience of German forestry schools.

Finally, in 1824, the French state established the *École forestière* at Nancy in Lorraine. According to the act of foundation, twenty-four students between the ages of eighteen and twenty-two were to be selected by competitive examination in mathematics, chemistry, physics, geography, French history, and German. The school opened early in 1825. Tuition charges were twelve hundred francs. The course was two years in length, with theoretical work in biology, drawing, and forest management in the fall, winter, and spring, and practical exercises in the summer. One half the places in the state forestry service were to be reserved for graduates of the new school, the other half to be kept for those who rose in the service through the old apprenticeship system of learning on the job. A law of 1837 closed all future appointments to the state forestry service except to graduates of the school. This in turn was undone by an ordinance of 1844, which restored the original ruling of 1824. A law of 1827 provided that secondary schools of forestry for students younger than nineteen years were to be opened in those parts of France that were most heavily wooded. This was never carried out. The Nancy school improved very rapidly during the July Monarchy; the entrance examinations were made more difficult, and the students admitted increased in number and very much improved in quality. At the same time the teaching staff and the equipment were greatly enlarged. By the 1840's the Forestry School at Nancy was considered as good as any in Europe.[38]

In the field of mining education the German states, as we have seen, had definitely taken the lead in the eighteenth century. Toward the middle of that century efforts were made to introduce technical education, including instruction in mining, into some of the German universities. For example, courses in applied chemistry and applied mechanics, were started at three universities (cf. Chap. 2, ftn. 28). Objections from the faculties soon stopped such courses.[39] In the meantime a number of German states opened elementary mining schools. The French government had opened its first mining school in 1783. It was closed during the Revolutionary era, and then reopened in 1816. This was an excellent, advanced school chiefly for graduates of the *École polytechnique*. It admitted few students, and most of its graduates became government mining inspectors. In the same year, 1816, the state authorized the opening at Saint-Étienne of a more elementary school for the training of mining engineers. This *École des mineurs* started in 1818 with a director, three teachers, and a small

[38] This account is based on C. Guizot, *L'Enseignement forestière en France, L'École de Nancy* (Nancy, 1898), a careful study based on the archives of the Nancy school. Cf. also *American Journal of Education,* 1870, p. 574.

[39] W. E. Wickenden, ref. 21, p. 44. In 1799 a *Bauakademie* was opened by the Prussian government in Berlin. It had ambitious aims, i.e., to educate all types of engineers, as the *École polytechnique* was training them in France. But it took pupils as young as fourteen years, and its courses were very elementary. A similar school was opened in Prague in 1806, and somewhat more advanced ones were started in 1815 in Vienna, in 1822 in Berlin and Darmstadt, and in 1823 in Dresden. Not until the opening of the *Polytechnische Hochschule* in Karlsruhe in 1825 did any German state have a good advanced school of engineering. In some of the South German states, the governments started small evening classes for skilled works. These were organized in imitation of the British Mechanics Institutes and Dupin's classes for workers in France. For the whole situation in Germany, cf. Wickenden, *op. cit.,* pp. 44–50; A. Hermann, *Über Polytechnische Institute* (Nuremberg, 1826); and Saint-Marc Girardin, ref. 7.

number of students. These first students, whose ages ranged from fifteen to twenty-five years, had to pass an elementary admissions examination in arithmetic, algebra, geometry, and drawing. As time went on, the entrance examinations were made more difficult, and the number of teachers increased. The instruments, the library, and the mineralogical collections of the former mining school at Pesey were brought to the new school at Saint-Étienne. The first director had, during the *Empire,* been the head of a mining school at Geislautern. The courses for the first-year students included geology, metallurgy, and mechanics; those for the second year covered statistics, descriptive geometry, stereotomy, mechanics as applied to all types of mining operations, chemistry, mineralogy, and drawing. Much practical work in mathematical calculations, in drawing, in geological field trips and visits to mines and factories was included in the work of both years. After 1836 a course was added in railroad construction and management. Men trained in the Saint-Étienne school helped to build the first large coke furnaces and the first big steel mills in France.[40]

As the school at Saint-Étienne within a decade forged ahead to the position of an excellent institution of very advanced standing, the government in 1845 opened a more elementary mining school at Alais in the *Département* of Gard. This *École des maîtres mineurs* was to train workmen already employed in mines to become foremen, defined as "a workman, one who possesses practical knowledge sufficient to superintend and guide the workmen, and enough theoretical knowledge to

[40] On the school at Saint-Étienne, cf. *Bulletin des lois,* Ord. Aug. 2 1816 and Ord. May 7 1831; *Le centenaire de l'école nationale des mines* (Saint-Étienne, 1921), esp. pp. 11ff., with a list of distinguished graduates, and pp. 19–43 for a summary of the history of the school; V. Guillermin and M. Gillot, *L'École nationale des mines de Saint-Étienne* (Saint-Étienne, 1921); Barnard, ref. 32, pp. 425ff.; the serial, *Correspondance des élèves d'école royale des mineurs* (Saint-Étienne, 1827ff.); and A. L. Dunham, "The Development of Coal Mining in France, 1815–1848" in *Papers Michigan Academy of Science, Arts and Letters* (1941).

understand and to execute the orders of the directors of the mines." Candidates had to prove, by a certificate from a mining director, that they had labored in a mine as a common worker for at least one year, and then had to pass an examination in reading, writing, and arithmetic. The course at Alais covered two years, with work in the school in the winter and practical exercises in mining operations in the summer. At Saint-Étienne all the pupils were day students; at Alais, all had to live in the school. The courses given at Alais resembled those given at Saint-Étienne, though the subjects were handled with less thoroughness. Emphasis was laid on advanced arithmetic, plane and solid geometry, physics, chemistry, mineralogy, geology, and practical mining processes. While tuition at the Saint-Étienne school was free, at Alais some students paid tuition, whereas others were on state scholarships or scholarships supplied by private companies.[41]

4. Advanced Schools of Civil Engineering

The *École polytechnique,* founded earlier in the Revolutionary era, was in spite of many setbacks due to the wars of the *Empire* widely recognized as the leading technical school of Europe. After 1815, with the return of peace, its courses and equipment were improved and extended and the hopes and programs of its founders realized. The school continued to be governed by a *Conseil d'instruction* made up of members of the faculty; each member of this body presided over the school for a month. The *Conseil d'instruction,* in turn, was supervised by a *Conseil de perfectionnement* made up of important teachers in the school, notable scientists, and government officials. This body proved very useful; its members were interested in the school but still detached enough to have a per-

---

[41] *Bulletin de la société d'encouragement pour l'industrie nationale,* 1846, p. 514; 1847, pp. 709–10; Barnard, ref. 32, p. 426; and Audiganne, ref. 21, p. 881.

spective on the whole situation, especially in the matter of the relation of the *École polytechnique* to the still more advanced *écoles d'application*.

The system of teaching with lecturers and *répétiteurs,* invented by Monge and Fourcroy, was continued. The *répétiteurs* were usually young men who hoped later to obtain positions as professors. Their position somewhat resembled that of the tutors at Oxford and Cambridge and the *Privat-Dozenten* of the German universities, though they never gave lectures. They met the students individually or, more usually, in groups of five or six, for questioning and discussion. For the positions of professors, *répétiteurs,* and pupils the competition was very keen. From 1815 on the *École polytechnique* seems to have attracted more ability than any school in France. Its graduates were in great demand for positions in the army, navy, public works, mining, and industry.

As the *École polytechnique* during the first half of the nineteenth century was recognized as the outstanding technical school of the world and as it was imitated in every country from Russia to the United States, its history deserves a detailed consideration. Napoleon had, in 1804, put the school under a military regime. This was ended in 1816 when the direction of the institution was transferred from the Ministry of War to that of the Interior. In 1822 some military drill was reintroduced, but the school remained under the Ministry of the Interior till 1831, when it was restored to the Ministry of War after an investigation by a commission headed by Arago.[42]

[42] A. Fourcy, *L'histoire de l'École polytechnique* (Paris, 1828), pp. 331ff. *École polytechnique: Livre du centenaire* (3 vols., Paris, 1894–1897), Vol. I, pp. 114–15. G. Pinet, *Histoire de l'École polytechnique* (Paris, 1887) contains a detailed description of the organization of the school at various stages of its history, a discussion of the interests and activities of the students, and a series of fifty important documents and statistical tables. Cf. also references to the *École polytechnique* in the notes to Chapter Three. One of the best discussions of the curriculum is in H. Barnard, *Military Schools and Courses,* etc. (2nd ed., New York, 1872), pp. 13–134. Cf. also G. de Santillana, "Positivism and the Technological Ideal in the 19th Century," M. A. F.

The entrance examinations were very stiff, and students who intended to take them usually had extra tutoring during their last years in secondary schools. The examinations were in arithmetic, elementary and advanced algebra, plane and solid geometry, plane and spherical trigonometry, statics, conic sections, drawing, and, finally, Latin translation, and French composition. No technical school in the world before 1850 demanded as much. And yet complaints were made that the entrance examinations did not include calculus, physics, mechanics, descriptive geometry, and chemistry. Calculus and physics were required later in the advanced *École d'application* for artillery at Metz, for ship construction at Brest, and for the *École des ponts et chaussées* in Paris, while descriptive geometry, physics, mechanics, and chemistry were required for those who would later enter the advanced *École des mines*. The entrance examinations were partly written and partly oral. They were given by a traveling board of examiners who went about from 1 August to 10 October to a series of specified towns scattered over France. The examiners also held examinations for the military school at Saint-Cyr, the *École de marine,* and the forestry school.

Of 14,782 candidates who took the final entrance examina-

Montague, ed., *Studies in the History of Science Offered to George Sarton* (New York, 1947). There is a large contemporary literature discussing the merits and demerits of the *École polytechnique.* For hostile criticism of the school, cf. de Chambray, *De l'école polytechnique* (Paris, 1836); and for a defense of the school, cf. G. D. E. Bugnot, *L'école polytechnique* (Paris, 1837). Among the complaints made were that the courses were too theoretical, that the students were driven too hard, and that the entrance examinations were too difficult. Cf. also the following contemporary accounts and discussions: P. Doré, *De la nécessité et des moyens d'ouvrir des nouvelles carrières pour le placement des élèves de l'École polytechnique* (Paris, 1830); P. de la Madelaine, *De l'admission à l'École polytechnique et des abus* (Paris, 1833); and A. Bobin, *Questions concernant les jeunes gens que l'on destine à l'École polytechnique* (Paris, 1842). There is an interesting study of the economic and social status of the families of the students in the *École polytechnique,* A. Daumard, "Les élèves de l'école polytechnique de 1815 à 1848," *Revue d'histoire moderne,* 1958.

tion for the *École polytechnique* between 1794 and 1836, 5,628 were admitted to the school.[43] The average number admitted each year in the period 1796 to 1831 was a hundred and thirty-four; from 1831 to 1850 the average rose to three hundred and one. In 1836, the number of applications was six times the number of places open that year; this seems to have been typical. The students were drawn mostly from the middle class. They were able and only moderately well to do, and were struggling for a position in life. As the *École polytechnique* was an obvious road to a successful career with an assured though low income, it can be understood why the competition for entrance was so keen and why the competition for a high place in one's class after the students had entered the school was sharp and even bitter.

Having passed the entrance examinations, the students admitted were asked to declare for what public service they were preparing. The choice was wide; for the army there were the artillery, the engineers, munition manufactures, and the general staff; for the navy, the naval artillery, maritime engineers, and hydrostatic engineers; for civil engineering, the corps of bridges and highways and that of mining inspectors; after 1830 there were added the corps of telegraph and later that of

[43] *Annuaire de l'École polytechnique* (Paris) 1836, pp. 100–01; 1837, pp. 78–79, 94–101, 176–84, 196; also G. D. E. Bugnot, *op. cit.,* p. 9. Further details on entrance examinations may be found in A. Fourcy, *op. cit.,* p. 375; Ministère de la Guerre, *Instructions pour l'admission à l'École polytechnique en 1852,* and by the same ministry, *Programmes des connaissances exigées pour admission,* etc., 1852. Both these works seem to exist in the United States only in the New York Public Library. Cf. also Barnard, ref. 42, pp. 47, 66–70; and Military Education Commission, *Accounts of Systems of Military Education in France,* etc. (London, 1870), pp. 19–21; Bache, ref. 7, pp. 544–46. The *Annuaire de l'École polytechnique,* which was published from 1833 to 1846, is a mine of information about all aspects of the school, as are the annual *Programmes de l'enseignement de l'École polytechnique* and the *Rapports par le Conseil de perfectionnement de l'École polytechnique.* The New York Public Library is the only place in the United States that has any number of these reports. The only complete file I could locate in France was in the library and archives of the *École polytechnique.*

railroad inspectors, and finally that of the administration of the state tobacco monopoly. Students who entered without declaring their intentions were on graduation allowed to compete only for places in any given public service with students in the class admitted to the school in the same year. More and more, after 1815, the students declared their intentions on entering, and critics of the school always complained that too many declared for artillery and military engineering. It was very difficult for the student to change his choice afterwards, unless he stood near the top of his graduating class.[44]

The standards of scholarship in the institution were kept high, first because of the keen competition to enter the school, which probably gave it the most able student body of an advanced school of any type in the world, and second because the students knew that on leaving the school the first positions they obtained either in the government services or in the advanced *écoles d'application* would depend on the quality of their work in the *École polytechnique*. Even for those who served for a time in one of the state services and later went into private industry, their record in the *École polytechnique* counted heavily in the kind of positions they could obtain.

The courses in the school continued to be modeled on those given before the Revolution at the famous engineering school at Mézières and at the *École des ponts et chaussées* in Paris. The basic courses, taken by all students, were in the first year calculus, descriptive geometry, physics (especially heat and electricity), mechanics, chemistry (especially of metals), astronomy, geodesy, French composition and literature, German, and drawing. The first year's work was divided into three portions of unequal length, two of them of about four months each, with an additional two weeks of review, private study, and examinations. The third portion of two months at the end of the school year was devoted to a general review, private

[44] *Annuaire de l'École polytechnique,* (Paris, 1837), p. 63; Lamé and Clapeyron, ref. 19, pp. 29–30.

study, and examinations. In accordance with this arrangement, the four hardest subjects were distributed. Analysis and descriptive geometry, the staple work of the school — its "Latin," as it was called — came in the first four months. Then there was the pause for private study, review, and examinations. This ran to about the middle of March. For the next four months, attention was centered on mechanics and geodesy, with a similar pause at the end. During both these first two periods, physics and chemistry were also studied and examinations on them were given. Evening classes were in the meantime held in French literature and German, and in landscape and figure drawing. As a general rule, there was only one difficult lecture each day. The final portion of the year was devoted to private study and final examinations. During this period of four weeks and more, no lectures were given. The final examinations of the first year usually occupied the time from the first to the twenty-fifth of September, and the new term began in late October.

In the second year a continuation of analysis with mechanics in place of descriptive geometry was central in the work of the first four months. Then came private study, review, and examinations. Next there were four months of stereotomy, the art of war, and topography. Chemistry and physics were also studied, and in the evenings French literature and German as well as figure and landscape drawing. The course in physics laid emphasis on the theory and methods of timber and masonry construction, on road building, and after 1835 on railroad construction, mechanics (especially dynamics and hydrostatics), and physics (especially acoustics, optics, and heat). The chemistry taught in the second year was organic chemistry. We have now brought the pupil nearly to the end of his academic career. Most students left the school on completing the two-year course. Those who were allowed to stay a third year varied their course according to the service into which they planned to go later. Laboratory exercises were given in connection with all the courses in physics and chemistry, and in the second and third year factory visits, outdoor surveying, and map making were made parts of the course.[45]

The highest authority in disciplinary matters were the two "commandants"; the highest authority in matters of study was the "director of studies." The latter was appointed by the king (in the period 1815–1848) on the joint nomination of the *Conseil d'instruction* of the school and the *Académie des sciences.* The large *Conseil de perfectionnement,* appointed by the *Conseil d'instruction,* acted as a sort of advisory board of trustees; it was made up of the military commandants, the director of studies, one of the entrance examiners, five members of the board of final examiners, three of the *Académie des sciences,* three professors of the school, and one member of each of the branches of the public service into which the graduates of the *École polytechnique* entered.

The basis of teaching in the *École polytechnique* were lectures, often with demonstrations, given by the professors who were usually about fifteen in number. These, together with the assigned reading, laboratory work, and practical exercises, were carefully gone over by the twenty to twenty-five *répétiteurs.* The lectures were given to large groups, and these were broken up into small groups for the work with the *répétiteurs.* Even the studying was done in special study rooms presided over by *répétiteurs,* who were present to answer questions. Frequent quizzes, mostly oral, were given by the *répétiteurs,* but the longer written examinations were set by the professors, who also from time to time examined the elaborate notebooks

---

[45] Military Education Commission, ref. 43, pp. 24–29, 35–41; Bache, ref. 7, pp. 550–53; A. Fourcy, ref. 42, pp. 376–79. After 1816 the courses in civil engineering, fortification, and the art of war were all transferred to the special *écoles d'application* to which they belonged. Bache, *op. cit.,* p. 548. For a typical day's schedule at the *École polytechnique,* cf. Bache, *op. cit.,* p. 556; Barnard, ref. 42, pp. 72–178; *Military Education Commission, op. cit.,* pp. 23–24, 441–42; for the distribution of time for longer periods, cf. *Annuaire de l'École polytechnique,* 1837, pp. 241–55.

kept by the students. Every exercise was graded; each student could always tell whether he was gaining or losing in his academic status. And, in the final reckoning, every portion of his studies told for or against him. So during the whole course the prospect of his final position in the public services would rarely be absent from a student's thought. He knew all along that upon his position in the final class list depended much of his fortune for life.

The whole teaching method combined the carefully prepared lecture of the German university professor with the close personal questioning and direction of the English college tutorial system. The professors were among the most eminent scientists in France. During the Bourbon Restoration, Arago taught mathematics, Gay-Lussac chemistry, and Ampère mechanics. In selecting the professors it was the practice to pick men who were themselves active in scientific research, the theory being that a teacher who was not doing original scientific work himself could not stimulate his students. At the same time, the professors were supposed to be advancing science through their own research. And the system of *répétiteurs* allowed a scientist to go on with his research while he was lecturing. He was relieved of all burden of looking after details of the students' work. In some cases, the *répétiteurs* later became professors in the school. The American A. D. Bache, after traveling all over Europe, found the *École polytechnique* in the late 1830's the best equipped school in the world in physical and chemical apparatus, mathematical instruments and models, and casts and models for drawing. He also found the faculty and the student body without a rival.[46]

The students had to work very hard and were allowed few privileges. Except for some military drill there was but little

[46] *École polytechnique, Livre du centenaire* (3 vols., Paris, 1894–1897), Vol. I, p. 46; Bache, ref. 7, pp. 546–47, 556–57, 560–61; Military Education Commission, ref. 43, pp. 21–24; Barnard, ref. 42, pp. 70–72; there were sometimes quarrels among the various governing groups of the *École polytechnique;* for an example, cf. *Annuaires* (1843–1846).

physical exercise. There was nothing of the English love of games, or the gymnastics of the German schools. The students were supplied with billiard tables, but games of dice or cards were strictly forbidden even though not played for money. Nothing could be eaten except at fixed mealtimes; the bringing in of any provisions or liquor was prohibited. No smoking was allowed except during recreation hours. Except for Wednesdays and Sundays, the students usually worked eleven and a half hours a day. They rose at six, and lights had to be out at ten P.M. The introduction into the school or its dormitories of newspapers and periodicals was not allowed; even books relating to the subjects of instruction were not permitted unless especially sanctioned by the authorities. The students were allowed to receive visitors by special permission only and, except on Wednesday afternoons and all day Sunday, were not permitted to leave the school grounds.[47]

The tuition costs varied; by 1850 the charge for board and instruction was about eight hundred francs, and the cost of a uniform and other personal equipment was about a hundred and twenty dollars. Whole or part scholarships were available for all the students admitted provided they could prove that their parents were unable to maintain them. Usually about one third of the students received financial aid. The school was thus really open to all students of talent who wanted such a type of education so long as they had the necessary preliminary training.

The final examinations each year, oral and written, were given by a special board of examiners; two were appointed by the ministry in charge of the school, on recommendation of the *Conseil d'instruction* and the *Académie des sciences,* and three were appointed annually by the *Conseil d'instruction.* In the students' final rating, mathematics courses counted most.

---

[47] Bache, *op. cit.,* pp. 557–59; *Annuaire,* 1837, pp. 217–32, 270–78, including details about payment of students' bills, and about their clothing. Cf. also *Military Education Commission, op. cit.,* pp. 31–35.

Few failed, for the extreme severity of the entrance examinations meant that only well-qualified candidates were admitted. In 1836, for example, only five in the first-year course, and eight in the second-year course were required to repeat a course, and no one was dropped from the school.[48]

Having graduated from the *École polytechnique,* the students were then distributed to the various government services, for entering some of which they would have first to enroll in one of the specialized *écoles d'application.* The first choices went to the students who graduated with the highest marks, regardless of their declaration on entering the school of the service for which they wished to prepare. Such choices varied from one period to another. If a student did not choose to enter the government service he was not obliged to do so, though pressure was usually brought to get the graduates into government positions. That more students did not choose positions in private industry seems to have been due to the extraordinary *esprit de corps* that the school had built up. In the period 1795 to 1836, almost 1700 graduates entered the artillery, 917 the military engineers, 25 the general staff, 108 the geographical engineers, 19 the state munition manufactures, 119 the infantry, 55 the naval artillery, 118 the naval engineers, 13 the naval hydrographical engineers, 105 the general navy, 196 the corps of mines, 118 the corps of bridges and highways, and 7 the state tobacco manufactures. In 1836, of 120 graduates only 9 did not enter one of the public services. Henry Barnard, an American, writing about the *École polytechnique* early in the second *Empire,* found the state services selected by the students in the following order: first, roads and bridges and mines (very nearly on an equality), munition manufactures, naval architects, army engineers, artillery, general staff, hydrological corps, tobacco administration, telegraph, general navy, and last, naval artillery. Evidently there was a good deal of variation in the popularity of the several services. This was

[48] Bache, *op. cit.,* pp. 547, 553–55.

in part due to the different salaries — frequently changed — attached to the various public services. For some positions in the public services, graduation from the *École polytechnique* was sufficient, but for most of the services the students went first to one of the *écoles d'application* before entering government service.

In spite of its high reputation, the *École polytechnique* in the period 1815 to 1850, as we have seen, was much criticized. On the scientific side, the criticism was usually directed against the great emphasis on mathematics in the whole program of the school, and on the large amount of purely theoretical work in most of the courses. It was claimed that much of the mathematics taught would never be used in any of the *écoles d'application* nor later in the government services. Some thought it might even be better to go back to the situation prevailing before the *École polytechnique* was founded and to have candidates for each public service trained in a special school which they would enter directly on leaving secondary school. The greatest complaint was about those who entered the various branches of the army rather than about those who entered some sort of civil engineering or some branch of the navy. Moreover, it was pointed out by the critics that there was no necessary co-ordination between those who got high grades in advanced mathematics courses and those who were needed in government services. No one seems to have objected — as they would now — to the omission of all the social sciences and the comparative neglect of most of the humanities.[49]

[49] Bache, *op. cit.,* pp. 542–45. In a report of 1851, the writer, who is a severe critic of the school, says that the top twenty per cent of each class were very exceptional men, the next sixty per cent were good students, but the last twenty per cent were "men who are not very well fitted for any public service." Assemblée nationale, *Enquête sur la situation des services de la marine militaire* (2 vols., Paris, 1851), Vol. 1, pp. 299–300. In the period 1795 to 1830, about one hundred graduates eventually went into teaching, *Annuaire de l'École polytechnique,* 1837, p. 78. The role played by the graduates occupies the whole third volume of the *École polytechnique: Livre du centenaire.* There is a complete table of all the graduates for the

Everyone assumed that a professional school like the *École polytechnique* should be almost exclusively professional. As against those who criticized the courses as being too theoretical, there were more who praised just this side of the work of the school. They liked to point out that the great progress in France in both theoretical and applied science was due to the influence and inspiration of the *École polytechnique*. From the proceedings of the *Académie des sciences* to the evening courses for working men and to the popular books and periodicals on applied science, the influence of the graduates of the *École polytechnique* was everywhere increasingly evident. Some of those who praised the school said it should admit more students, some of whom could enter diplomacy as commercial agents or could become subprefects in the state administration. Some thought some able students were refused admittance because of trick mathematic questions in the entrance examinations. This in their opinion also led to distortions in the teaching of mathematics in the best secondary schools. The great interest in the *École polytechnique* and its work is shown in the number of articles, pamphlets, and books that appeared regarding it.[50]

The *École polytechnique* was also under fire because it was regarded by the Conservatives as a hotbed of liberalism and radicalism. The school was closed in 1815 because of the hostility of the students to the restored Bourbon regime, and it was not reopened until the next year. Many of the students were Liberal, Monarchist, or Republican in sentiment. They

years 1795 to 1853 in *École polytechnique, Répértoire ou renseignements sur les élèves,* etc. (Paris, 1855). A list of all the graduates by name and the services they entered is in *Tableau historique et chronologique de l'école polytechnique depuis sa fondation* (2nd ed., Paris, 1828).

[50] For attacks on the *École polytechnique* and for its defense, cf. works referred to in note 42 and also Lamé and Clapeyron, ref. 19, esp. pp. 94–104; for a plea to enlarge the curriculum and to extend electives, cf. *Gazette spéciale de l'instruction publique,* 21 Feb. 1839; Barnard, ref. 42, pp. 13–46 contains a good estimate of the worth of the criticisms of the school and describes reforms made after 1850.

liked to sing the forbidden *Marseillaise;* some, after 1820, joined the Liberal secret society, the *Carbonari.* When the Duc d'Angoulême, the King's nephew, visited the school, a large group of students cried, *"Vive la Charte"* (the Charter of 1814). Some students at the school kept alive and furthered the ideas of social utility as they had been expounded in the eighteenth century. Many of these young men had dreams of building a better society, just as they were learning to build a bridge. So the *esprit polytechnicien* was bent on increasing commerce and developing production, at the same time increasing social welfare. The ideas of Saint-Simon and his followers, of Comte, and of Fourier stirred many a student in the school. About sixty of the students fought against the government troops in the July revolution of 1830. This brought great acclaim to the school from Liberal circles; poems were written about the brave *polytechniciens* fighting at the barricades, cheek by jowl with the masses, and Lafayette praised them to the skies. Again in 1848 the *polytechniciens* were active in the revolution which overthrew Louis Philippe.

The influence of Saint-Simonianism seems to have been particularly strong, and graduates of the *École polytechnique* furnished some of the leaders and missionaries of the Saint-Simonian School. Saint-Simon, himself a close friend of Monge, one of the founders of the *École polytechnique,* in 1797 moved into a house across the street from the school, and from then till his death in 1825 he was on close terms with some members of the faculty. Saint-Simon's views that a democratic and scientific age was succeeding a royal, feudal, and ecclesiastical age, that science would ameliorate the condition of all mankind, that society should be organized on the basis of social utility, and that an elite of scientists and engineers should rule society and the state squared with many of the aims of the students of the *École polytechnique.* Comte, Saint-Simon's secretary and the founder of Positivism, was a graduate of the school, and Enfantin, one of the leaders of the

Saint-Simonian School, was a former student. *Polytechniciens* flocked to the meetings of the *Saint-Simoniens* and read their journals, first the *Producteur* and later the *Globe*. Many of the graduates, though they never were Socialists, had the general spirit of social amelioration and became leaders in railroad building, the opening of factories, the inauguration of the Suez Canal, and in extended colonization in Africa. They also helped to break down inertia and routine methods in manufacturing and in many of the state services. In 1830 a group of graduates founded the *Association polytechnique* (with the motto, "For the fatherland, for the sciences, and for glory") to give courses to workingmen in mathematics, bookkeeping, and applied chemistry and physics. In 1848, a split-off from this, the *Association philotechnique,* extended even further these efforts at popular education. So this famous school played a leading role in the whole life of France. And all over the world its courses and its methods of instruction were the model for all types of higher technical education.[51]

The *écoles d'application* for which by 1850 the *École polytechnique* prepared were the following: four military schools —the artillery and engineering school at Metz, the infantry

[51] G. Pinet, "L'École polytechnique et les Saint-Simoniens," *Revue de Paris,* 15 May 1894; G. Weill, "Les républicains et l'enseignement," *Revue internationale de l'enseignement,* 15 Jan. 1899; Fourcy, ref. 42, pp. 331–37; *École polytechnique: Livre du centenaire,* Vol. 1, pp. 44–47; and G. de Santillana, "Positivism and the Technological Ideal in the Nineteenth Century" in M. A. F. Montague, ed., *Studies in the History of Science Offered to Sarton* (New York, 1947). Many of the higher technical schools from Japan through the United States to Russia were modeled on those at the *École polytechnique.* Crozet, a graduate of the *École polytechnique,* was a teacher at both the Virginia Military Institute and at West Point, and he translated Monge's treatise on descriptive geometry into English, cf. W. Couper, *Crozet* (Charlottesville, Va., 1936), and S. Forman, *West Point, a History of the Military Academy* (New York, 1950). Thayer at West Point and Greene at Rensselaer Polytechnic Institute spent their best efforts in introducing the methods of the *École polytechnique* into the United States. On the influence on German engineering schools, cf. Wickenden, ref. 21, p. 14, and F. Schnabel, *Die Anfänge des technischen Hochschulwesens* (Munich, 1925).

and cavalry school at Saint-Cyr, the staff school at Paris, and the cavalry school at Saumur; four naval schools — the naval school at Brest, the naval artillery school at Paris, the naval architectural school at Paris, and the hydrographic engineering school; the *École des ponts et chaussées;* the *École des mines;* the munitions school; several small schools for the administration of the state tobacco service (conducted in the manufacturing plants); and finally several schools for the state telegraphic service. The military and naval schools will be discussed later under the general topics of military and naval education. From the point of view of higher instruction in the fields of civil engineering the two most important of the *écoles d'application* were the *École des ponts et chaussées* and the *École des mines,* both in Paris.[52]

The *École des ponts et chaussées* had already been well organized before the *École polytechnique* was founded. When it was made an *école d'application,* the courses were reorganized and the level of instruction raised. About half of the students were not graduates of the *École polytechnique.* They were admitted after very severe examinations in drawing, advanced mathematics, and physics. The course in the *École des ponts et chaussées* lasted three years. The winter term ran from the first of November to the first of May. The months from May to November were spent in field work when construction was going on. Those admitted were given their instruction free. The principal practical courses were in road, bridge, canal, and later in railroad construction. The theoretical courses were chiefly in mathematics, chemistry, physics, and geology. The social standing of the graduates was high, taking precedence over army colonels at state functions. The first half of the nineteenth century saw an enormous amount of road, bridge, and canal building, the extensive draining of marshlands, the improvement of harbors, and, finally, railroad construction.

[52] Barnard, ref. 32, p. 421, and in the same journal, pp. 421–26 for *écoles d'application.*

In all of these subjects courses were given at the *École des ponts et chaussées,* and much of the work was either supervised or inspected by graduates of the school.[53]

In the building and supervising of this sort of projects, hundreds of engineers were engaged. Most of these had been trained not in schools but in the old apprenticeship system of learning their profession on the job. Before 1850 we are still in a period when the two methods of training, apprenticeship and school instruction, ran side by side. The term "civil engineer" had come into common use in the second half of the eighteenth century, but the position was not clearly defined even by 1850. In England, though an *Institute of Civil Engineers* was founded in 1817, Telford, the leading civil engineer of the period, thought that an engineer was best trained by the apprenticeship system. It was the French who took the lead by insisting that school training was the best way to start an engineer on his career. In the end, the French idea prevailed everywhere, and by 1850 the influence of French practice was beginning to be evident in countries as far removed from France as Russia, Turkey, Portugal, Brazil, and the United States.

The advanced *École des mines* at Paris was also a pre-Revolutionary foundation. It had been closed during the Consulate, though the mining schools in the provinces remained open. When it was reopened in 1816, it was raised to the position of an *école d'application.* Like the *École des ponts et*

---

[53] *Annuaire de l'École polytechnique,* 1837, p. 294. *École polytechnique: Livre du centenaire,* Vol. 3, pp. 7–18, 50–51, 57; A. Gibb, *The Story of Telford* (London, 1935), pp. 208–10; J. W. Roe, *English and American Tool Builders* (New Haven, 1916), p. 2; for the great economic changes in France in the period 1815 to 1850, changes which lay back of the advances in technical education, cf. F. B. Artz, *France under the Bourbon Restoration* (Cambridge, Mass., 1931), Chap. 3; H. Sée, *Histoire économique de la France* (2 vols., Paris, 1939–1942); and A. L. Dunham, *The Industrial Revolution in France 1815–1848* (New York, 1955); the last is especially useful. On the earlier history of the *Ponts et Chaussées,* cf. J. Petot, *Histoire de l'administration des ponts et chaussées,* 1599–1815 (Paris, 1958).

chaussées, it was well housed and well equipped in excellent buildings in Paris. Both schools were considered in the first half of the nineteenth century as the best of their kind in the world. Part of the students of the *École des mines* were graduates of the *École polytechnique,* others came from the mining schools in the provinces, and some were admitted on the basis of a stiff entrance examination. To all those admitted the instruction was free. The course covered two or three years of theoretical and applied mathematics and science and in addition German and English. The summers were used for practical exercises. For those who were to spend three years in the school, a preparatory first-year course covered calculus, advanced mechanics, descriptive geometry, physics especially as applied to gases, steam, heat, and optical problems, general chemistry, drawing, German, and English. The first year of the regular course was chiefly devoted to the study of the principles of mining operations, metallurgy, mineralogy, paleontology, English, and German, and the last-year courses included further instruction in mining methods, industrial construction, mining laws and administration, drainage, and again English and German. Much practical work in laboratories and drawing rooms was required. And the work done in the summer, some of it outside France, was carefully supervised, and each student had to submit a long written report. More elementary schools of mining were, as we have seen, at Saint-Étienne, and after 1846 at Alais. Most of the graduates of the advanced *École des mines* at Paris either became government mining inspectors or worked as engineers for private companies. The graduates were much sought after.

There was the same close connection between the state *Corps de mines* and the school that existed between the *Corps de ponts et chaussées* and the *École des ponts et chaussées.* In both cases however the number of civil and mining engineers educated was not sufficient to meet the growing needs of French mining construction and industry. In practice, the graduates of the *École polytechnique* who went on for further study in the *École des ponts et chaussées* and the *École des mines* almost universally went into government service. But nearly half of the students in each school were not graduates of the *École polytechnique*. These *externes,* as they were called, usually found employment with private companies. Still, the supply of trained engineers after 1815 always remained insufficient. The French theory had always been that, while you could not give all engineers a school training, to train some who would be active in every field of engineering would raise the level of practice all along the line. This theory was ultimately accepted all over the world. As one enters the second half of the nineteenth century, the balance tips steadily in favor of those whose training had been, at least in part, in engineering schools, so that in the twentieth century nearly all engineers have some school training.[54]

To meet the need for training engineers for industry, a group of private capitalists founded in 1829 the *École centrale des arts et manufactures*. In view of the long prevalent belief in France that the government should open schools for all types of special training, it is surprising that the state had not earlier started a school for the training of engineers for manufacturing. In search for reasons for this, we may notice that

---

[54] *Gazette des écoles,* 11 July 1830; *Annuaire de l'École polytechnique,* 1843–46, p. 369; Bache, ref. 7, pp. 562–63; A. Griscom, *A Year in Europe,* 2nd ed. (2 vols., New York, 1824), Vol. 1, p. 192. On *École des mines,* cf. L. A. Guillon, "Historique de l'école des mines," *Annales des mines* 1889. The first important mining school in the United States, established in 1864 at Columbia University, was modeled on the French *École des mines.* Wickenden, ref. 21, pp. 11–12. On relations of the *École polytechnique* and the administration of the state tobacco monopoly after 1831, cf. *École polytechnique: Livre du centenaire,* Vol. 3, pp. 261–79; M. d'Ocagne, *Les grandes écoles de France* (Paris, 1887), part on "Écoles des manufactures de l'état." For the graduates of the *École polytechnique* who went to the state munitions works, cf. *Annuaire de l'école polytechnique,* 1837, pp. 68, 284. For the advanced training of telegraph and railroad engineers, cf. *École polytechnique, Livre du centenaire,* Vol. 3, pp. 281–93; *Annuaire de l'École polytechnique* (1843), pp. 373–76.

before the Revolution French manufactures were far less mechanized than were those of England. In France, hand-workers turned out the fine luxury articles, such as clocks, watches, brocades, furniture, and porcelain which furnished the most lucrative French exports. And where trained engineers were most needed, in the army, the navy, mining, and public works, the French provided the best school training in Europe. After the outbreak of the Revolution, the need for more trained engineers of all sorts was recognized, but it was believed that the *École polytechnique* and other schools would supply these in sufficient numbers. These schools, however, failed to furnish enough engineers, but by this time France was involved in wars, and the supply even of trained army and navy engineers was quite insufficient. With the return of peace in 1815, the commercial competition with England became keen, and France soon began to expand industrially. By 1820, there were demands for more trained engineers everywhere. As we have seen, the periodical literature of the Restoration is full of such demands. But the restored Bourbon government was conservative — even reactionary — and very clerical, and unfavorably disposed toward the leaders of the manufacturing class and toward all efforts to extend education. Moreover, the students of the *École polytechnique* and of some of the other technical schools showed their hostility to the Bourbon government, so that the government seems to have had the notion that all technical education was, in itself, hostile to the rule of "the throne and the altar." At best, the Bourbon government did little to interfere with the existing technical schools, and in some cases even provided funds for their improvement, but it was indifferent or hostile to the founding of new ones.

So it was left to private initiative to found the advanced *École centrale des arts et manufactures.* Of the four men chiefly responsible for the opening of this new school, three were scientists: one was a graduate of the *École polytechnique,* one a graduate of the *École normale,* and the third had received an education in theoretical science at the *Université de Genève.* They had frequently met at the *Athénée,* a society which conducted lectures and discussions on science, industry, commerce, economics, and literature. The principal capitalist involved was Lavallée. He became the first director, and the three young scientists the first teachers. The enterprise had the enthusiastic backing of the *Conseil général des manufactures,* a sort of early chamber of commerce, and of the *Société d'encouragement pour l'industrie nationale,* though neither of these bodies furnished funds. The avowed purpose of the school was to train engineers for industry so as to raise the productivity of French manufactures that they might better compete with those of England. There were good higher schools in France for advanced training in medicine, law, theology, and art, and for educating mining, road, military, and naval engineers, but no adequate provision existed for educating civil and industrial engineers. So the new school was set up as what its second director called a *"Sorbonne industrielle."* [55]

The organization of the school's management, its system of entrance examinations, its curriculum, and its methods of construction showed the influence of the *École polytechnique.* To be sure that the entering students had an adequate background, entrance examinations were given in arithmetic, algebra (including quadratic equations), logarithms, plane and solid geometry, drawing, and French composition. The entrance examinations in Paris were given by a special examiner

---

[55] C. de Comberousse, *Histoire de l'École centrale des arts et manufactures* (Paris, 1879), Vol. 13, pp. 16–28; this account is based on a study of the archives of the school. Cf. also F. Pothier, *Histoire de l'École centrale des arts et manufactures* (Paris, 1887), esp. the documents in the Appendix; L. Guillet, *Cent ans de vie de l'École centrale des arts et manufactures* (Paris, 1929), pp. 1–16, 44, 63–65, 91–93, 106–83; this is an excellent monograph. There is an interesting article on the need of such a school in *Le Globe,* 8 Oct. 1828, and a good contemporary account of the plans for the school in A. de Férussac, ed., *Bulletin des sciences technologiques,* 1829, Vol. 11, pp. 290–94.

attached to the school, in other parts of France by a professor of mathematics in a local secondary school, and in foreign countries by a mathematics teacher in a certified university. To take the entrance examination, students had to be at least fifteen, and, after 1835, sixteen years old. The tuition was seven hundred francs a year, raised to eight hundred in 1830. The curriculum in the school shows clearly that the founders were sympathetic with those who thought the courses in the *École polytechnique* laid too great an emphasis on higher mathematics and on theoretical physics. The mathematics, physics, and chemistry taught were all related to practical exercises in laboratories and in shopwork. Courses were given in descriptive geometry, general applied physics and industrial mechanics, steam engines, machine construction, industrial chemistry, building construction, mining methods, metallurgy, business methods and management, drawing, and, after 1834 railroads. Shopwork, such as was given in the *écoles des arts et métiers,* was not much used, but models of machines were taken apart, drawn, and then reconstructed, and laboratory exercises were given in physics and chemistry.

All the students did not, as in the *École polytechnique,* take the same courses; some courses were required of all students while others were chosen according to the student's special interests. The full course took three years. The courses were much more thorough than those offered in the *Conservatoire des arts et métiers,* and much more advanced than those given in the *écoles des arts et métiers.* As soon as the school acquired funds, the best scientists were hired as teachers. They gave the main lecture courses, and the work of the students was carefully supervised by *répétiteurs,* as in the *École polytechnique.* Each student had among his duties the preparation of eight projects a year, complete with drawings, specifications, and estimates of each. On the first *Conseil de perfectionnement,* which met once a year as a sort of advisory board of trustees, were some of the leading scientists, bankers, and manufacturers of France, including Chaptal, Arago, Laffitte, Casimir-Périer, and Ternaux. This body, however, met less frequently in the 1830's, and was finally dropped.

The school opened in 1829 with one hundred and forty students, of whom forty-eight were more than twenty-one years old. A few men over thirty left their businesses to attend. The pre-eminence of France in technical education is shown in that quite a number of foreigners were attracted: Spaniards, Italians, Germans, and Swiss, and even some Greeks and Americans. The revolution of 1830, followed by the cholera epidemic of 1831–32, made the first years somewhat difficult, but the school got out of debt by 1837. In 1836–37, the government of the July Monarchy, which was far more favorable to industry and to industrial education than had been the Bourbon government of Charles X, created a number of scholarships and a substantial loan fund for students. From 1832 to 1837, a hundred and twenty-seven students were graduated; from 1838 to 1847, four hundred and fifty-six received diplomas. By 1840 there were three hundred students registered in the school, and by 1850 there were forty teachers (lecturers and *répétiteurs*). In 1848, a group of graduates helped to found the *Société des ingénieurs civils*. When Lavallée retired from the directorship in 1857, he refused the offer made by a private corporation of one million francs for his interest. Instead, he donated his interest to the state, asking only for pensions for himself and his colleagues. The French State accepted the offer and made arrangements to take over the school in 1857.[56]

For the years 1829 to 1851, the graduates were distributed in the following occupations: agriculture, 18; architecture, 39; railroads, 119; teaching, 42; textile manufactures, 36; public

---

[56] De Comberousse, ref. 55, pp. 34–38, 49–65, 66–100, 109–126; L. Playfair, *Industrial Education on the Continent* (London, 1852), pp. 27–54. On page 124 of Comberousse, there is a list of eminent graduates; the work also contains a list of professors and other personnel. The names of all the students up to 1889 is in *Les anciens élèves de l'École centrale des arts et manufactures* (Paris, 1889).

works, 53; industrial chemistry, 57; general civil engineering, 56; machine manufacture, 30; metallurgy and mining, 79; and commerce and miscellaneous manufactures, 522. In all branches of French industry and commerce, the former students and graduates of the *École centrale* played an important role. In the same period, 1829 to 1851, over six hundred foreigners from twenty nations had studied in the *École centrale*. And out of 4,560 students admitted up to January 1864, one fourth were foreigners.[57] The great popularity of the *École centrale* shows that there was a demand for the sort of training it offered. The *écoles des arts et métiers* and related schools were steadily increasing the number of trained skilled workmen and shop foremen. The *École centrale* supplied the higher theoretical knowledge without which manufacturers and their chief aides could not direct their establishments or control the managers and foremen whom they employed.

On the other hand, time showed that the *École polytechnique* and the *écoles d'application* could not supply the needs of industry. The entrance examination of the *École polytechnique* excluded all but a few of the most brilliant students; at the same time its courses were considered by industrialists as too theoretical; its training, including the preparatory and advanced studies, covered seven years of work. Writing in 1851 one critic declared, "During an existence of over twenty years, the *École centrale* has fully justified the expectations of

---

[57] Playfair, *op. cit.*, p. 28; the best description of the courses is on pp. 27ff. of this work; in Bache, ref. 7, pp. 567–68; and in H. Barnard, *Systems, Institutions and Statistics of Scientific Instruction* (New York, 1872), pp. 462–74. There is an interesting comparison between the work of the *écoles des arts et métiers* and that of the *École centrale* in *Bulletin de la société d'encouragement pour l'industrie nationale*, 1833, p. 197. The annual prospectus of the *École centrale*, a complete file of which I consulted in the *Bibliothèque Nationale*, shows the point of view of leaders of the business world of France, and would be very useful to any student of nineteenth-century economic history. The necessity of meeting the competition of England, the desire to create a more powerful middle class in France, and a general exuberance over the possibilities of applying science to industry run through these documents.

its founders. Besides the four principal groups of courses studied, i.e., the mechanical arts, the chemical arts, metallurgy, and architecture and construction, it instructs its students in all the pursuits of industrial labor. Since chemistry has left laboratories to enter workshops and to perfect there the results of manufacturing processes, since the physical world has been searched for means of employing steam and heat, which have become such powerful agents of production, industry has ceased to be abandoned to empiricism. Every manufacture has asked from science methods quicker, surer, and more economical. The *École centrale des arts et manufactures* satisfies this demand."[58]

5. Military Instruction

If, on the one hand, the various revolutionary governments between 1789 and 1815 have started new military and naval

[58] C. Lavallée, "L'École centrale" in *Revue des deux mondes,* 15 May 1872, 418–28; H. Barnard, *National Education in Europe* (2nd ed., New York, 1854), p. 408; and Barnard, ref. 57, pp. 467–74. The curriculum and teaching methods of the *École centrale* were copied in every country of the western world and, after 1870, in Japan. Wickenden, ref. 21, pp. 17–18, 63–64. As late as 1867 one English scientist wrote, "There is nothing whatever corresponding to the *École centrale* in England." Barnard, ref. 57, p. 472. In a *Summary of Opinions concerning Engineering Curricula* (Lancaster, Pa., 1926), p. 24, published by the American *Society for the Promotion of Engineering Education,* the following conclusions read like a summary of what the *École centrale* tried to do from its inception: "1. Moderate diversity of training but tending away from too much specialization; 2. dominance of scientific and broadly technical content; 3. inclusion of a well-defined core of required subject matter in common; 4. inclusion at all stages of subjects of purely cultural value; 5. due emphasis on the economic aspects of engineering . . . and management; 6 . . . coördination of related subjects; and 7. thoroughness rather than completeness of detail." For a discussion of twentieth-century trends in technical education between the two World Wars, cf. the *Summary of Opinions* etc. referred to above, and three other publications of the same society, *A Study of Evolutionary Trends in Engineering Curricula* (Lancaster, Pa., 1927), *Opinions of Professional Engineers concerning Educational Policies and Practices* (Lancaster, Pa., 1927), and W. C. John, *A Study of Engineering Curricula* (Lancaster, Pa., 1927).

schools, they have on the other hand played havoc with both, first by endlessly changing the organization and regulations of these schools, and second by allowing and sometimes encouraging the students to leave before completing their courses. The coming of peace in 1815 allowed the government to consolidate and stabilize the whole educational order through all the ranges of the educational regime.

When the situation settled down after 1815, it became the custom — later embodied into law — to choose one third of the army officers of the line, two thirds in the scientific corps, and the whole of the general staff from among those who had had advanced professional training in some army school, including the *École polytechnique*. The remainder were taken from the ranks, but these rarely rose above the grade of captain. Many army outfits maintained a small school for the instruction of commissioned and noncommissioned officers who had no special military schooling.[59]

In most of the special military schools there was a *Conseil d'instruction* composed of officers and teachers of the institution. This *Conseil* exercised a general supervision over the courses of instruction and had the right to suggest alterations and improvements in it. The financial business of each school was managed by another board, the *Conseil d'administration*, and there was generally a third board, the *Conseil de discipline,* to look after questions of discipline. The result of all these arrangements was to give the various officers and professors of each school a dominant voice in the general management of the institution. All military schools were under the general direction of the Ministry of War. For each branch of

[59] H. Barnard, *Military Schools* (New York, 1872), pp. 149–50, 273. Cf. P. Chalmin, *L'Officier français de 1815 à 1870* (Paris, 1957), and by the same author, "Les écoles militaires françaises jusqu'en 1914," *Revue historique de l'armée*, 1954; P. Lyet, "Les écoles militaires de France," *ibid.*, 1954, a series of articles covering most of the military schools of France; also R. Girardet, *La Société militaire dans la France contemporaine, 1815–1939* (Paris, 1953).

the military service he appointed an advisory committee, the *Comité consultatif.*

The most elementary military school was the *Prytanée militaire,* moved in 1808 to La Flèche. It was commonly considered a charitable institution, intended to give a free or partly free education to the sons of officers and noncommissioned officers. Founded during the Revolutionary era, there were by 1859 four hundred pupils, of whom three fourths were educated entirely at the expense of the state. They ranged in age from ten to nineteen years, the majority being under fifteen years of age on entrance. The course did not differ greatly from that given in the *lycées.* It included Latin, the German, English, Italian languages, French literature, history, geography, mathematics, physics, chemistry, biology, and the drawing of maps and fortifications. This last and the military drill required were about the only strictly military features. Out of over four thousand pupils educated at La Flèche between 1814 and 1866, one thousand and sixty-seven went on to the advanced military school at Saint-Cyr, forty-six went to the *École polytechnique,* and twelve to the navy. The others went directly into the army or entered civilian professions.[60]

The main advanced military school for officers of the line was the *École militaire* at Saint-Cyr, founded during the Revolutionary era, and still flourishing in the twentieth century. Students admitted to the school had to pass entrance examinations, mainly in mathematics, which were less severe than those for the *École polytechnique.* These examinations were held during the summer, in Paris and in a series of provincial cities, by a board of four permanent examiners, a military officer, and three civilians. The competition for entrance was keen; for three hundred vacancies in each begin-

---

[60] Barnard, *Military Schools, op. cit.,* pp. 251, 257–58, also note 91 in Chap. 3; Buisson, ref. 2, articles "Prytanée français" and "Prytanée militaire de la Flèche."

ning class there were often as many as a thousand candidates. About fifteen, each year, came from the *Prytanée* at La Flèche. Students entered the school at the ages of eighteen to twenty-one, though men already in the army could be admitted up to twenty-five years. The state supplied scholarships and other aid for those who could not afford to attend otherwise. About one third received state aid.

The course lasted two years, though it could in special circumstances be extended to three years. It included advanced mathematics, chemistry, physics, map making and drawing, and a series of courses on military history, army administration, fortification, and on the attack and defense of places, all with practical exercises. In the instruction, *répétiteurs* were used, as in the *École polytechnique*. Lectures formed the basis of instruction and the classes were large, except for the language courses which were kept small. About five times as many students elected to study German as elected to study English. Study was supervised by the *répétiteurs*. After each lecture the students were marched to the study rooms where they worked, with a teacher or a *répétiteur* always present to answer questions.

The first-year studies were general and were supposed to complete the student's *lycée* education. The second-year courses were more specialized. Unannounced examinations were given frequently to keep the students on their toes. More general examinations, announced a week ahead, were given from time to time. At the end of each year, classes stopped for the last three weeks, and there was a period of intense reviewing before the final examinations began. The first-year students were examined by professors of the school; the second-year students, by outside examiners. All examinations were oral. The competition in examinations was keen because the rating of a student among his fellows was very important both in being admitted to advanced army schools and in obtaining places in the army. Those admitted to the school had to agree to serve five years after graduation. Those who failed or were dismissed had to enter the army as common soldiers.

The students slept in large barracks of sixty beds each. They had to make their own beds, clean their uniforms and shoes, and sweep out the rooms. They arose at five in the morning, and lights had to be out at night at nine o'clock. The visitor to the school got the impression — with all the military drill and practical exercises — that it was a large depot for the training of recruits with an educational department attached. As a result of the drill and practical exercises, however, students on joining a regiment were at once fit for duty. The practical exercise included some experience in infantry, cavalry, and artillery. The advantages of this showed up in the Crimean War (1853–56) where it was possible to transfer French officers from one service to another on short notice.

In every class there was a military officer to maintain discipline. The regulations for the students' conduct were very severe, resembling those in the *École polytechnique*. The number of students in the school varied from time to time, but there were usually about six hundred. Some of the graduates went on to the Cavalry School at Saumur or to the General Staff School. Most of them, however, went directly into the army.[61]

In 1826 the French government established a cavalry school at Saumur. It was, says Barnard, soon "considered the most perfect and extensive kind in Europe — perhaps the only one really deserving the title, the others being merely schools of equitation." [62] Students admitted were either graduates of the military school at Saint-Cyr or had passed an entrance examination. The course lasted one year, and there were ordinarily about four hundred students in the school. The courses were

[61] A. Lubet, *Le Bahut, album de St. Cyr* (Paris, 1860), pp. 35–92, 109–83. The work contains a wealth of details on the Saint-Cyr school. Cf. also Barnard, ref. 59, pp. 225–44, and unsigned article in *American Journal of Education,* Vol. 7, 1872, pp. 287ff.

[62] Barnard, *op. cit.,* pp. 241–44.

entirely military, including army regulations in both peace-time and war, cavalry tactics, equitation "comprising all the theoretical and practical knowledge required for the proper and useful employment of the horse," and methods of breeding.

The other higher military schools were primarily *écoles d'application* for graduates of the *École polytechnique,* as the *École d'état major* in Paris, founded in 1818. The model of the Staff School was an English school at High Wycombe, the success of which in providing the English army with a highly trained general staff in the Peninsula War had been noticed by French officers. Some of the students came from the *École polytechnique,* more from Saint-Cyr; a few were admitted on examination from the army. The course lasted two years, and the school had usually about fifty students. About nine hours a day were spent in lectures and study halls. The day's work began at six, half-past six, or seven, depending on the season, and continued until five, with short breaks for meals. No instruction was given in military history, gymnastics, swimming, musketry or artillery; students were supposed to have learned these elsewhere. A considerable portion of each day was devoted to out-of-doors exercises: riding, fencing, drill, and drawing. Lectures lasted an hour and a half, and there were usually only two lectures a day. The courses covered a wide variety of subjects: descriptive geometry, physical and military geography, geodesy, artillery, fortifications, military law and administration, veterinary science, and German. The students had the rank of second lieutenants, and on passing the final examination were raised to the rank of first lieutenant. It was customary for graduates of the *École d'état major* to spend two years in the infantry, two years in the cavalry, and one year in the engineers or artillery. After five years of such apprentice training, when a man was usually about twenty-seven, he was eligible for a staff appointment. The organization of the school somewhat resembled that of the *École polytechnique,* though there was no *Conseil d'instruction* and no *répétiteurs*. Eight months were devoted to study in the school, three months to outdoor studies and practical exercises, and one month to examinations.[63]

The most important of the military *écoles d'application* was the *École du génie et d'artillerie* at Metz. This brought together two schools founded during the Revolution, one at Metz and one at Châlons-sur-Marne. Students usually entered the school at the age of twenty-one after graduating from the *École polytechnique* with the provisional rank of second lieutenant. A few students who had not been enrolled in the *École polytechnique* were admitted by examination. The course at Metz lasted two years; students who lost time because of illness were allowed to stay three years, as were also those who failed the final examination. The commandant of the school held his position for five years, and was taken alternately from the artillery and the engineers. The directing general staff of the school was appointed for five years by the Minister of War. They acted as a sort of board of trustees. The school was directly ruled by a council made up of the commandant, the director of studies, and selected professors of engineering and artillery. All the students took certain courses, as those in German, swimming, and horsemanship, topography and geodesy, including military drawing and surveying, field fortification, general military art and legislation, permanent fortification, the attack and defense of fortified places, accompanied by a sham siege, architecture as applicable to military buildings and fortifications, and the theory and practice of artillery. Other courses were given separately for the engineers and for the artillery. Nearly two thirds of the course was

[63] Barnard, ref. 59, pp. 245–58. Military Education Commission ref. 43, pp. 119–46. This is the fullest account of the Saint-Cyr school in the first half of the nineteenth century. Various special army schools were set up, as for example a school of musketry which was founded in 1842. The course lasted four months; the chief school was at Vincennes, but branches were set up in principal garrison towns. Barnard, *op. cit.,* pp. 259–64. Regimental schools for artillery and engineering were also maintained.

common to both branches. The most remarkable thing about the curriculum was the absence of mathematics courses; the students were expected to have their mathematics before they entered the school.

Instruction was by means of lectures; there were no *répétiteurs* as in the *École polytechnique*. As a part of their work, students were given special projects for which they had to prepare drawings and a full report, including estimates of cost. Lectures began at ten A.M., and usually lasted an hour and a half. They were followed by supervised study in special study halls and by periods when the students were questioned orally. No classes were held for six weeks before the final examinations which came at the end of each year's work. The faculty consisted of the following professors: one for the application of mathematics to artillery and to military construction, one for mechanics as applied to machines, one for permanent fortifications and for the attack and defense of places, one for architecture and military construction, one for geodesy and topography, and finally one for applied physics and chemistry. Instructors of lesser rank, and usually younger, taught drawing, horsemanship, swimming (for those who could not swim), German, and dancing (for those who wanted it). Only the German and drawing instructors were civilians. In the summertime, practical exercises were undertaken in the field.

The discipline was less severe than in the *École polytechnique*. Students were allowed to take occasional meals in approved restaurants in town, and they could stay up at night till eleven o'clock. They were allowed freely to go to the theater. They were also permitted in their free time to read anything they cared to bring into the school. There were usually about one hundred and sixty students in the school at Metz; each year about forty of them went into the land artillery, ten into marine artillery, and thirty into the engineers. The competition at the school was less keen than at the *École polytech-*

nique. The students were said generally to arrive at Metz somewhat exhausted after the severe course of study to which they had been subjected during the previous two years. Moreover, the future career of the graduates of the *École polytechnique* was determined more by what they had done there than by their achievement in the school at Metz.[64]

A small *École de pyrotechnie militaire* was founded at Metz in 1824 for research in study of artillery and of methods of improving munitions. The students were mostly graduates of both the *École polytechnique* and the *École du génie et d'artillerie.* The government maintained a school of military gymnastics for about three hundred students near Vincennes. The course lasted six months, and trained teachers of gymnastics for all army schools.[65]

A comparison with military education in other countries shows them less advanced than the French. The *Royal Military Academy* at Woolwich in England, for artillery and engineering officers, arose out of a school for ordnance training organized in 1741. The *Royal Military College* for officers in infantry was founded near London in 1799 and moved to Sandhurst in 1812. In 1799 Count Rumford founded a school for civil engineering training, the *Royal Institution of Great Britain.* None of these schools did work as advanced as that done at the *École polytechnique,* to say nothing of the *écoles d'application.* Britain still depended largely on the old apprenticeship system for training all types of civil and military engineers. The *United States Military Academy* at West Point grew out of an act of Congress of 1802. The great initiator in this school was Sylvanus Thayer, its superintendent from 1819 to 1833, who modeled the curriculum and methods of instruction on those of the *École polytechnique.* The high

[64] Barnard, *op. cit.,* pp. 138–220; Military Education Commission, ref. 43, pp. 46–73, 443–87; *Annuaire de l'École polytechnique,* 1843, p. 351, *ibid.,* 1837, p. 282; *Bulletin des lois,* ord. of 5 June 1831.

[65] *École polytechnique: Livre du centenaire,* Vol. II, 465; Barnard, *Military Schools,* ref. 59, pp. 265–72, 259–64.

standards he set were of immense influence in the fields of the teaching of mathematics and the physical sciences. Many of the graduates of West Point became professors of mathematics in American colleges, universities, and technical schools. Following West Point, other technical schools were established: 1824, *Rensselaer Polytechnic Institute,* with twenty-five students in a rented house; 1839, *Virginia Military Institute;* 1845, the *Naval Academy* at Annapolis; and in 1847, the *Lawrence Scientific School* at Harvard, and the *Sheffield Scientific School* at Yale. All these American schools followed the French plan in placing mathematics, including descriptive geometry, drawing, and theoretical physics and chemistry before the practical work of applying them.[66]

6. Naval Education

The government continued as before to maintain a series of naval schools for theoretical and practical training for both the state navy and the merchant marine. On an elementary level there were established, in 1824, five naval apprentice schools, one in each of the five naval stations of France. The instruction was partly given by older teachers and partly by the more advanced pupils to those less advanced. The best one was at Rochefort, where the teaching was under the supervision of the *Frères des écoles chrétiennes.* The regulations for these elementary naval schools were frequently changed, and for some years certain of the schools were closed. These schools were mostly attended by youths in the locality, and the theoretical instruction and practical exercises, both on land and on shipboard, were elementary. The pupils usually entered the merchant marine.[67]

[66] *Study of the Evolutionary Trends in Engineering Education* (Lancaster, Pa., 1927), p. 19–23; E. R. Mann, *A Study of Engineering Education* (New York, 1918), pp. 2–20; Wickenden, ref. 21, pp. 4–9, 24–29; E. V. Wills, *Growth of American Higher Education* (Philadelphia, 1936), pp. 101–02.

[67] *American Journal of Education,* Vol. 21, 1870, p. 581.

In 1825 the Ministry of Marine established in each of the ports of France an elementary naval school which offered courses in geometry, mechanics, and navigation. In addition some elementary naval schools were set up by the town governments in various parts of France. In all, seventy such schools were established. All the courses were lecture courses, many of them given by graduates of the *École polytechnique*. The whole enterprise was a rather superficial missionary undertaking. Many of these courses were given in the evening. The schools varied greatly in the courses offered and in the quality of work done. It is estimated that by 1840 about five thousand pupils were doing work in these schools. Many of the pupils entered the merchant marine, though some went into manufacturing. Instruction was free for the students admitted. These had to be thirteen years old, but few entered before they were twenty to twenty-two. Usually one professor had charge of all the instruction. Theoretical courses were given in algebra, geometry, trigonometry, astronomy, navigation, the use of nautical instruments, nautical tables, ship construction, and French composition. Practical instruction included rigging, management of sails, knowledge of geography and seacoasts, currents and tides, and gunnery.

In 1810 two more advanced naval schools had been started at Brest and Toulon. They were united in 1816 and moved to the inland city of Angoulême, where food prices were low and the political atmosphere conservative. In 1827 the *École navale* was moved to Brest. This *École navale* was, for the navy, roughly the equivalent of the *École militaire* at Saint-Cyr for the army. About forty-five students were taken each year, and the course lasted two years. Some time after the school was moved to Brest it had attached to it a training ship, the "Borda," on which part of the instruction was given. To enter the school, the applicants had to be between fourteen and seventeen years of age and had to pass examinations in arithmetic, algebra, geometry, plane trigonometry, physics, chemistry, geography, drawing, and English. The candidates had also to prepare an essay in French and do a translation of Latin. There were usually about a hundred and twenty-five pupils. Preference was given to sons of naval officers and of other officials who had served "the king with zeal and fidelity." Some scholarships were available. The instruction in the school was usually given by eleven or twelve professors, and the subjects studied included astronomy, physics, chemistry, and the elements of navigation, with some instruction in history, geography, drawing, French literature, and English. The course lasted three years. In the courses in navigation there were taught the elements of naval architecture, the theory and practice of managing a ship, and gunnery and small arms as used in naval operations. The school sessions began the first of October and lasted till April. The older pupils aided in advising and helping the younger ones. The discipline was severe, and the boys rose every morning throughout the year at five; lights were out at nine. Part of the instruction was given on land, part on shipboard. At times, the pupils were taken to the shipyards to see vessels in process of construction or repair and to the workshops in the arsenal of Brest. Among the practical exercises given throughout the year were those in rowing and sailing small boats in all sorts of weather. Attached to the *École navale* was an additional training ship, the "Orion," on which cruises were taken in the summertime. A general examination was given, after some weeks of review, at the end of each school year. If a student failed an examination, he was allowed to repeat it once. After finishing the three-year course with satisfactory grades, the students received commissions in the state navy.[68]

The most advanced naval school was an *école d'application* primarily for graduates of the *École polytechnique,* the *École*

[68] *Le Globe,* 10 Oct. 1826; *American Journal of Education,* Vol. 21, pp. 587–88.

du génie maritime in Paris.[69] There were usually about thirty students in this school, of whom eight were foreigners, and the course lasted two and a half years — three winters in Paris, and two summers in the dockyards. They usually entered at the age of twenty or twenty-one. Since the students already had had a good general scientific training, the courses were eminently practical. The principal courses given were in ship construction, the strength of materials, drawing, and English for the first year. For the second year, the instruction centered on applied mechanics, accounting, naval artillery, technology of naval workshops, and again drawing and English. In their work in the dockyards the students were carefully instructed, and each one had to keep an elaborate journal with drawings. The pupils could select the port to which they would go according to their standing in the class. At the end of two and a half years, they were examined on the work of the whole course. Those who passed were given commissions in the state navy. Any who failed to pass were allowed a third year of study, but failing in that they were definitely rejected.[70]

J. R. Soley, an American who carefully studied French naval education, including a number of quite small naval schools not included in this account, summed up his impressions as follows: "It was remarked by Captain Hore, the naval attaché in Paris, that the English have no system of naval education, and the French have too much! The fault of 'too much system' means a sacrifice of results to methods, an effort which looks rather to the perfection of the machinery of instruction than

---

[69] The regulations of the school were frequently changed. This account is a composite one that does not try to trace all the shifts in regulations, cf. A. de Crisenoy, *Our Naval Schools and Naval Officers* (2 vols., New York, 1873), Vol. 2, pp. 119–206; and J. R. Soley, *Report on Foreign Systems of Naval Education* (Washington, 1880), pp. 109–39, 322–33. The accounts in de Crisenoy and Soley are dense with detailed information about every aspect of the *École navale.*

[70] Soley, *op. cit.,* pp. 140–43.

to the work done by this machinery. But the injurious effects are felt rather in minor details and in exceptional cases than in the general result. In most cases, the naval educational system, though highly organized is sufficiently elastic to meet the wants of individual cases. In the French naval schools, there is certainly, in matters of theoretical and practical instruction, much greater flexibility than is to be found in those of almost any other nation. The system of oral teaching, without the restrictions of textbook, and supplemented by individual explanation and interrogation cannot be other than an elastic one. Discipline, however, is overdone." Soley's whole report, though based on a study of naval schools later than 1850, still applies very well to conditions before the middle of the century. The total impression of his whole report is very favorable to French naval education as being the best in the world.[71]

7. Conclusion

The governments of the Bourbon Restoration (1814–1830) and of the July Monarchy (1830–1848) were conservative; the first more so than the second. And in neither case did the national government show much interest in scientific and technical education. But these enterprises, which had made some progress during the seventeenth and eighteenth centuries and had received a strong push forward during the Revolutionary era, now forged ahead in spite of government indifference and even hostility. Two contributing factors to this were the relative internal peace, only slightly disturbed by the July Revolution of 1830, and the growing industrialization of France to which the technical schools made important contributions.

In 1850 Paris was still the world's leading center of engineering education. Great Britain could boast of but three strug-

[71] Soley, *op. cit.*, p. 152.

gling centers of engineering education, each with a single professor in charge. Before 1880 virtually everything in Britain was left to private or local enterprise. Few understood that theoretically trained men were necessary to apply the advances in science to industry effectively. Such effort as was exerted was concentrated on giving some training in science to workingmen. This was largely inspired by welfare motives and was a wholly unsatisfactory scheme of technical education. At the same time, higher technical education and research were almost stifled from lack of support. The United States had a few schools of engineering recently organized after French models, but all still in a rather rudimentary stage of development. Germany, not yet united, was in the early stages of her industrialization with eight rapidly developing polytechnical schools, three mining academies, and numerous technical schools of lower rank. Switzerland had not yet established her advanced federal polytechnic school, but had a few excellent cantonal schools of middle rank. France had greatly strengthened her position in the first half of the nineteenth century by improving old schools and opening new ones at various levels of instruction. Yet by 1850 the long period of French ascendancy was drawing to a close. Though increasingly industrialized, her rate of industrial advance began to fall behind that not only of Great Britain but also of Germany. France was entering upon a phase of a stable population, and, by the nature of her luxury industries in which hand-finishing played a major role, there was less pressure than in England and Germany to penetrate foreign markets.

While the French engineering schools, especially the *École polytechnique* and its *écoles d'application,* and the *École centrale des arts et manufactures* maintained their high intellectual traditions unimpaired, they came to be rivaled by the Swiss *Polytechnic School* and later by the rapidly advancing schools of Germany and America in enrollment, material equipment, and financial resource. The rising stream of foreign students now went first to Switzerland, then to Germany. The days of outstanding French leadership in all types of technical education were rapidly passing.[72]

[72] Wickenden, ref. 21, pp. 4, 22–23.